CURRENT ECONOMIC ISSUES

20TH EDITION

READINGS IN ECONOMICS, POLITICS, AND SOCIAL POLICY FROM
DOLLARS&SENSE

EDITED BY JAMES M. CYPHER, ROB LARSON, ALEJANDRO REUSS, CHRIS STURR,

AND THE *DOLLARS & SENSE* COLLECTIVE

CURRENT ECONOMIC ISSUES, 20TH EDITION

ISBN: 978-1-939402-27-1

Published by: Economic Affairs Bureau, Inc. d/b/a *Dollars & Sense*
89 South Street, LL02, Boston, MA 02111
617-447-2177; dollars@dollarsandsense.org.
For order information, contact Economic Affairs Bureau or visit: www.dollarsandsense.org.

Current Economic Issues is edited by the *Dollars & Sense* collective, which also publishes *Dollars & Sense* magazine and the classroom books *Microeconomics: Individual Choice in Communities*, *Real World Macro*, *Real World Micro*, *America Beyond Capitalism*, *The Economic Crisis Reader*, *The Economics of the Environment*, *Grassroots Journalism*, *Introduction to Political Economy*, *Labor and the Global Economy*, *Real World Banking and Finance*, *Real World Globalization*, *Real World Latin America*, *Real World Labor*, *Striking a Balance: Work, Family, Life*, *Unlevel Playing Fields: Understanding Wage Inequality and Discrimination*, and *The Wealth Inequality Reader*.

The 2016 *Dollars & Sense* Collective: Betsy Aron, Autumn Beaudoin, Sarah Cannon, Nina Eichacker, Peter Kolozi, John Miller, Jawied Nawabi, Kevin O'Connell, Alejandro Reuss, Dan Schneider, Zoe Sherman, Bryan Snyder, Chris Sturr, De'En Tarkpor, Jeanne Winner, and Will Whitham.

Co-editors of this volume: James M. Cypher, Rob Larson, Alejandro Reuss, and Chris Sturr

Cover design: Chris Sturr.

Cover photos: Energy Department workers Brian Lawson and Kenesaw Burwell install solar panels, June 4, 2012 (Dennis Schroeder, public domain); protesters rallying as part of Iceland's "Kitchenware Revolution," Austurvöllur Square, October 11, 2008 (OddurBen, Creative Commons Attribution-Share-Alike 3.0 Unported license); Container ship CSCL Globe, Euromax Terminal Yangtzehaven, Rotterdam, January 11, 2015 (kees torn, Creative Commons Attribution-Share-Alike 2.0 license).

Production: Chris Sturr

Printed in U.S.A.

CONTENTS

Chapter 1

FROM CRISIS TO STAGNATION

Article 1.1

TRUMP AND NATIONAL NEOLIBERALISM

BY SASHA BREGER BUSH
January/February 2017

The election of Donald Trump portends the completion of the U.S Government's capture by wealthy corporate interests. Trump's election is widely seen in terms of a dispossessed and disenfranchised white, male working class, unsatisfied with neoliberal globalization and the insecurity and hardship it has unleashed, particularly across regions of the United States that were formerly manufacturing powerhouses (like the Rust Belt states of Pennsylvania, Michigan, Ohio and Wisconsin, four states believed to have cost Hillary Clinton the election). While there is much truth to this perspective and substantial empirical evidence to support it, it would be a mistake to see Trump's victory wholly in these terms.

This election appears to be a key stage in the ongoing process of American democratic disintegration, though in my opinion Trump's election does not signal the beginning of a rapid descent into European-style fascism. Instead, the merger of state and corporate interests is proceeding along an already-established trajectory. American democracy has been under attack from large and wealthy corporate interests for a long time, with this process accelerating and gaining strength over the period of neoliberal globalization (roughly the early 1970s to the present). This time period is associated with the rise of powerful multinational corporations with economic and political might that rivals that of many national governments.

I am persuaded by the argument that the U.S. political system is not democratic at all, but rather an "inverted totalitarian" system. Political commentator Chris Hedges notes: "Inverted totalitarianism is different from classical forms of totalitarianism. It does not find its expression in a demagogue or charismatic leader but in the faceless anonymity of the corporate state." Citing the American political theorist Sheldon Wolin, Hedges argues that our inverted totalitarian system is one that retains the trappings of a democratic system—e.g. it retains the appearance of loyalty to "the Constitution, civil liberties, freedom of the press, [and] the independence of the judiciary"—all while undermining the capacity of citizens to substantively participate and exert power over the system.

1

In my view, what Trump's election has accomplished is an unmasking of the corporate state. Trump gives inverted totalitarianism a persona and a face, and perhaps marks the beginning of a transformation from inverted totalitarianism to totalitarianism proper. By this I mean that I think we are entering a period in which our political system will come to look more obviously totalitarian, with ever fewer efforts made to conceal its true nature and with the demagoguery that we typically associate with this form of politics. In spite of this, it makes no sense to me to call the system toward which we are heading (that is, if we do not stand up and resist with all our might right this second) "fascism" or to make too close comparisons to the Nazis. The European fascists put their faith in the power of the state to remake society. I do not see this on the horizon for the liberal-capitalist US, where feelings of hatred and distrust towards an oversized federal government helped to elect Trump. Whatever totalitarian nightmare is on our horizon, it will be uniquely American: a kind of "corporate" or "market-based" totalitarianism that is unique in world history. With its orientation towards the needs of the marketplace and big business, it will resemble in many ways the system that we've been living under for decades. If the pre-Trump system of inverted totalitarianism solidified in the context of global neoliberalism, the period of corporate totalitarianism that we are entering now seems likely to be one characterized by what I call "national neoliberalism."

Trump's Election Doesn't Mean the End of Neoliberalism

Trump's election represents a triumph of neoliberal thinking and values. Perhaps most importantly, we should all keep in mind the fact that Americans just elected a businessman to the presidency. In spite of his Wall Street background and billionaire status, Trump successfully cast himself as the "anti-establishment" candidate. This configuration—in which a top-one-percenter real estate tycoon is accepted as a political "outsider"—is a hallmark of neoliberal thinking. The fundamental opposition between market and government is a central dichotomy in the neoliberal narrative. In electing Trump, American voters are reproducing this narrative, creating an ideological cover for the closer connections between business and the state that are in store moving forward. (Indeed, Trump is already using the apparatus of the U.S. federal government to promote his own business interests). As states and markets further fuse in coming years, this representation of Trump and his administration—as being anti-government—will help immunize his administration from accusations of too-cozy relationships with big business. Trump's promises to "drain the swamp" by imposing Congressional term limits and constraints on lobbying activities by former political officials will also help to hide this relationship. (Has anyone else noticed that Trump only addresses half of the "revolving door," i.e., he plans to limit the lobbying of former politicians, but not the political roles of businessmen?)

Trump's Contract with the American Voter, his plan for the first 100 days in office, discusses policies and programs many of which are consistent with neoliberal thinking. (I interpret the term "neoliberalism" to emphasize at its core the importance of private property rights, market-based social organization, and the dangers of government intervention in the economy.) Trump's plan redirects the activities of the U.S. government along the lines touted by neoliberal "market fundamentalists" like Milton Friedman, who advocate limiting government's role to market-supportive functions like national defense (defense stocks are doing very well since the election) and domestic law and order (Trump's proposals have a lot to do with altering immigration policy to "restore security"). Trump also plans to use government monies to revitalize physical infrastructure and create jobs. Other government functions, for example, health care provision and education as well as protecting the environment and public lands, are open for privatization and defunding in Trump's agenda. Under Trump, the scope of federal government activities will narrow, likely to infrastructure, national defense, and domestic policing and surveillance, even if overall government spending increases (as bond markets are predicting).

Trump also seems content to take neoliberal advice in regard to business regulation (less is best) and the role of the private sector in regulating itself (industry insiders understand regulatory needs better than public officials). Trump's plan for the first 100 days specifies "a requirement that for every new federal regulation, two existing regulations must be eliminated." As of the time of this writing, his selection of cabinet appointees illustrate a broad willingness to appoint businesspeople to government posts. As of mid-December 2016, a Goldman Sachs veteran, Steven Mnuchin, has been appointed Secretary of the Treasury; billionaire investor Wilbur Ross, Secretary of Commerce; fossil-fuel-industry supporter and Oklahoma Attorney General Scott Pruitt, EPA administrator; fast-food mogul Andrew Puzder, Secretary of Labor; Exxon-Mobil CEO Rex Tillerson, Secretary of State. Trump's business council is staffed by the CEOs of major U.S. corporations including JP Morgan Chase, IBM, and General Motors. To be fair, the "revolving door" between government and industry has been perpetuated by many of Trump's predecessors, with Trump poised to continue the tradition. But this is not to say that neoliberalism will continue going in a "business as usual" fashion. The world is about to get much more dangerous, and this has serious implications for patterns of global trade and investment.

Trump's Election Does Mean the End of Globalism

The nationalism, xenophobia, isolationism, and paranoia of Donald Trump are about to replace the significantly more cosmopolitan outlook of his post-WWII predecessors. While Trump is decidedly pro-business and pro-market, he most certainly does not see himself as a global citizen. Nor does he intend to maintain the United States' extensive global footprint or its relatively open trading network. In other words, while neoliberalism is not dead, it is being transformed into a geographically more fragmented and localized system (this is not only about the U.S. election, but also about rising levels of global protectionism and Brexit, among other anti-globalization trends around the world). I expect that the geographic extent of the U.S. economy in the coming years will coincide with the new landscape of U.S. allies and enemies, as defined by Donald Trump and his administration.

Trump's Contract with the American Voter outlines several policies that will make it more expensive and riskier to do business abroad. All of these need not occur; I think that even one or two of these changes will be sufficient to alter expectations in business communities about the benefits of certain cross-border economic relationships. Pulling the United States out of the TPP, along with threats to pull out of the Paris Climate Agreement and attempts to renegotiate NAFTA, is already signaling to other countries that the new administration will not be interested in international cooperation. A crackdown on foreign trading abuses will prompt retaliation. Labelling China a currency manipulator will sour relations between the two countries and prompt retaliation by China. As Trump goes forward with his anti-immigration and anti-Muslim rhetoric and policies, he will alienate the United States' traditional allies in Europe (at least until Europe elects its own nationalist and xenophobic leaders) and communities across the Global South. The U.S. election has already undermined performance in emerging markets, and bigoted rhetoric and policy will only increase anti-American sentiment in struggling economies populated largely by people of color. Add to this the risk of conflict posed by any number of the following: his antagonizing China, allying with Russia, deploying ground troops to stop ISIS, and pulling out of the Korean DMZ, among other initiatives that seem likely to contribute to a more confrontational and violent international arena. All of this is to say that Trump will not have to intervene directly in the affairs of business in order to make it less international and more national. The new global landscape of conflict and risk, combined with elevated domestic spending on infrastructure and security, will bring U.S. business and investment back home nonetheless.

National Neoliberalism and State-Market Relations

Fascist states are corporatist in nature, a state of affairs marked by a fusion of state and business functions and interests. In the fascist states on the European continent in the 1930s and 1940s—systems that fall under the umbrella of "national socialism"—the overwhelming power of the state characterized this relationship. Political theorist Sheldon Wolin writes in Democracy, Inc., in regard to Nazi Germany and Fascist Italy (as well as Stalinist Russia), "The state was conceived as the main center of power, providing the leverage necessary for the mobilization and reconstruction of society."

By contrast, in Trump's America—where an emergent "national neoliberalism" may be gradually guiding us to a more overt and obvious corporate totalitarian politics—we can expect a similar fusion of state and market interests, but one in which the marketplace and big business have almost total power and freedom of movement. State and market in the U.S. will fuse further together in the coming years, leading some to make close parallels with European fascism. But it will do so not because of heavy handed government dictates and interventions, but rather because domestic privatization initiatives, appointments of businessmen to government posts, fiscal stimulus, and the business community's need for protection abroad will bring them closer. Corporate interests will merge with state interests not because corporations are commanded to, but rather because the landscape of risk and reward will shift and redirect investment patterns to a similar effect. This may be where a budding U.S. totalitarianism differs most starkly from its European cousins.

Of course, it helps that much of the fusion of state and market in the United States is already complete, what with decades of revolving doors and privatization initiatives spanning the military, police, prison, healthcare and educational sectors, among others. It will not take much to further cement the relationship.❏

Sources: Associated Press, "Trump's foreign policy plan includes boots on the ground against ISIS," *PBS Newshour*, Aug. 16, 2016 (pbs.org); Kristen Bellstrom, "Trump's Pick for Secretary of Labor: 'Ugly' Women Don't Sell Burgers," *Fortune*, Dec. 9, 2016 (fortune.com); Jackie Calmes, "What is Lost by Burying the Trans-Pacific Partnership?" *New York Times*, Nov.11, 2016 (nytimes.com); Szu Ping Chan, "From Brexit to the rise of protectionism: is the world facing an era of permanent low-growth?" *The Telegraph*, Oct. 10, 2016 (telegraph.co.uk); Shawn Donnan, "WTO Warns on Rise of Protectionist Measures by G20 Economies," *Financial Times*, June 21, 2016 (ft.com); Ben Geier, "Even the IMF Now Admits Neoliberalism Has Failed," *Fortune*, June 3, 2016 (fortune. com); Chris Hedges, "Sheldon Wolin and Inverted Totalitarianism," Common Dreams, Nov. 2, 2015 (commondreams.org); Michael Hirsh, "Why Trump and Sanders Were Inevitable," *Politico*, February 28, 2016 (politico.com); Ben Jacobs and Pengelly, Martin, "Donald Trump on North Korea going to War: 'Good luck, enjoy yourself folks'," *The Guardian*, April 2, 2016 (theguardian. com); Jake Johnson, "Blame the Neoliberals," Common Dreams, Nov. 10, 2016 (commondreams. org); Rich Lowry, "The Anti-Establishment Front-Runner," *Politico*, Oct. 21, 2015 (politico.com); Gene Marcial, "Trump Victory Boosts Demand for Trump Stocks," *Forbes*, Nov. 13, 2016 (forbes. com); Nolan D. McCaskill, "Trump transition website promotes his brand," *Politico*, Nov. 10, 2016 (politico.com); Chris Mooney; Brady Dennis; and Steven Muffson, "Trump names Scott Pruitt, Oklahoma attorney general suing EPA on climate change, to head EPA," *The Washington Post*, Dec. 7, 2016 (washingtonpost.com); Steven Muffson and Brady Dennis, "Trump Victory Reverses US Energy and Environmental Priorities," *Washington Post*, Nov. 9, 2016 (washingtonpost.com); Damian Paletta; Carol E. Lee; and Jeremy Page, "Donald Trump's Message Sparks Anger in China," *Wall Street Journal*, Dec. 5, 2016 (wsj.com); Sally Pipes, "Under Trump, Americans Can Finally Put Obamacare Behind Us," *Forbes*, Nov. 14, 2016 (forbes.com); Mercedes Schnelder, "Donald J. Trump's 'Vision' for Education," *HuffingtonPost.com*, Nov. 13, 2016 (huffingtonpost.com); Michael Shear, et al., "Trump Unveils High-Powered and Well-Heeled Business Council, and Invites Filipino Strongman to White House," *New York Times*, Dec. 2, 2016 (nytimes.com); Jeffery Smith, "This Is the Most Important Market Reaction to Donald Trump's Victory," *Fortune*, Nov. 9, 2016 (fortune. com); Karin Strohecker, "Emerging Markets-Strong dollar, higher US yields make stocks, currencies suffer," *Reuters*, Nov. 14, 2016 (reuters.com); Steven Swinford and Ben Riley-Smith, "Trump-Putin Alliance Sparks Diplomatic Crisis as British Ministers Demand Assurances from US over Russia," *The Telegraph*, Nov. 12, 2016 (telegraph.co.uk); Donald Trump, "Donald Trump's Contract with the American Voter: 100-day Action Plan to Make America Great Again," DonaldJTrump.com, 2016; Sheldon Wolin, *Democracy Inc: Managed Democracy and the Specter of Inverted Totalitarianism*, (Princeton: Princeton University Press, 2008); John Ydstie, "Trump Picks Steve Mnunchin to Lead Treasury Department," NPR, Nov. 30, 2016 (npr.org); Jim Zarroli. "Trump Taps Billionaire Investor Wilbur Ross for Commerce Secretary," NPR, Novmber 30, 2016 (npr.org).

Article 1.2

ARE WE STUCK IN A PERIOD OF ECONOMIC STAGNATION?

BY ARTHUR MacEWAN
July/August 2016

> Dear Dr. Dollar:
> Is it really true (or likely) that the U.S. and world economies are enter-
> ing an extended period of slow economic growth—that is, stagnation?
> —*Aaron Shields, Maplewood, N.J.*

Nowadays, among economists at least, everyone seems to be pessimistic about the future course of the economy. Larry Summers, a star among mainline econo-mists, secretary of the treasury in the 1990s, and advisor to Barack Obama in more recent years, is perhaps the most prominent figure giving voice to the specter of stag-nation. Most recently, in the March/April 2016 issue of *Foreign Affairs*, after review-ing the current poor performance of the U.S. and other economies, Summers wrote:

> The key to understanding this situation lies in the concept of secular stag-
> nation. ... The economies of the industrial world, in this view, suffer from
> an imbalance resulting from an increasing propensity to save and a decreas-
> ing propensity to invest. The result is that excessive saving acts as a drag on
> demand, reducing growth and inflation.

Summers goes on to say that weak growth and investment can be temporarily over-come and demand maintained only by "dangerous levels of borrowing," as in the early 2000s. The result was the housing bubble, the catalyst for the Great Recession.

Summers is not alone. A recent and much-cited book by Northwestern University economist Robert Gordon, *The Rise and Fall of American Growth*, makes a comple-mentary argument. Gordon maintains that economic expansion from 1870 to 1970 was driven by five realms of innovations: electricity, chemicals and pharmaceuticals, the internal combustion engine, urban sanitation, and modern communications. He does not see any current development—particularly not information technology—that matches the impact on economic growth of any one of these five.

Gordon's analysis, with periods of growth depending on major innovations, is similar to the Marxist analysis by the late Paul Sweezy, which has been contin-ued and given emphasis now by his followers at *Monthly Review* magazine. Sweezy viewed capitalism as creating excess capacity, with investment creating new pro-ductive capacity which outstripped the demand for the products. Thus, this very success of capitalist production tended to undermine the basis for new invest-ment. Further, the lack of sufficient demand was also a product of capitalists' success—i.e., their ability to keep wages low. Sweezy referred to this phenomenon as "over accumulation," where the success of capitalist production tended to cre-ate stagnation and undermine capitalist production—a prime contradiction of the system. For Sweezy, then, the normal state of capitalism is stagnation, and periods of growth were to be explained only by epoch-changing innovations—the steam engine, the railroad, and the automobile.

Poor Performance

The current focus on stagnation is a response to the poor performance of the U.S. economy so far in the 21st century. Since 2001, the annual growth of per capita GDP (adjusted for inflation) has been less than 1%. By comparison, the average annual growth rate from 1870 to 2007 (the onset of the Great Recession) was twice that. Of course, the years since 2001 include the Great Recession. But most recessions have been balanced by sharp upward recovery, with a growth rate substantially above the average. (See table below.)

Not so this time. Since the nadir of the Great Recession in 2009, average annual growth of per capita GDP has been only about 1.3%. Moreover, in the years leading up to the Great Recession, even meager growth (about 1.7% per year) was attained only by the rise of debt and the housing bubble. These early-21st-century years saw a high level of debt-based construction, but there was limited investment in plant and equipment, which might have attenuated stagnation.

Further, both the severity of the Great Recession and the slow growth in the 21st century have been part of a longer-term development. Whereas annual average GDP per capita growth was 2.5% in the 1950 to 1973 period, it dropped to below 2% in the 1973 to 2007 years, just before the Great Recession and slow recovery. (Though this drop is significant, the growth rate of around 2% is in line with the average over the last 150 years.) Furthermore, as compared to recessions in the 1950 to 1973 period, recessions since 1973 have been substantially more severe (in terms of depth and length), with the Great Recession being the worst.

The Current Situation

While the grand theories of stagnation—the tendency in capitalism for savings to outpace investment, the absence of major innovations, and over-accumulation—are important, there are also some more particular factors that have contributed to slow

---

Economic Growth in the United States, Over the Long Run and Since 1950
Average Annual Rates of Growth of Gross Domestic Product Per Capita

1870-2015	1.94%
1950-1973	2.50%
1973-2001	1.97%
1973-2007	1.92%
2001-2015	0.96%
2009-2016	1.30%*

* Preliminary and approximate

Sources: Bureau of Economic Analysis (bea.gov) and Charles I. Jones, "The Facts of Economic Growth," Hoover Institution (hoover.org).

economic growth in the United States and other "advanced" countries during the 21st century.

Lack of government demand creation. The well-known government response to recessions has been to run a fiscal deficit, enhancing aggregate demand. While the Obama administration did respond to the Great Recession with a stimulus program, it was clearly too small—thanks in no small part to advice from Summers, but also because of the anti-deficit mania that has become so widespread among politicians and the public.

Lack of public spending on physical and social infrastructure. Over the last several decades, government at all levels has failed to spend sufficiently on infrastructure, both physical (roads, bridges, public transport) and social (schools, training programs, public health). Without strong infrastructure through public investment, private investment is inhibited.

Rising economic inequality. With economic inequality rising ever since the 1970s, consumer demand has been weakened. Also, the rich, who get a larger and larger share of income, tend to save more. Both phenomena contribute to Summers' point regarding savings outstripping investment opportunities.

The set of these factors, so clear in the United States but also evident in other advanced economies, is tied up with the dominant ideology of neoliberalism and its opposition to government spending (except for the military). Neoliberalism seems to work very well for large firms and wealthy individuals, shifting the distribution of income increasingly in their favor. However, it also prevents actions that would counter the stagnation tendencies of capitalism.

It seems unlikely that the U.S. economy—or the economies of other high-income countries—can limp along indefinitely at the slow rate of economic growth that has prevailed in the 21st century. When combined with the high degree of economic inequality that exists in the United States, continuing stagnation, which would carry with it insufficient job growth and a degradation of jobs and pay for many people, would generate considerable economic and political instability.

So what are the options? It is conceivable that the stagnation would be alleviated by an abandonment of the three neoliberal principles that have exacerbated stagnation in recent years. After all, the depression of the 1930s, followed by World War II, did lead to a rather different operation of capitalism in the United States, with a larger role for government and less inequality. However, there are also options that would involve a more dramatic break with U.S. capitalism, either a break to the right or a break to the left. In the 2016 presidential campaigns, Donald Trump and Bernie Sanders roughly personified these two options. Which way things actually do move in the coming period will depend in part on decisions among the elite groups in this country, whether or not they will stick to neoliberalism regardless of the obvious dangers it presents to them. But the future course of the economy will also depend on popular political action. Unions, social justice organizations, the environmental movement, and community groups can affect the developments, but so can the Tea Party and similar organizations on the right. ❑

Sources: Lawrence H. Summers, "The Age of Secular Stagnation," *Foreign Affairs*, March/April 2016; Robert Gordon, *The Rise and Fall of American Growth: The U.S. Standard of Living Since the Civil War*, 2016.

Article 1.3

RECOVERY DENIED
Growth and Prosperity Continue to Go Their Separate Ways

BY JOHN MILLER
May/June 2014

> The big story continues to be the rapid, healthy growth that hasn't returned since the Great Recession. …
>
> According to Congress's Joint Economic Committee, average growth over the 19 quarters of this recovery has been 2.2%. … The average for all post-1960 recoveries is 4.1%. … The average for the Reagan expansion was 4.9%. …
>
> These are huge differences in foregone prosperity. …
>
> The main White House growth plan is to have government borrow more money to spend more on the transfer payments that didn't stimulate the economy the last time. …
>
> Americans will be receptive to an agenda to lift the middle class with growth, not redistribution.
>
> —"The Growth Deficit," *Wall Street Journal*, May 1, 2014.

A "growth deficit" surely has been one of the hallmarks of the U.S. economy since the end of the Great Recession. But the *Wall Street Journal* editors must not be paying attention if they think that doubling down on the pro-rich, free-market policies initiated during the Reagan administration is going to restore of "forgone prosperity" for most people.

It's not just a growth deficit that has plagued the U.S. economy, but also an equality deficit. The economic growth there has been during "this not so great recovery," as the editors call it, has gone overwhelming to the very richest and has done less to improve the economic well-being of the rest than during any economic recovery in the last sixty years.

This is not just a matter of a single recovery delayed. Economic growth and prosperity for most people parted company some three decades ago. Chanting the *Journal* editors' mantra of "growth not redistribution" will only drive them further apart, resigning all but the super-rich to an economic slump that persists even during economic recoveries.

Recovery Delayed

This recovery has surely been delayed. According to National Bureau of Economic Research (NBER), the nation's arbiter of the business cycle, the Great Recession ended back in June 2009. By the official scorecard, the current recovery will hit the five-year mark this June, making it longer than the average recovery (58 months). But the economy has grown at about half of the pace of the average recovery since 1960, as the editors report, and is the slowest of all recoveries since 1950.

Some of that dismal growth record should be attributed to the severity of the Great Recession, the worst economic crisis since the 1930s. Typically, recoveries from financial crises have been protracted. That this recovery seems to conform to the historical pattern, however, is cold comfort for those waiting for the economic suffering of the Great Recession to subside.

To undo the economic suffering inflicted during a recession, a recovery must first create enough jobs to replace those lost in the downturn. That is admittedly a large undertaking this time around. Still, no recovery has taken longer to replace the jobs lost in the previous recession. By this June, more than six years since the onset of the recession, the recovery will finally get back to the pre-recession level of employment. That's longer than the four years the "jobless" recovery took to replace the jobs lost in in the

A Date with a Business Cycle

Let's look more closely at what economists mean when they declare that a recession is over and a recovery is underway. This will help show why that announcement is unlikely to mean that happy days are here again for most people, especially those looking for work.

The National Bureau of Economic Research (NBER) tracks the ebb and flow of economic activity over a business cycle—from the low point ("trough") of a recession to high point ("peak") of an expansion, and back again. In the first phase of the cycle, the expansion, the economy grows. In the second, it contracts. The NBER has identified nine complete business cycles in the U.S. economy since World War II.

The NBER's business-cycle-dating committee, a group of seven economists, has no rigid rules for determining the start or end of a business cycle. The members study a broad array of macroeconomic indicators, including Gross Domestic Product (GDP), industrial production, employment, real income, trade, several interest rates, and personal income, as well as several composite indices, including the index of coincident indicators, which measures employment, income, output, and sales. In short, they eyeball the data.

Economists traditionally define a recession as two consecutive quarters of negative real growth, or declining output, as measured by GDP. But applying even this shorthand definition is not easy. In December 2008, for instance, the economy had not yet suffered two consecutive quarters of negative economic growth. Nonetheless, mounting monthly job losses convinced the NBER to declare that a recession had begun a whole year earlier, in December 2007. The economy had lost jobs every month from December 2007 on—already the longest period of uninterrupted job-loss since the Great Depression.

Determining when a recession finishes and an expansion begins isn't any simpler. Economists generally date the expansion back to when the economy begins to grow again,recouping the output lost during the recession.In September 2010, the NBER declared that the Great Recession had ended—reached its trough—back in June 2009,. But even itsannouncement cautioned that "economic activity is typicaly below normal in the early stages of the expansion, and it sometimes remains so well into the expansion."

That has surely been the case this time. Economic growth returned to the U.S. economy beginning in the third quarter of 2009. But job losses continued until March 2010,. And much milder 2000 recession, and much longer than the then-record three years it took to replace the jobs lost in the 1991 recession. But replacing the jobs lost in the recession is not enough to close the jobs gap. Each month, approximately 125,000 people enter the labor force in search of work. These new entrants must be able to find jobs before unemployment returns to pre-recession levels. The Hamilton Project, a policy group dedicated to restoring broad-based economic growth, calculates that if the economy were to add 208,000 jobs a month, matching the best year of job creation in the 2000s, it would still take until August 2018 to close the jobs gap.

And that says nothing of the quality of the jobs created. A study conducted by the National Employment Law Project (NELP) compared the distribution of the jobs lost during the Great Recession to those created during the recovery (as of

nearly five years later the recovery has yet to replace the jobs lost during the Great Recession, the official "headline" unemployment rate remains elevated, and millions more have dropped out of the labor force altogether or are working part-time even though they want full-time jobs.

Economic expansions are supposed to improve our life-chances, not just swell the economy. That has not happened in this economic recovery, even some five years after the NBER declaredthat the crisis was officially over.

U.S. BUSINESS CYCLES, 1949-2014

Trough	Peak	Trough	Expansion (months)	Contraction (months)	Full Cycle (months)
Oct 1949	July 1953	Aug 1954	45	13	58
Aug 1954	July 1957	Apr 1958	35	9	44
Apr 1958	May 1960	Feb 1961	25	9	34
Feb 1961	Nov 1969	Nov 1970	105	12	117
Nov 1970	Dec 1973	Mar 1975	37	16	53
Mar 1975	Jan 1980	July 1980	57	6	63
July 1980	July 1981	Nov 1982	12	16	28
Nov 1982	July 1990	Mar 1991	93	8	101
Mar 1991	Mar 2001	Nov 2001	120	8	128
Nov 2001	Dec 2007	June 2009	73	18	91
June 2009	NA	NA	60*	NA	NA

Source: Economic Cycle Research Institute, National Bureau of Economic Research.

*Through June 2014

Sources: "Determination of the December 2007 Peak in Economic Activity," National Bureau of Economic Research, Dec. 11, 2008, www.nber.org/cycles/dec2008.html; and, "The June 2009 trough was announced September 20, 2010," http://www.nber.org/cycles/sept2010.html.

2012). They looked at three equal-sized groups of occupations: low-wage jobs (paying median hourly wages from $7.69 to $13.83), mid-wage jobs ($13.84 to $21.13), and high-wage jobs ($21.14 to $54.55). Their results were striking. While three-fifths (60%) of the jobs lost in the Great Recession were in mid-wage occupations, just over one-fifth (22%) created during the recovery were in these occupations. The exact opposite held for low-wage jobs. These accounted for more than one-fifth (21%) of the jobs lost, but nearly three-fifths (58%) of the jobs created, with the biggest job gains in retail sales and food preparation.

No wonder inflation-adjusted hourly pay, for all but the top 10% of wage workers, were lower in 2013 than in 2009 (at the beginning of the recession). The median real household income in June 2013, meanwhile, was an alarming 4.4% lower, as reported by the Sentier Research Group.

Recovery Enjoyed

For the best off, the last five years have surely not been times of forgone prosperity. Just how well have they done during the recovery? By the end of 2013, corporate profits had risen so far that *WSJ* reporter Justin Lahart fretted about the "The Next Problem: Too Much Profit." What is driving profits to new record highs? "The tight lid companies have put on costs," answers Lahart. "They've been slow to hire and slow to raise wages."

It's clear that record profits have come at the expense of wages (and jobs), judging from the profit share of Gross Domestic Product (GDP). Corporate profits now stand at 11.1% of GDP, the highest share since 1948. Meanwhile, employee compensation (wages and benefits) has fallen to its lowest share.

Stock market investors have also done quite well. Stock values have surpassed their pre-recession peaks. But this is of little help for most households. Less than one-half of households own any stock, even indirectly through retirement accounts.

This tale of two recoveries has led to the greatest concentration of economic gains on record. From 2009 to 2012, 95% of income gains went to the richest 1%, those with incomes over $394,000, as economists Emmanuel Saez and Thomas Piketty have documented. That was greater than the 65% share that went to the top 1% during the 2002-2007 recovery prior to the Great Recession or even the 70% share during the 1923-1929 recovery before the Great Depression.

Reagan's Revenge, Recovery Denied

The Reagan recovery might have boasted a high rate of economic growth, as the *Journal* editors note, but that hardly suggests that Reagan's free-market, pro-rich tax policies would restore broad-based economic growth.

One reason the economy grew more quickly during the Reagan recovery is that the 1982 recession did much less damage than the Great Recession. Another is that, in practice, Reagan's economic policies were more Keynesian than Obama's. In the Reagan recovery, real per capita government spending grew twice as quickly (2.6% per year) as during the Obama administration (1.3%). On top of that, state and local government spending, adjusted for inflation and population, increased during the first half of the 1980s—while it declined from 2008 to 2012.

Nonetheless, Reagan's anti-government, "free-market" ideology took hold, saddling the economy with jobless recoveries that benefit almost exclusively the super rich, fail to replace middle-income jobs, and make inequality far worse. In their recent book Getting Back to Full Employment, economists Dean Baker and Jared Bernstein explain that, between the 1950s and 1970s, slack labor markets with high unemployment occurred about one-third of the time. Since Reagan, from 1980 to 2013, slack conditions have prevailed more than twice as often. And that's made a difference for inequality. When Reagan took office, the richest 1% pulled down about 10% of the nation's income, less than one half of 22.5% they get today.

The Reagan legacy includes pro-rich tax cuts that have reduced government revenues and kept government spending in check, union-busting labor relations that have eroded the bargaining power of workers, deregulation that paved the wave for financialization, and "free-trade" policies that have made it easy for companies to threaten offshoring unless workers make concessions, In its most recent *Global Wage Report*, the International Labor Organization found that wages as share of output in developed economies have dropped steadily since 1990. The most important drivers of the decline, in declining order of importance, are financialization, two institutional factors (smaller size of government and declining union density), and globalization.

If those long-term trends don't convince you that the *Journal* editors' preferred policies led to the separation of growth and prosperity, consider this: In the early 2000s, we conducted a full field test of those polices under the George W. Bush administration. The result was an economic recovery that added fewer jobs than even the Obama recovery, left the economy in the throes of the worst economic crisis since the 1930s, and increased the economic chasm between the super-rich and the rest of us.

Trying those same policies again will only be a way to ensure that, for most of us, it will be not just a recovery delayed, but recovery denied. ❑

Sources: Paul Krugman, "Reagan was a Keynesian," *New York Times*, June 7, 2012; Dean Baker and Jared Bernstein, "Getting Back to Full Employment," Center on Children and Families at Brookings, March 2014; Justin Lahart, "The Next Problem: Too Much Profit," *Wall Street Journal*, March 27, 2014; "The Low-Wage Recovery and Growing Inequality," National Employment Law Project, August 2012; "Global Wage Report 2013/13," International Labour Organization, 2013; "Evolution of the "Jobs Gap" and Possible Scenarios for Growth," The Hamilton Project at Brookings, May 2, 2014; Heidi Schierholz, "Six Years From Its Beginning, The Great Recession's Shadow Looms Over the Labor Market," Economic Policiy Institute, January 2014.

Article 1.4

THE COSTS OF AUSTERITY
Unemployment and Economic Losses in the Neoliberal Era

BY GERALD FRIEDMAN
January/February 2015

Full employment, the simple idea that government should ensure that everyone of working age can find work, was a central feature of policy in the New Deal era—from the 1930s through the mid-1970s. Since the start of neoliberal era, however, economic policy has emphasized low inflation even at the cost of slower economic growth and higher unemployment. Dismissing an earlier full employment target of 4%, neoliberal policy makers have sought to keep unemployment at a rate no lower than the so-called Non-Accelerating Inflation Rate of Unemployment (or NAIRU), around 5.5%. This policy has succeeded at lowering inflation, which has averaged less than 3% a year since the mid-1970s, compared with 4% a year for the 1948-74 period. This one percentage point drop in the inflation rate, however, has come at a steep human toll in higher unemployment—the average unemployment rate has been over 6.5% since 1974, compared to 4.7% between 1947 and 1974—as well as a huge loss in economic output.

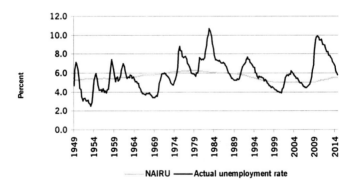

**FIGURE 1: ACTUAL UNEMPLOYMENT RATE VS.
NON-ACCELERATING INFLATION RATE OF UNEMPLOYMENT**

Unemployment has been high in the neoliberal era. From 1947 to 1974, policy makers sought to keep unemployment low, with a full-employment target rate ultimately set at 4% during the Kennedy administration. While unemployment rates were above this level in most years, the economy did reach full employment during the early and mid-1950s and in the 1960s. Since the 1970s, however, policy makers have abandoned the full-employment target and seek only to hold unemployment to the NAIRU, or a level sufficient to prevent wage and price inflation. Even this level has been reached only briefly since 1974—for a few months in 1978, briefly at the end of the 1980s and in 2006, and most significantly in the late 1990s.

FIGURE 2: GDP, ACTUAL AND TREND, 1947-2014

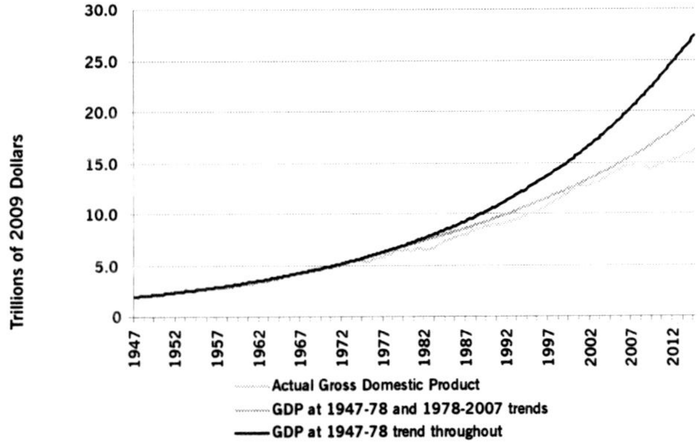

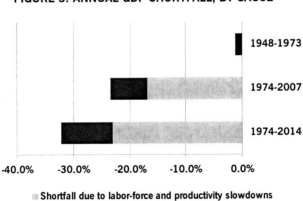

Trillions in potential output have been lost. Output is lost when workers are unemployed and when they give up on finding jobs. In addition, higher unemployment and stagnant wages have slowed the long-term growth in income by reducing the incentive for businesses to increase productivity. The rate of growth in output per worker has slowed from about 2.2% per year for 1947-1978 to 1.6% per year for 1978-2007. In the graph, the top line shows what GDP would have been each year had productivity growth continued at the 1947-1978 rate and there had been full employment. Beginning in 1978, the middle line shows what GDP would have been had growth continued at the 1978-2007 rate and there had been full employment. The bottom line shows actual GDP.

FIGURE 3: ANNUAL GDP SHORTFALL, BY CAUSE

Even before the Great Recession hit, our income was much less than it could have been. Higher unemployment, a slowdown in the growth of the labor force, and a slowdown of labor productivity growth long predate the Great Recession. In the 1948-73 period, unemployment lowered output by a little more than 1% below the trend capacity, an annual loss of $43 billion in inflation-adjusted terms (chained 2009 dollars). By 2014, however, compared with growth at the earlier rate, our losses have surged to nearly a third of output, with an average annual shortfall of over 20% of GDP for the 1974-2012 period as a whole (over $2 trillion per year, in 2009 dollars). This lost output is divided between two causes: 1) the slowing in the trend growth of income (due to the size of the labor force and the output per worker) and 2) the direct cost of higher unemployment.

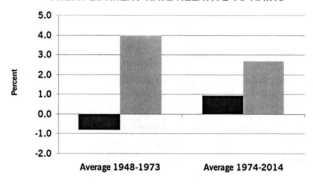

FIGURE 4: REDUCTION OF INFLATION AND INCREASE OF UNEMPLOYMENT RATE RELATIVE TO NAIRU

Higher unemployment has done little to slow inflation. By reducing wages and therefore demand for goods, higher unemployment reduces inflation. But the relationship is weak and the effect is relatively small. Higher unemployment rates of the 1974-2014 period compared to the 1948-1973 period account for a decline in the annual inflation rate of only 0.3%, out of a total decline of 1.3%. For this small reduction in annual inflation, we have lost trillions of dollars of output.

FIGURE 5: INCOME GROWTH, BY INCOME GROUP, TWO PERIODS

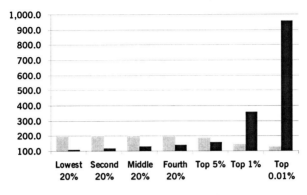

1947-1974 ■ 1974-2007

Index = 100.0 for beginning of each period. Figures are for upper limit of ech quintile (20% group) listed, lower limits of top 5%, top 1%, and top 0.01%.

The rich have done better since 1974. High unemployment rates have weakened the bargaining power of workers and their unions, leading to lower wages and an erosion of benefits. Higher unemployment, therefore, has redistributed income from working people to their employers and owners of capital. Under what some historians call the "New Deal order," lasting into the 1970s, incomes doubled for most Americans, but increased only half as fast for the top 1%. Since 1974, income growth has fallen for working people because of longer periods of unemployment and stagnant wages. Capital income, however, has grown and the richest American have done much better. During this period, high unemployment has helped incomes explode for the richest Americans, even while hardly increasing for the poorest 40% of households. ❏

Sources: Congressional Budget Office data, accessed through Federal Reserve Bank of St. Louis (fred.gov); Bureau of Labor Statistics (bls.gov); Bureau of Economic Analysis (bea.gov); U.S. Bureau of the Census (census.gov); Thomas Piketty and Emmanuel Saez (eml.berkeley.edu/~saez/)

Chapter 2

FISCAL POLICY

Article 2.1

SURVIVING IN THE AGE OF TRUMP

BY DEAN BAKER
November 2016

I will claim no special insight into the politics that led to Trump's election. I was as surprised as anyone else when not just Florida and North Carolina, but also Pennsylvania, Michigan, and Wisconsin started to turn red. But that's history now. We have to live with the fact of President Trump and we have to figure out how to protect as much as possible of what we value in this country from his presidency.

This won't be easy when the Republicans control both houses of Congress and will soon be able to appoint a new justice to the Supreme Court to again give them a right-wing majority. But there are still points of pressure.

Most importantly, the people in Congress want to get re-elected. Pushing unpopular policies like privatizing Social Security or Medicare, or taking away insurance by ending Obamacare, will be horrible albatrosses hanging over their heads the next time they face voters. This reality has to constantly be put in their faces. It is easy for politicians to push nonsense stories about eliminating trillions of dollars of waste, fraud, and abuse. It is much harder to get away with taking away your parents' Social Security check or the health care insurance that pays for your kid's insulin.

The other point of pressure is that we know (even if the folks who report the news don't) that Trump got elected by making many promises that he will not be able to keep. Rebuilding an economy in which the benefits of growth are broadly shared is a great idea, but Donald Trump is not going to bring back the coal mining jobs lost in West Virginia, Kentucky, Ohio and elsewhere. These jobs were not lost because of environmentalists concerned about the future of the planet; they were lost because of productivity growth in the industry (think of strip mining replacing underground mining). We should make sure that people regularly are informed about President Trump's progress in bringing back coal mining jobs to Appalachia.

Before getting into some specific issues, it is worth noting that not everything Trump says he wants to do is bad. He says that he wants a big infrastructure program. This is badly needed both to modernize our infrastructure and also to create jobs. Trump's proposed tax cuts will provide a boost to demand that will generate jobs as well. It's horribly targeted in giving most of the benefits to the rich, but it will still lead to more consumption and therefore more demand and jobs. This may finally give the economy enough stimulus to restore the labor market to its pre-recession strength. That will be good, especially since the beneficiaries of the job growth and the stronger labor market will be disproportionately African American and Hispanic and less-educated workers. Now, I will get to some specifics.

Social Security

During the campaign Trump distinguished himself from other Republicans by saying there was no reason to cut benefits or to raise the retirement age. (The age for full benefits is already being raised to 67 by 2022.) In spite of this commitment, many Republicans, most importantly House Speaker Paul Ryan, have long wanted to cut and privatize Social Security. They are likely to try to enlist Trump into this effort.

There are two points here. First, the retirees and near retirees who are most dependent on Social Security are core Republican voters. If the Republicans want to cut their benefits, this fact has to be in their face in every way we can possibly bring it home. Undoubtedly, the proposal will be phased in so that current retirees and those near retirement will be largely protected. Fortunately, the history here is that people identify with the program. In part, they probably don't believe that they really will be shielded from cuts, but they also see Social Security as a good program which they want their children and grandchildren to benefit from as well.

The other point is that if Trump goes along with plans to cut or privatize Social Security, this is a huge breach of faith with voters. Many of Trump's supporters said they liked him because he spoke his mind, unlike a typical politician. Making a commitment to protect the country's most important social program, and then turning around and reversing it once you get into the White House, is just about the most sleazy politician's flip flop imaginable. This should be a career-ending move for Trump and any of his accomplices.

Medicare

The basic story here is the same as with Social Security; it is also a hugely popular and tremendously effective program. There is one notable difference. Since the nature of the benefit is more complicated (coverage of most of seniors' health care costs), it is possible to make major cuts without calling them cuts. This is the trick behind Paul Ryan's plan for privatizing Medicare which he characterizes as "modernizing" the program.

In this area it will be important to highlight what privatization would actually mean. It will require seniors to deal with insurance companies who will profit by denying them care. It would also end Medicare as we know it. It is bad enough that younger healthier people have to struggle with insurers to pay bills. Subjecting our elderly parents and grandparents to this treatment is a cruel trick. We have to do our best to make everyone know that this is the Republican agenda.

Obamacare

One of Trump and the Republican's central pledges has been to get rid of Obamacare. This is a vote winning pledge primarily because no one knows what Obamacare is. The Republicans have been allowed to paint it as death panels denying care for old people and a mandate requiring people to buy insurance they don't want. Very few people, including many of the people directly benefitting, know that Obamacare is the program that has allowed 20 million people to get health care insurance.

It is also the program that has made it possible for people with serious health conditions to be able to get insurance at relatively affordable prices. This is a great thing by itself, but it has also allowed millions of workers to leave jobs they dislike without worrying about getting health insurance for themselves and their families. This is seen most clearly in the sharp increase in the number of voluntary part-time workers. These are workers who say that they prefer working less than full-time jobs; jobs that generally don't provide health care insurance.

There has been an unprecedented rise in the number of people voluntarily working part-time since the exchanges went into operation in January of 2014. The number of people who have chosen to work part-time is up by almost 1.9 million since Obamacare went into effect. The number involuntarily working part-time has fallen by almost the same amount. Disproportionately the people benefitting have been young parents who are presumably choosing to have more time with their kids. Most people would probably think this is a good thing.

Anyhow, no one knows the positives of Obamacare largely because the political consultants tell Democratic politicians not to talk about it. But when President Trump looks to dismantle the program, it will be very important that people understand that this is taking away health care insurance from their family members, friends, and neighbors.

There were problems in implementing Obamacare; there will undoubtedly be many more problems in undoing it, especially since the end result will leave most people in a much worse situation. It is important that everyone know that real people are being hurt by the repeal. This means highlighting stories like parents of kids with diabetes being unable to afford insulin and comparable horror stories. Older people with heart conditions and cancer survivors will no longer be able to get affordable insurance. This is the Republican replacement for Obamacare and everyone must know it.

Immigration

Donald Trump has told the public that the undocumented workers in this country are rapists and drug dealers. In reality, they are the people who work their asses off cleaning toilets in hotel rooms and in wealthier people's homes. They are people doing the dishes in restaurant kitchens and picking vegetables in the hot sun. Many of the people who Donald Trump has pledged to deport have been here ten or twenty years. Many have kids who are U.S. citizens. Some have started businesses and are employing other people.

This is the reality of the undocumented population. We have to do everything we can to drive these facts home. We have an ally in the business community. They don't want to see millions of their workers randomly grabbed up and thrown out of the country. This is why there has been so much Republican support for immigration reform. While we are not likely to see immigration reform under President Trump, it is certainly possible that a Republican Congress would act to put a brake on the worst attacks on immigrants.

Regulation

Trump has pledged to reverse regulations in a wide range of area, including regulations on the financial industry and environmental regulation. In some cases, there may be legal remedies for efforts to undo regulation through executive action, but the courts will be uncertain allies at best and a Republican Congress will be happy to grant full legal authority in many cases.

The best hope here is to educate the country about the consequences. While some regulations are undoubtedly overly burdensome, they exist for a purpose. Most of us are old enough to remember the sleazy practices and outright fraud involving mortgage loans and mortgage backed securities that helped to inflate the housing bubble. Dodd-Frank provided some checks on such practices but hardly put an end to abuses in the financial sector, as folks familiar with John Stumpf and Wells Fargo know. The Wall Street gang is sufficiently greedy that they will quickly take advantage of deregulation to further stuff their pockets at the public's expense. We have to make sure to get our flashlights out.

There is a similar story on environmental regulation. Most of these measures have been well worth their cost. This is another case where it is easy to hate regulation in the abstract, but to actually value the specific regulations that protect the environment and people's health. Even Donald Trump's supporters are appalled that the kids in Flint have lead in their drinking water. Donald Trump's agenda here is about putting a lot more lead in folks' drinking water. Most people would not think this is good, at least if they understood that what was at issue.

On global warming we will have to do everything we can at the state and local level and use private initiatives to promote conservation and clean energy. Maybe someone can put a huge thermometer showing global average temperatures on a building in view of the White House. This is a huge problem and we have to find some way to get the U.S. on board with international efforts to reduce greenhouse gas emissions.

Anyhow, those are some cheap thoughts on how we can best get through a Trump presidency. Hopefully, they are helpful. I will also toss in a word about how we got here. There has been to my mind a very silly debate about whether Trump supporters are driven by racism, xenophobia, and misogyny or whether they are driven by economic factors.

I consider this debate silly since both are obviously important in my view. Racism, xenophobia, and misogyny are deeply rooted in society and few of us can claim to be completely devoid of these sentiments. The question is how these hatreds can come to be the defining feature of political life for large numbers of people and here I think the economic policies of the last four decades have played a crucial role.

I would argue that we have pursued policies that have been deliberately designed to shift income upward over this period. It is understandable that the losers from these policies would be looking to lash out at the winners. Voting for Trump was a way these people could spit in the face of the people who they see as wrecking their lives.

It's not pretty, but the best way to respond is to give them real ways to improve their lives and stop having all the benefits from growth go to those at the top. Trump is not going to help the people who have been left behind, and we have to make this fact as clear as possible. But we should also be showing them policies that will have substantial and direct effects in improving their lives. ❏

Source: Dean Baker, *Rigged: How Globalization and the Rules of the Modern Economy Were Structured to Make the Rich Richer* (Center for Economic Policy Research, 2016).

Article 2.2

TAXING THE WEALTHY AND THE ART OF SOPHISTRY

BY JOHN MILLER
November/December 2016

> [Trump] would collapse the individual income tax brackets from seven to three, with rates of 12%, 25% and 33%. ...
>
> The 33% top marginal rate is still too high, but ... Mr. Trump is explicitly selling "a working- and middle-class tax relief proposal." ...
>
> Faster growth means lifting the oppressive burden of government of the Obama years.
>
> —"Trump and the Art of Growth," *Wall Street Journal*, Sept. 16, 2016
>
> Though she defeated Bernie Sanders in the primary, [Clinton] is adopting the socialist's deathtax rate structure. She'd tax all estates over $10 million at 50% ... and go to 65% on assets above $500 million.
>
> The [estate] tax confiscates assets and punishes a lifetime of investment and thrift. The desire to pass along assets to heirs is also a motivation for many entrepreneurs.
>
> —"Clinton's 65% Killer Death Tax," *Wall Street Journal*, Sept. 22, 2016

If you're for cutting taxes on the wealthy, we're for you. If you're for increasing taxes on the wealthy, we're against you. That's "the art of growth." *Wall Street Journal* style.

Well, Picassos they're not, at least as far as the art of growth goes.

The *Wall Street Journal* editors are pushing positions that find little support even among mainstream economists, hardly the sworn enemies of the rich. A 65% tax on the estates of the super-rich is not going to kill economic growth, and lowering taxes on the incomes of the super-rich is not going to breathe new life into today's sluggish economy.

What is indisputable is that a plan like Trump's will reduce the progressiveness of the federal income tax, making today's ever-worsening inequality yet worse. A plan like Clinton's would increase the progressiveness of the federal income tax, reducing inequality without threatening economic growth. To insist otherwise is the art of sophistry, not the art of growth.

To see why, let's take a closer look at the Trump and Clinton tax proposals, what the evidence actually says about how taxing the wealthy affects economic growth, and what economists actually have to say about it.

Taxes and the Historical Record

The Trump tax plan would lower the top income tax bracket from 39.6% to 33%, eliminate the alternative minimum tax (which since 1969 has collected income taxes from high-income taxpayers who otherwise would have paid very little in income tax), cut the corporate income tax by more than half, and do away with the estate tax. With those and other pro-rich measures, close to half of the benefits of the Trump tax cut—some 44%—would go to the richest 1%, according to the analysis of Citizens for Tax Justice, showering an average tax cut of $88,410 to these taxpayers all with adjusted gross incomes in excess of $428,713 in 2013. The Trump proposal would cut tax revenues by $6.2 trillion over the next decade, more than twice as much as the Reagan tax cut in the 1980s and the Bush tax cuts of the 2000s (both corrected for inflation).

The Clinton tax proposal would increase tax revenues by $1.4 trillion over the next decade, with those additional revenues coming nearly exclusively from taxes on the well-to-do. Clinton proposes to levy a "fair share" surcharge of four percentage points on taxpayers with over $5 million of adjusted gross income, pushing their marginal tax rate up from 39.6% to 43.6%. She would also replace the alternative minimum tax with the Buffett rule, which would require all taxpayers with adjusted gross income in excess of $1 million to pay no less than a 30% of their total income in federal income taxes. Her plan would also raise taxes on capital gains from assets held less than six years, and boost the top tax rate on estates over $500 million (paid by just two in every 10,000 taxpayers) from 40% to 65%. Altogether, 77.8% of the burden of the Clinton tax increases would fall on the richest 1% of taxpayers (and 91.6% on the richest 10% of taxpayers), says the Tax Policy Center.

The tax rates on the wealthy proposed by the two presidential candidates are not outside the range of the historical record of the United States, despite the editors' muttering about Clinton's socialist death tax and the enormity of Trump's tax cut. Given the fervor with which the editors preach that lowering taxes on the wealthy is the key to our economic salvation, you might be surprised to learn that faster economic growth rates and lower taxes on the wealthy are not closely correlated.

That much is clear even at first glance. The U.S. economy grew most quickly when taxes on the wealthy were at their highest, not their lowest. During the 1960s, the only decade in which the annual growth rate averaged 4%, the top estate tax rate was 77% throughout the decade and the top income tax rate was as a high as 91% and never lower than 70%. For instance, in 1960 a 91% marginal tax rate was levied on married families with income above $400,000 (or $3.25 million in 2016) and only on their income above $400,000. In addition, during the four decades that the U.S. economy expanded 3% a year, the top tax rates on the wealthy varied widely. During the 1980s, the top income tax rate was as low as 28% and the top estate tax rate was just 55%. In the 1950s those rates were 91% and 77%. But the economy grew an identical 3.09% a year during both decades. And over the last fifteen years, when top tax rates have been quite low by historical standards, the U.S. economy has grown more slowly than during any of the five decades from 1950 to 2000.

International comparisons also fail to show that cutting taxes on the wealthy is the key to increasing economic growth. For instance, when economists Thomas Piketty, Emmanuel Saez, and Stefanie Stantcheva compared economic growth rates and changes in the top marginal income tax rate of 18 OECD countries during the 1960-2010 time period, they found that, "cuts in top tax rates do not lead to higher economic growth." The United States, for instance, cut its top rate by over 40 percentage points during that period, and its per capita income grew just over 2% annually. In Germany and Denmark, which barely changed their top income tax rates, growth rates were also just over 2% per year.

Blowing Up Trickle Down

In their recent study of the "Effects of Income Tax Changes on Economic Growth," Brookings Institution economists William Gale and Andrew Samwick conclude that, "it is by no means obvious that tax rate cuts will ultimately lead to a larger economy."

They explain their results this way. Tax cuts offer the potential to raise economic growth. With lower taxes workers keep more of what they earn in wages, savers get more after taxes, and investors make more money on their investments after taxes. In this way, tax cuts provide an incentive to work more, save more out of income, and to throw more money into investments. Economists call this the "substitution effect" because, for instance, as after tax wages (the reward for work) go up, workers will substitute income (from working more) for leisure time. But at the same time, tax cuts dull the incentive to work, save, and invest by reducing the need to engage in productive economic activity. With lower taxes, workers can earn the same income working fewer hours, save as much as before while consuming more, and investors can make as much money as before while investing less. Economists call this the "income effect" because, for instance, with higher after-tax wages workers can afford to work fewer hours and take more time off (leisure) without a loss of income. For Gale and Samwick this leaves the net effect of income tax cuts on growth "theoretically uncertain."

Economist Jane Gravelle with the non-partisan Congressional Research Service finds that the effect of estate taxes on the size of economy and economic growth is likewise uncertain. On the one hand, a lower estate tax makes it cheaper for people to leave money to their heirs. That might encourage them to work harder and save more. On the other hand, a lower estate tax allows people to make the same after-tax bequest with a smaller amount of savings, which might persuade them to work and save less. On top of that, to the extent that a lower estate tax increases the size of bequests after taxes, recipients may work and save less. All of this convinces Gravelle that the effect of changes in the estate tax on savings and output "would be negligible."

When Congressional Research Service economist Thomas Hungerford examined these issues, he found that, "The top tax rates appear to have little or no relation to the size of the economic pie, but there may be a relationship to how the economic pie is sliced."

Unlike the effect of cuts in the top tax rates on economic growth, there is good evidence that lower taxes on the rich and greater economic disparities go hand in hand. Using IRS data, Hungerford reports that the average tax paid by the top 0.1% of U.S. families fell to 25% in 2009, just half of the 50% they paid in 1945. At the same time their share of income more than doubled from 3.3% in 1945 to 7.0% in 2009 in the midst of the Great Recession, before reaching 7.9% in 2015.

Clinton's tax proposal would combat rising inequality by increasing taxes on those at the top. She doesn't offer tax cuts for those with modest incomes. But she does pledge to improve their economic position by using the revenues from her tax increases to pay for affordable childcare (including doubling the child tax credit), paid family leave, debt-free college, and infrastructure spending.

The Trump tax plan, on the other hand, would not just be a "big league" (as he says) reduction of the tax burden of the rich. It would also strip the government budget of 15% of its revenues over the next decade. On top of that, the Trump proposal would raise the taxes of 7.8 million families with children by replacing personal exemptions with a standard deduction penalizing families with three or more children, repealing the head-of-household filing status that had reduced the taxes of single parents, and raising the bottom tax bracket from 10% to 12%. Hardest hit would be single parents with school-age children and no child care costs, some with as little as $16,000 of income.

How to Slice the Economic Pie

The real art of growth is in figuring out how to expand the economic pie and at the same time make the slices more equal. This can be done, but only if we reject the art of sophistry practiced by the *Wall Street Journal* editors and parroted by Trump and his ilk.

The economic evidence is clear. Reducing the tax burden on those with the largest slices hasn't made the economic pie any bigger. When that message trickles down, we all will be better off. ❑

Sources: "The Distributional and Revenue Impact of Donald Trump's Revised Tax Plan," Citizens for Tax Justice, Sept. 9, 2016; Jim Nunns, Len Burman, and Joe Rosenberg, "An Analysis of Donald Trump's Revised Tax Plan," Tax Policy Center, October 11, 2016; Richard Auxier, Len Burman, Jim Nunns, and Jeff Rohaly, "An Updated Analysis of Hillary Clinton's Tax Proposals," Tax Policy Center, Oct. 11, 2016; "Effects of Income Tax Changes on Economic Growth," by William G. Gale and Andrew R. Samwick, Economic Studies at Brookings, Sept. 2014; Thomas Piketty, Emmanuel Saez, and Stefanie Stantcheva, "Optimal Taxation of Top Labor Incomes," National Bureau of Economic Research Working Paper 17616, 2011; Thomas L. Hungerford, "Taxes and the Economy: An Economic Analysis of the Top Tax Rates Since 1945," Congressional Research Service Report for Congress, Sept. 14, 2012; Jane G. Gravelle, "Economic Issues Surrounding the Estate and Gift Tax," Congress Research Service Report for Congress, April 24, 2007; Lily L. Batcheider, "Families Facing Tax Increases Under Trump's Latest Tax Plan," Social Science Research Network, Sept. 24, 2016; Bureau of Economic Analysis; "Historical Highest Marginal Income Tax Rates," Tax Policy Center; "A Historical Look at Estate and Gift Tax Rates," CCH: A Wolters Kluwer Business.

Article 2.3

THE GREAT TAX-CUT EXPERIMENT
Has cutting tax rates for the rich helped the economy?

BY GERALD FRIEDMAN
January/February 2013

Since the late 1970s, during the Carter Administration, conservative economists have been warning that high taxes retard economic growth by discouraging productive work and investment. These arguments have resonated with politicians, who have steadily cut income taxes, especially those borne by the richest Americans. The highest marginal tax rate, which stood at 70% by the end of the 1970s, was cut to less than 30% in less than a decade. (The marginal rate for a person is the one applied to his or her last dollar of income. A marginal rate that applies to, say, the bracket above $250,000, then, is paid only on that portion of income. The portion of a person's income below that threshold is taxed at the lower rates applying to lower tax brackets.) Despite increases in the early 1990s, the top marginal rate remained below 40%, when it was cut further during the administration of George W. Bush. These dramatic cuts in tax rates, however, have not led to an acceleration in economic growth, investment, or productivity.

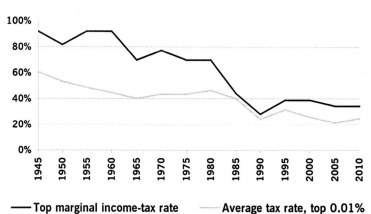

FIGURE 1: FEDERAL TAXES ON RICHEST AMERICANS,
MARGINAL AND AVERAGE RATES, 1945-2010

—— Top marginal income-tax rate   ·········· Average tax rate, top 0.01%

The federal government has been cutting taxes on the richest Americans since the end of World War II. The average tax paid by the richest taxpayers, as a percentage of income, is typically less than the top marginal rate. Some of their income (the portion below the threshold for the top marginal rate, any capital-gains income, etc.) is taxed at lower rates. Some is not subject to federal income tax because of deductions for state and local taxes, health-care costs, and other expenses. The decline in the average tax rate for the richest, however, does follow the cuts in the top marginal income-tax rate.

FIGURE 2: TAX REVENUE AS A PERCENTAGE OF GDP, 2008

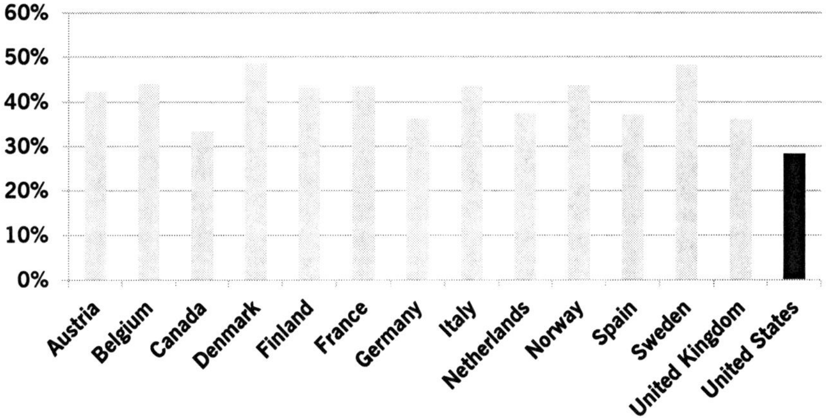

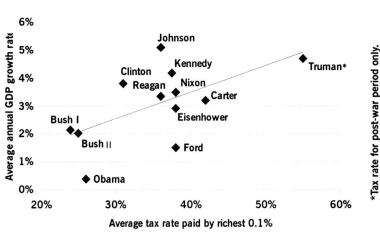

Americans pay a smaller proportion of total income in taxes than do people in any other advanced capitalist economy. As recently as the late 1960s, taxes accounted for as high a share of national income in the United States as in Western European countries. After decades of tax cuts, however, the United States now stands out for its low taxes and small government sector.

FIGURE 3: AVERAGE TAX RATES ON RICHEST AND REAL GDP GROWTH, BY PRESIDENT, 1947-2010

On average, the economy has grown faster during presidential administrations with higher tax rates on the richest Americans. Growth was unusually slow during George W. Bush's two terms (Bush II) and during Obama's first term, when the Bush tax cuts remained in effect. On average, every 10 percentage-point rise in the average tax rate on the richest has been associated with an increase in annual GDP growth of almost one percentage point.

FIGURE 4: TOP MARGINAL TAX RATE AND INVESTMENT, 1963-2011

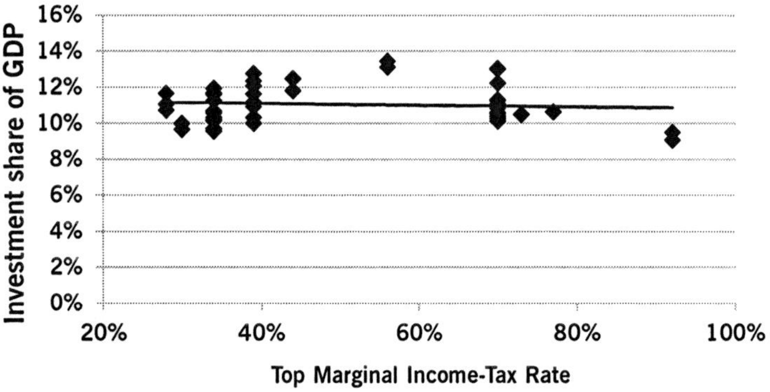

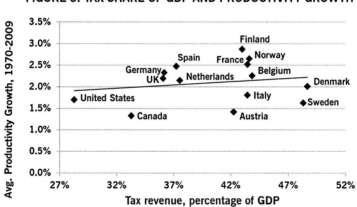

Cutting taxes on the richest Americans has not led them to invest more in plant and equipment. Over the past 50 years, as tax rates have declined, there has been no increase in investment spending as a percentage of GDP. (The flat trend line shows that changes in the highest marginal income-tax rate have not affected investment much, one way or the other.) Instead, the investment share of the economy has been determined by other factors, such as aggregate demand, rather than tax policy.

FIGURE 5: TAX SHARE OF GDP AND PRODUCTIVITY GROWTH

Despite lower and declining tax rates, especially on the rich, the United States has had slower productivity growth over the last several decades than other advanced economies. Overall, lower taxes are associated with slower growth in GDP per hour worked. A 10 percentage point increase in taxes as a share of GDP is associated with an increase in the productivity growth rate of 0.2 percentage points. ❑

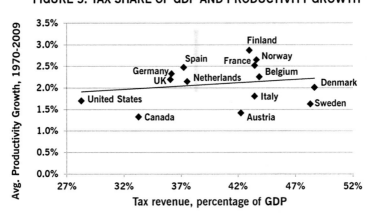

Sources: Tom Petska and Mike Strudler, "Income, Taxes, and Tax Progressivity: An Examination of Recent Trends in the Distribution of Individual Income and Taxes" (Statistics of Income Division, Internal Revenue Service, 1997); Thomas Hungerford, "Taxes and the Economy: An Economic Analysis of the Top Tax Rates Since 1945" (Congressional Research Service, 2012); *Economic Report of the President, 2012*; Bureau of Economic Analysis (bea.gov); Organization of Economic Cooperation and Development, OECD STAT.

Article 2.4

THE $17 TRILLION DELUSION

BY MARTY WOLFSON
January/February 2014; updated November 2016

$17,000,000,000,000

President Obama boasted last week that he had signed legislation to lift "the twin threats" to our economy of government shutdown and default. But what was done to fix the problem of growing debt that leads Washington to repeatedly raise the debt ceiling? Nothing. In fact, by Friday, the U.S. debt had rocketed past $17 trillion. What does this mean? At $17 trillion, this number has passed total U.S. gross domestic product (GDP), the measure of all that is produced in the economy.

Since Obama took office, the national debt has increased from about $10.6 trillion to more than $17 trillion—a 60 percent increase. ...Meanwhile, entitlement spending—the key driver of spending and debt—remains unaddressed.

> —"Debt Hits $17 Trillion," The Foundry: Conservative Policy News Blog from the Heritage Foundation, October 21, 2013

Shortly after the ceiling on federal debt was raised on October 17, 2013, the conservative Heritage Foundation notified its readers that the outstanding debt of the United States had "rocketed past $17 trillion," and that "entitlement spending—the key driver of spending and debt—remains unaddressed." The three assumptions in that statement—that the true measure of our debt is $17 trillion, that the cause of the buildup of debt is entitlement spending, and that therefore the appropriate policy to "address" this problem is to cut Social Security benefits and other "entitlements"—are endorsed by many politicians and policy pundits in Washington. But they're all wrong as economic analysis and disastrous as policy recommendations.

Seventeen trillion dollars certainly sounds like a big, scary number, especially when national debt clocks tell us that this translates into more than $53,000 for every person in the United States. But it is the wrong number to focus on.

The $17 trillion figure is a measure of "gross debt," which means that it includes debt owed by the U.S. Treasury to more than 230 other U.S. government agencies and trust funds. On the consolidated financial statements of the federal government, this intragovernmental debt is, in effect, canceled out. Basically, this is money the government owes itself. What is left is termed "debt held by the public." It is this measure of debt that is relevant to a possible increase in interest rates due to competition for funding between the private and public sectors. It is also the category of government debt used by the Congressional Budget Office and other analysts. (Of course, the full economic significance of any debt measure needs to be considered in context, in relationship to the income available to service the debt.) The total debt held by the public is $12 trillion.

The Social Security Trust Fund owns $2.7 trillion of the $5 trillion of Treasury securities held in intragovernmental accounts. In fact, Social Security is the largest single owner of Treasury securities in the world, surpassing even China's significant holdings of $1.3 trillion.

Social Security accumulated all these Treasury securities because of the way that its finances are organized. Social Security benefits to retirees (and to the disabled) are paid for by a payroll tax of 12.4 % on workers' wages (with 6.2% paid by the worker and 6.2% paid by the employer), up to a limit, currently $113,700. If, in any year, Social Security revenue is greater than what is needed to pay current retiree benefits, the surplus must, by law, be invested in Treasury securities (most of which are "special obligation bonds" issued only to the Social Security Trust Fund).

Since 1983, workers have been paying more in Social Security taxes than what was needed to pay retiree benefits. A special commission, appointed by President Reagan and chaired by future Federal Reserve Chair Alan Greenspan, recommended several changes to increase the revenue received by the Social Security Trust Fund. Most prominent among these changes was an increase in the payroll tax rate to its current level of 12.4%, although the Commission also recommended reductions in benefits, including a gradual increase in the retirement age from 65 to 67. The effect of the changes would be to create significant surpluses in the Social Security Trust Fund. The thinking was that, if in the future payroll taxes fell below benefits, the Trust Fund could draw upon the accumulated surpluses to pay benefits.

Therefore, the $2.7 trillion of Treasury securities held by the Trust Fund came about not because entitlements are out of control and the government has been forced to borrow to meet retiree benefits, but rather because future retirees have paid more taxes than necessary to meet benefit obligations. Workers have essentially been prepaying into the Trust Fund in order to provide for their future benefits.

So it makes no sense to try to solve the supposed problem of too much government debt by cutting benefits for current and future Social Security recipients. These workers were asked to help keep Social Security solvent by paying increased payroll taxes. As a result, the gross federal debt increased. It would be totally unfair and irrational to cut benefits now because these workers had sacrificed in the past. That would be hitting them with a double burden, the second burden of benefits cuts incurred because there was the first burden of overpaying payroll taxes into the Trust Fund.

What's more, the strategy the Heritage Foundation advocates would make the alleged problem they are claiming to address even worse. That's because cutting benefits would mean that payroll taxes would more easily meet retiree benefits, and so the surplus accumulating in the Social Security Trust Fund would be greater. Since the Trust Fund is required by law to invest its surpluses in Treasury securities, a greater surplus translates into more bonds being accumulated by the Trust Fund, and therefore a higher gross federal debt (assuming that Treasury borrowing from other sources remains the same). So cutting Social Security benefits in order to reduce the $17 trillion debt would produce the contradictory result that the debt would be even higher than it would have been without the benefit cuts. Even if Congress decided to reduce overall borrowing in step with lower Social Security benefits, there would still be no positive effect on federal debt: the lower borrowing would be balanced by the increase in Treasury securities held by the Trust Fund. Thus, in neither case would the goal of reducing outstanding gross federal debt be achieved.

Despite the 1983 changes to Social Security, the Trustees, the board that oversees Social Security, stated in their 1995 annual report that the 75-year projection of Social Security finances was no longer in "close actuarial balance" and that the long-range deficits should be "addressed." In 2002, they began to be more specific: "Bringing Social Security into actuarial balance over the next 75 years could be achieved by either a permanent 13-percent reduction in benefits or a 15-percent increase in payroll tax income, or some combination of the two."

Of course, the assumptions used by the Trustees, their policy approach, and the need for benefit cuts are all a matter of dispute. However, had benefits been cut by 13% beginning in 1996, total reductions would have totaled $1 trillion by 2012. So the Trust Fund would have accumulated that much more in Treasury securities, and the gross debt would actually have increased to $18.2 trillion.

In reality, the bonds in the Social Security Trust Fund are primarily a political accounting device to remind us that we as a society have promised a certain level of benefits to Social Security retirees. It is true that at some point the Trust Fund will most likely need to redeem the bonds in order to pay full benefits to retirees. And it is true that the government will need to raise the funds to do this, either by borrowing from the public (selling Treasury bonds) or through increased tax revenue. But this is the case because we promised benefits to these retirees, not because there is a certain level of bonds in the Trust Fund. The benefits would be due retirees whether or not there are bonds in the Trust Fund.

So the real issue is whether or not society will keep its commitment to retirees. The agenda of those who say we have to cut benefits is really that they don't want to meet this commitment. We should recognize that this is their agenda, and not let them hide behind the smokescreen of supposedly out-of-control federal debt.

Update, November 2016

Two years later, the numbers are somewhat different, but the analysis remains the same. Instead of $17 trillion, the gross debt at the end of 2015 was $18.1 trillion. Treasury securities held in intergovernmental accounts remained at $5.0 trillion and public debt increased to $13.1 trillion.

The Social Security Trust Fund increased its holdings of Treasury securities slightly, to $2.8 trillion, compared to China's holding of $1.2 trillion. The payroll tax is still 12.4%, but the wage ceiling is now $118,500. Had Social Security benefits been cut by 13% starting in 1996, they would have amounted to $1.2 trillion by 2015.

Therefore cutting benefits would actually have increased gross debt to $19.3 trillion at the end of 2015. Such a policy makes the supposed debt problem worse and continues to be unfair and punitive to workers who have already contributed so much. So the real question remains: will we keep the commitment we have made to retirees? ❑

Sources: Congressional Budget Office, "Federal Debt and the Statutory Limit," November 20, 2013; Financial Management Service, United States Department of the Treasury, "Monthly Treasury Statement," October 2013; United States Department of the Treasury, "Treasury International Capital System, Monthly Foreign Holders of Treasury Securities," October 2013; The Annual Report of the Board of Trustees of the Federal Old-Age and Survivors Insurance and Federal Disability Insurance Trust Funds, various years; Office of the Chief Actuary, Social Security Administration, Statistical Tables, Benefit Payments by Calendar Year.

Article 2.5

WHAT COULD SANDERS HAVE DONE?
The Dynamic Effects of Seven Sanders Initiatives

BY GERALD FRIEDMAN
November/December 2015; updated December 2016

No one should be surprised by the popular support that Sen. Bernie Sanders (I-Vt.) attracted in his run for president as a democratic socialist. Nor should we be surprised that he drew attacks charging that his policies would have bankrupted the United States. Sanders' proposals for infrastructure, early-childhood education, higher edu-cation, youth employment, family leave, private pensions, and Social Security would have totaled over $3.8 trillion over 10 years. While this is a large number, it would be barely 6% of federal spending for 2017-2026. Apart from any benefits these programs would bring directly, their cost would be reduced in four ways: Two operate by offsetting current spending and tax policies—either by replacing existing federal spending or reducing tax breaks currently subsidizing private spending. The other two, which account for over 70% of the cost reduction, would have been "dynamic effects" by increased economic growth—boosting tax revenues and reducing federal safety-net spending when the economy expands.

FIGURE 1: ADDITIONAL SPENDING AND OFFSETING COST REDUCTIONS

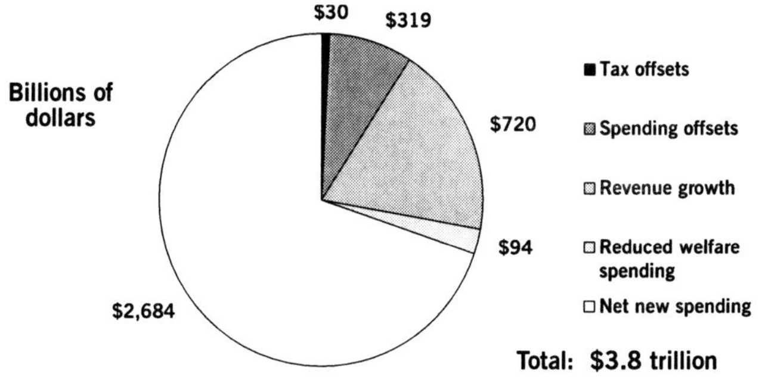

Billions of dollars

$30 $319

$720 ■ Tax offsets

$94 ▨ Spending offsets

☐ Revenue growth

☐ Reduced welfare spending

☐ Net new spending

$2,684

Total: $3.8 trillion

A quarter of new spending could have been offset by savings and by faster economic growth. The ongoing effects of the Great Recession that began in 2007 have left many resources underutilized. By putting unemployed workers and discouraged workers (who have stopped looking for jobs) back to work, the Sanders program would have increased economic activity and government revenues while reducing spending on safety-net programs like Supplemental Nutrition.

Taking these dynamic effects into account, the net cost to the public treasury would have been about $2.7 trillion, instead of $3.8 trillion, over 10 years. That is, over a quarter of the total tab would have been offset by reductions in other forms of government spending and by increased tax revenue derived from faster economic growth.

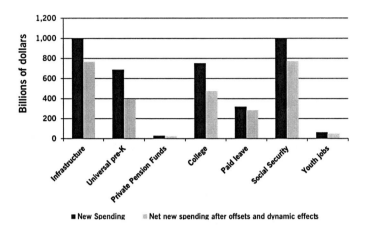

FIGURE 2: NEW SPENDING PROGRAMS AND NET COSTS AFTER OFFSETS AND DYNAMIC EFFECTS

Each of the seven spending proposals would have had offsets and dynamic effects. Universal childcare and free college tuition, for example, would replace existing spending on programs for childcare assistance and much of the spending on Pell Grants for students at public colleges, spending on infrastructure would off-set some required maintenance spending, and raising Social Security benefits would allow some seniors to avoid dependence on Supplemental Nutrition (SNAP) and other safety net programs. The programs would also have increased tax revenues by eliminating some existing "tax expenditures"—tax breaks that subsidize private spending—like deductions for employer-provided child care.

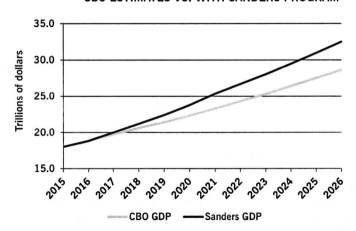

FIGURE 3: PROJECTED GROSS DOMESTIC PRODUCT (GDP), CBO ESTIMATES VS. WITH SANDERS PROGRAM

Sanders would have accelerated the recovery from the Great Recession. Nine years after the beginning of the Great Recession, the American economy remains depressed. While the economy has been growing steadily since the end of 2009, output remains substantially below capacity. Only 59% of the adult population is employed, down from over 63% before the recession and the lowest level in 30 years. I estimate that increased government spending in the Sanders program would increase GDP growth rates for 2017-2026 enough to have raised 2026 GDP by $4 trillion.

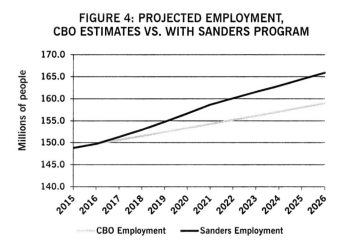

FIGURE 4: PROJECTED EMPLOYMENT,
CBO ESTIMATES VS. WITH SANDERS PROGRAM

The Sanders program would have added six million new jobs. The Congressional Budget Office (CBO) projects that, due to sluggish economic growth, the percentage of the working-age population employed will fall between now and 2026, from 59% to 57%. The Sanders program would have directly created jobs in infrastructure, in child- care services, in higher education, and for young people. It would also have created additional jobs indirectly, as the newly employed and others spend their additional income. All told, the program would have added six million jobs by 2026.

FIGURE 5: PROJECTED FEDERAL SPENDING, PERCENT OF GDP, CBO ESTIMATES VS. WITH SANDERS PROGRAM

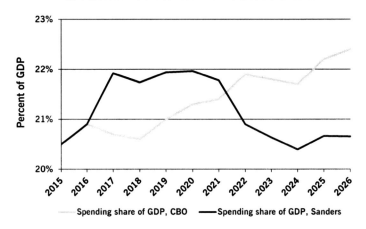

Spending share of GDP, CBO —— Spending share of GDP, Sanders

Government spending would have declined relative to GDP within the decade.
Federal spending would have initially increased faster than GDP under the Sanders
program. After 2021, however, federal spending would be lower as a percentage
of GDP than it would be under Congressional Budget Office (CBO) projections,
because of the strength of the economic recovery engendered by the Sanders stimulus.
This is actually a conservative estimate of the boost to GDP because it does not include
the productivity-raising effects of infrastructure spending and increased education. ❑

Sources: Laurence M. Ball, Daniel Leigh, and Prakash Loungani. "Okun's Law: Fit at Fifty?"
Working Paper, National Bureau of Economic Research, January 2013 (nber.org); Congressional
Budget Office, "Estimated Impact of the American Recovery and Reinvestment Act on
Employment and Economic Output from October 2012 Through December 2012," February
2013 (cbo.gov); Congressional Budget Office, "How CBO Analyzes the Effects of Changes in
Federal Fiscal Policies on the Economy," November 2014 (cbo.gov); "Friedman Analysis of HR
676: Medicare for All Would Save Billions—PNHP's Official Blog," accessed Jan. 24, 2014
(pnhp.org); Gerald Friedman, "An Open Letter to the *Wall Street Journal* on Its Bernie Sanders
Hit Piece," The Huffington Post, accessed Oct. 3, 2015 (huffingtonpost.com); Gerald Friedman,
"Universal Health Care: Can We Afford Anything Less?" *Dollars & Sense*, July/August 2011
(dollarsandsense.org); Keith Hall, "How CBO Will Implement Dynamic Scoring: Presentation
at the Heritage Foundation," Heritage Foundation: Congressional Budget Office, June 17, 2015
(cbo.gov); Laura Meckler, "Price Tag of Bernie Sanders's Proposals: $18 Trillion," *Wall Street
Journal*, Sept. 14, 2015 (wsj.com); Congressional Budget Office, "The 2015 Long-Term Budget
Outlook," accessed Sept. 21, 2015 (cbo.gov).

Chapter 3

MONEY, BANKING, AND FINANCE

Article 3.1

ABOLISHING THE FED IS NO SOLUTION TO A REAL PROBLEM

BY ARTHUR MacEWAN
July/August 2012

> Dear Dr. Dollar:
> Is the Federal Reserve, the Fed, as important to the operation of the economy as it seems? How does it work? If it is so important, how can anyone take seriously politicians such as Ron Paul, who calls for the Fed's abolition?
> —*Tom Prebis, Cleveland, Ohio*

Yes, the Federal Reserve, the central banks of the United States, is a powerful institution, important to the operation of the economy. By regulating the supply of money and influencing (if not fully determining) interest rates, the Fed has a major impact on the overall level of production, employment, and inflation. Also, the Fed has a large role (along with some other agencies) in regulating the operations of banks.

Yet the Fed is structured in a very undemocratic way. Although it derives its authority from Congress, its actions do not have to be approved by Congress, the president or any other segment of the government. Its funding is not set by Congress, and the members of its Board of Governors (the controlling group), though appointed by the president and approved by Congress, have terms that span multiple presidential and congressional terms. Also, while the Fed regulates the banks, bankers have a special role in the operation of the Fed. Some seats on the boards of directors of the twelve regional branches are reserved for bankers, giving them formal capacity to influence the Fed's policies, including its regulation of the banks.

Not surprisingly, the Fed has exercised its regulation of the banks with "a light hand." And its overall regulation of the economy—through affecting the money supply and interest rates—has often sacrificed employment to maintain the profitability of business in general and the banks in particular.

The Banks' Man at the Fed

To get some useful insight on the undemocratic and pro-business bias of the Fed, consider:

Jaimie Dimon, the head of JPMorgan Chase, is a member of the Board of Directors of the Federal Reserve Bank of New York. Cheek by jowl with Wall Street, the N.Y. Fed plays a major role in the dealings between the Fed and the large private banks. As the financial meltdown became apparent in 2008, the N.Y. Fed was fully involved in the actions that the Fed and the Treasury took in their efforts to manage the crisis.

Dimon's bank is one of the country's largest, with $19 billion in after-tax profits in 2011. In 2008, the bank received $25 billion in the government's bank bailout. Perhaps the bailout saved the economy from a more severe economic crisis, but it also saved the bankers—Dimon and the others—along with their absurd salaries. Other means of saving the system—such as temporary nationalization of the big banks (to say nothing of a permanent nationalization)—were never on the Fed's agenda.

Dimon has become one of the most vociferous and aggressive opponents of bank regulation. In 2012, he has frequently been in the news because his bank experienced a huge loss—at least $3 billion and perhaps as much as $9 billion—in a complex and risky operation, exactly the kind of banking activity that regulation is supposed to prevent, and exactly the kind of activity that could generate another financial crisis. Dimon has not moderated his opposition to regulation.

Does anyone see anything wrong here? Does the metaphor "fox guarding the henhouse" seem appropriate?

It is only a slight simplification to say that the Fed is run by and for the country's banks. If one believes that the interests of the banks are the same as the interests of the rest of us, no problem. This is the line that Dimon peddles, claiming that the banks play a crucial role in allocating funds to the most productive activity, supporting economic growth and jobs. More regulation, he claims, would prevent banks from doing this good work. In the wake of the financial crisis, it is impressive that anyone can spew such nonsense with a straight face.

Regulating the Economy

The Fed plays its role of affecting the money supply and interest rates by, in part, loaning money to the banks and then regulating the extent to which the banks can use this money to make loans to the businesses and public. More loans means more money in circulation; more money in circulation tends to reduce interest rates (i.e., the price of money), which tends to induce economic expansion. Also, in regulating the banks' activities, the Fed is supposed to maintain economic stability—preventing the banks from undertaking excessively risky activities, which, by endangering the banks themselves, would undermine the operation of the whole economy.

In the period leading up to the financial crisis that emerged in 2007-2008, the Fed certainly operated "with a light hand" in regulating the banks. Indeed, Fed Chairman Ben Bernanke took a "what, me worry?" approach, denying the existence of the housing bubble and turning a blind eye to the signs of impending crisis.

Having failed to use its power to prevent the financial crisis, the Fed has in subsequent years attempted to push economic growth by acting to increase the money supply and to keep interest rates low. Its success in this direction has been limited partly because it has not pushed as hard as it could. Right-wing congressmen and others of their ilk have accused the Fed of encouraging inflation, and perhaps Bernanke and others on the Fed's Board of Governors share this inflation fear. In earlier periods, the Fed has often given attention to maintaining low inflation at the expense of higher unemployment.

The Fed's lack of success in promoting economic growth in the current period also results from the fact that private non-financial firms have been reluctant to make new investments, even with low interest rates. So instead of making new loans for productive, job-generating investment, banks have used the low-cost money from the Fed for their own speculative activity—the sort of activity that led to JPMorgan Chase's multi-billion dollar loss, but which can also make lots of money for the banks.

The Appeal of "End the Fed"

Given the Fed's history of frequently sacrificing employment in the name of preventing inflation, its support of banks and the role of bankers in affecting its operations, its failure to prevent the recent financial crisis, its role in bailing out the banks and the bankers, and its failure to act strongly enough in the current period, there is a good deal of animosity towards the country's central bank. Ron Paul and others have been able to use this popular animosity to promote a broader agenda of reducing government regulation of the economy. Their call to "end the Fed" is one more effort to push the idea that the economy works best when the government works least. One would think that this is a pretty hard line to swallow in light of recent experience, when the "light hand" of government regulation was a key element in generating our current economic malaise. Yet it seems to have appeal.

In advocating an end to the Fed, Paul has called for a return to the gold standard as a means to regulate the money supply without government involvement. Ironically, at the center of Paul's right-wing attack on the Fed has been the claim that it has debased our currency and is generating inflation; the gold standard would supposedly prevent this debasement. The argument is ironic because reality has often been the opposite of Paul's claim—at many times in its history Fed policies have kept inflation in check but generated high unemployment, which tends to keep wages down.

In any case, the problem with the Fed is not the existence of a government authority that regulates the country's money. Before the Fed started operating in 1914, economic crises had been at least as frequent and severe as in later years. The gold standard (which the U.S. abandoned in steps, especially in the 1930s and ultimately in 1971) certainly did not provide stability and general economic well-being. The problem is the *nature* of the regulatory authority, run as it is in the interests of the banks and bankers, in particular, and of business, in general. The right's effort to "end the Fed," however, would likely throw us into an era of even greater economic instability, having us jump out of the frying pan and into the fire.

What to Do?

So what should be done about the Fed? Unfortunately, the Fed is part of the general economic and political problems of the country, and we should not expect to have a central bank that serves people's real needs until we have a more democratic society, a society in which money does not dominate politics and in which economic policy is not organized around the idea that maintaining profits is always the first priority.

Still, doing something about the Fed could be one step in doing something about those general problems. To begin a process of change, Dimon and other bankers should be removed from their positions of authority within the Fed. The removal of bankers from their positions of special influence would need to be followed by larger changes in the way members of the boards of directors of the regional Federal Reserve banks are chosen, and ultimately also the way members of the Board of Governors of the Fed are selected. Also, the Fed could be given a stronger mandate to act in ways that would reduce unemployment. Most generally, the goal should be to subject the Fed to democratic control.

At the end of the day, changing the Fed—changing how the U.S. economy is controlled—is a part of the larger struggle to change power in the United States so that it is in the hands of most people instead of the very few. ❑

Article 3.2

WHY THE SHIFT FROM PRODUCTION TO SPECULATION?

BY ARTHUR MacEWAN
May/June 2014

Dear Dr. Dollar:
Why has our economy switched so greatly away from manufacturing that produces real goods and services that provide real value and towards speculative,
financial activity—everything from mergers and acquisitions to derivatives,
off-shore tax shelters, and other scams? —*Glen W. Spielbauer, Dallas, Tex.*

The rising role of finance has certainly had all of these impacts (the "scams" you
mention). Also, the switch to finance was at the center of the housing bubble,
the collapse of the bubble, and the onset of the Great Recession. The switch to
finance, however, was not a switch of the economy as a whole; that is, financial firms
do not account for a growing share of output (GDP) or employment. The long-term
decline in manufacturing has been balanced by the expansion of "services that provide real value"—education and health care, for example.

The switch to finance is a switch in terms of where profits are being obtained and,
along with the profits, very high salaries. In the late 1960s, profits of financial firms
accounted, on average, for less than 14% of all U.S. corporate profits. In the years 2000
to 2012, financial firms were taking in 30% of corporate profits. In 2004, they peaked at
42.5% of corporate profits. (See graph.) Financial firms' profits, however, have been vola-
tile: In 2008 their share plummeted to only 10.2%. The 2004 and 2008 figures represent
the highest and lowest shares of corporate profits obtained by the financial industry since
at least 1965. Since 2008, the financial share has risen back up to over 27%.

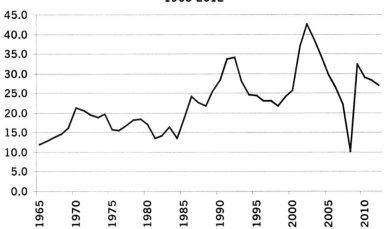

PROFITS OF FINANCIAL FIRMS, PERCENT OF ALL CORPORATE PROFITS, 1965-2012

Source: Economic Report of the President 2014, Table B-6.

Several factors, intertwined with one another, account for the rise of financial profits. One factor has been the generally slow growth of the U.S. economy since the 1960s. Slower growth reduced the opportunities within the United States for profitable investments in real production. So firms and people with money shifted towards financial investments.

At the same time as the economy was growing less rapidly, a larger share of income was being captured by people with high incomes—apparent in both the greater income inequality among households and the smaller share of income going to labor as opposed to capital (i.e., profits, rent, and other forms of property income). So as opportunities for profits from real investment were poor, firms and wealthy people had more money to invest.

These changes were both cause and effect of a shift in class power, as the high-income segment of the population had an increasing impact on government policy—both directly and through the corporations they controlled. They used this power to establish policies that weakened labor (e.g., undermining labor unions and the minimum wage) and gave greater leeway to the operations of firms (deregulation).

Deregulation was beneficial to firms in many sectors of the economy, but was especially important for the financial sector. Financial firms were able to undertake all sorts of highly risky—but also highly profitable—activities, such as the speculation in derivatives that set the stage for the Great Recession. Formal deregulation and the informal deregulation through lack of enforcement of still-existing regulations allowed the expansion of fraudulent activity, especially, for example, in making mortgages.

The rapid development of information technology also played a role. The advent of the computer age made it possible for financial firms to engage in actions that were not possible in an earlier era. For example, the explosion of the market for complex new financial instruments like "credit default swaps" and "collateralized debt obligations" and the advent of high-frequency trading in which nano-seconds matter could not have taken place without computer technology.

The switch to finance has been quite damaging. Speculative activity involves a real waste of resources—both capital and skilled labor that might be used for socially valuable production. Financial firms and their apologists claim that the firms make a socially valuable contribution by allocating capital to activities where it is most productive. But any examination of their activity shows that much, if not most, is no more productive than other forms of gambling—it is essentially rigged gambling. Also, the shift to finance has made a significant contribution to income inequality, with the firms' executives making up a substantial share of the infamous 1%. And along with all this, there is the role of finance in generating the Great Recession. Not a pretty picture. ❑

Article 3.3

IT'S TIME TO TREAT BANK CEOs LIKE ADULTS

BY DEAN BAKER
September 2016

The country's major banks are like trouble-making adolescents. They constantly get involved in some new and unimagined form of mischief. Back in the housing bubble years it was the pushing, packaging and selling of fraudulent mortgages. Just a few years later we had JP Morgan, the country's largest bank, incurring billions in losses from the gambling debts of its "London Whale" subsidiary. And now we have the story of Wells Fargo, which fired 5,300 workers for selling phony accounts to the bank's customers.

It is important to understand what is involved in this latest incident at Wells Fargo. The bank didn't just discover last month that these employees had been ripping off its customers. These firings date back to 2011. The company has known for years that low-level employees were ripping off customers by assigning them accounts—and charging for them—which they did not ask for. And this was not an isolated incident, 5,300 workers is a lot of people even for a huge bank like Wells Fargo.

When so many workers break the rules, this suggests a problem with the system, not bad behavior by a rogue employee. And, it is not hard to find the problem with the system. The bank gave these low level employees stringent quotas for account sales. In order to make these quotas, bank employees routinely made up phony accounts. This practice went on for five years.

As it became aware of widespread abuses, it's hard to understand why the bank would not change its quota system for employees. One possibility is that they actually encouraged this behavior, since the new accounts (even phony accounts) would be seen as good news on Wall Street and drive up the bank's stock price.

Certainly Wells Fargo CEO John Stumpf, as a major share and options holder, stood to gain from propping up the stock price, as pointed out by reporter David Dayan. In keeping with this explanation, Carrie Tolsted, the executive most immediately responsible for overseeing account sales, announced her resignation and took away $125 million in compensation. This is equal to the annual pay of roughly 5,000 starting bank tellers at Wells Fargo. That is not ordinarily the way employees are treated when they seriously mess up on the job.

Regardless of the exact motives, the real question is what will be the consequences for Stumpf and other top executives. Thus far, he has been forced to stand before a Senate committee and look contrite for four hours. Stumpf stands to make $19 million this year in compensation. That's almost $5 million for each hour of contrition. Millions of trouble-making high school students must be very jealous.

There is little reason for most of us to worry about Stumpf contrition, or lack thereof. His bank broke the law repeatedly on a large scale. And, he was aware of these violations, yet he nonetheless left in place the incentive structure that caused them. In the adult world this should mean being held accountable.

This is not a question of being vindictive towards Stumpf, it's a matter of getting the incentives right. If the only price for large-scale law breaking by the top executives of the big banks is a few hours of public shaming, but the rewards are tens of millions or even hundreds of millions in compensation, then we will continue to see bankers disregard the law, as they did at Wells Fargo and they did on a larger scale during the run-up of housing bubble.

There is another aspect to the Wells Fargo scandal that is worth considering. Insofar as the bank was booking revenue on accounts that didn't exist, it was also ripping off the banks' shareholders. The shareholders' interests are supposed to be protected by the bank's board of directors.

It doesn't seem the shareholders got much help there. It is a very prominent group, including Elaine Chao, a member of President George W. Bush's cabinet (and Senate majority leader Mitch McConnell's wife) and Frederico Peña, a member of President Bill Clinton's cabinet. Of course the board also includes Mr. Stumpf as chair.

It's hard not to wonder if the board ever asked questions about the large number of employees being fired for creating phony accounts. Did the board ever ask if they could get a CEO who was just as good for lower pay? For example, could they have paid Stumpf or his replacement half as much ($9.5 million a year) and gotten someone just as good, or would this person only have needed to fire 2,650 employees for ripping off the bank's customers.

The odds are that none of the board members asked these sorts of questions. After all, they were pocketing an average of more than $250,000 a year for very part-time work. They probably didn't give much thought as to whether they were serving shareholders well. In corporate America, and especially at the big banks, no one is expected to act like adults, they understand it is about stuffing your pockets at everyone else's expense. ❑

Article 3.4

THE FED RAISES INTEREST RATES ... BY PAYING THE BANKS

BY MARTY WOLFSON
January/February 2016

The business and financial press has been abuzz with speculation about when the Federal Reserve would begin raising interest rates. After the meeting of its Federal Open Market Committee (FOMC) on December 15-16, the Fed ended the suspense by announcing that it was raising its target federal funds rate by a quarter of a percentage point (to a range of 0.25 to 0.50%). Flying under the radar, though, was the Fed's use of a dramatically different method of raising interest rates. The new method involves paying billions of dollars to banks, primarily by paying interest on banks' reserves held at the Fed. The payments will reduce the amount of money that the Fed remits to the Treasury and, ultimately, to taxpayers.

Why Is the Fed Paying the Banks?

This new method is best understood when viewed in the context of the recent financial crisis. The collapse of the housing bubble in 2007 threatened both the financial system and the broader economy. The Federal Reserve began a campaign of aggressively reducing interest rates, lowering the interest rate that it controls, the federal funds rate, from its peak of 5.25% in September 2007 to just 2% in April 2008. The federal funds rate is an interest rate that banks pay when borrowing from other banks. Lower costs for the banks in turn lead to lower interest rates for business and consumer borrowing, thus encouraging greater spending, output, and employment.

In making these changes to the federal funds rate, the Fed used its classic method of changing the level of bank reserves. (See sidebar, p. 48.) It is this method that the Fed jettisoned when it announced its new procedures.

After the failure of Lehman Brothers in September 2008, financial markets became unsettled and many of the traditional funding sources for financial institutions dried up. Into this void stepped the Federal Reserve, which dramatically increased its lending and other interventions to help the banks. In the process, it pumped money into the banking system and expanded bank reserves, significantly beyond the level of reserves necessary to maintain its target for the federal funds rate.

On October 1, 2008, the Federal Reserve began to pay interest on bank reserves. Then-Fed Chair Ben Bernanke, in his recent memoir, gave this reason for the change: "The concern in 2008 was that emergency lending would lead short-term interest rates to fall below our federal funds target and thereby cause us to lose control of monetary policy."

In other words, without paying interest on reserves, banks would have so many excess reserves that did not earn any interest, and be so eager to gain at least some return on them, that the Fed would be unable to prevent them from lending at rates below the Fed's target for the federal funds rate (2% at that time). By paying interest on reserves, the Fed would eliminate banks' incentive to lend at rates below those it was receiving from the Fed.

This, however, is a curious explanation. The Fed dropped its target federal funds rate by 0.5% on October 8, 2008, and then by another 0.5% on October 29. On December 16, it lowered its target all the way to zero (a band of 0 to 0.25%), where it has stayed for seven years. Why was it concerned about the federal funds rate falling below its target rate when it was in the process of dropping its target rate to zero?

Moreover, in October 2008 the economy was moving into free fall. Real gross domestic product (GDP) fell at an annual rate of 8.2% in the fourth quarter of 2008 and unemployment was increasing rapidly. The Fed explained that it reduced the federal funds rate to zero "in order to provide stimulus to household and business spending and so support economic recovery." So why was the Fed giving the banks an incentive to keep their excess reserves at the Fed rather than lend them out?

The Fed's action can perhaps be understood by examining how it interprets its objectives. In addition to its mandates affecting employment and inflation, the Fed is also responsible for promoting financial stability. For the Fed, this means easing panic in financial markets, but also protecting the viability and profitability of the banks, especially those judged to be systemically important.

Promoting financial stability in the fall of 2008 meant the necessary step of intervening aggressively to prevent the collapse of the global financial system. But the Fed also interpreted it to mean bailing out large banks, even if the process did not sufficiently curtail the banks' power and risky practices. And it meant paying interest on reserves. Such payments directly boosted bank profitability, even if they may have come at the expense of the broader economy.

The Classic Method of Affecting Interest Rates: Change the Level of Bank Reserves

Banks are required to hold cash in proportion to the amount of their deposits. This cash is termed bank reserves. (Currently, the reserve requirement is 10% of the total amount deposited in checking accounts.) Banks hold some of this cash in their vaults in order to meet requests for withdrawals, but typically much of it is held as deposits with the Fed.

Some banks hold more reserves than they need to satisfy reserve requirements, but some find themselves with a deficit. Those banks needing reserves typically borrow them from banks with a surplus. The interest rate that banks charge to lend their reserves to other banks is called the federal funds rate.

When the Fed wants to lower the federal funds rate, as it did in 2007-08, it buys government securities and writes a check to the seller. When the seller deposits the check in a bank, the bank sends the check to the Fed, which then credits the bank with more reserves. A greater amount of reserves in the banking system reduces the need for borrowing to meet reserve requirements, and the federal funds rate falls.

Likewise, when the Fed wants to increase the federal funds rate, it sells government securities. The buyer gives a check to the Fed written on the buyer's bank, and the Fed reduces the amount of reserves the bank has on deposit with the Fed. The bank, now short of reserves, seeks to borrow them from other banks and is willing to pay an increased federal funds rate in order to do so.

The reserves not needed to meet reserve requirements are called excess reserves. Up to 2008, the Fed did not pay any interest on excess reserves. To earn interest, banks lent out the cash to businesses and consumers and thereby encouraged greater spending. In this way, excess reserves were usually kept relatively low.

The Implications of Quantitative Easing

With the federal funds rate at zero, the Federal Reserve began its program of "quantitative easing." This involved buying longer-term assets, U.S. Treasury securities as well as mortgage-backed securities. The Fed's stated objective was to reduce long-term interest rates so as to stimulate spending in housing and business investment.

There were three stages of quantitative easing, and interest rates did indeed fall. But, again, the Fed also had its eye on the banks. After the financial crisis, the demand for mortgage-backed securities fell, since massive numbers of mortgages were in default and payments on the securities were therefore down. As demand fell, the prices of the mortgage-backed securities plummeted. Many of the banks held large quantities of these securities. By purchasing so many of them, the Fed supported their prices and increased their value on the banks' balance sheets.

As a result of its quantitative easing programs, the Fed dramatically expanded its holding of assets. At the end of 2008, it owned less than half a trillion dollars in Treasury securities and no mortgage-backed securities. By November 2015, it held $2.5 trillion in Treasuries and $1.8 trillion in mortgage-backed securities. Because buying all these securities meant that the Fed's checks became reserves for the banks, and because the banks were paid for keeping these reserves with the Fed, excess reserves ballooned to $2.5 trillion.

The Fed's announcement on December 16 that it is raising its target for the federal funds rate does bring to the fore Bernanke's concern in 2008: how to increase the federal funds rate when there are so many excess reserves. The Fed ruled out any largescale reduction of excess reserves when it also announced on December 16 that it would not be reducing its large holdings of securities. By not selling securities, the Fed would not be accepting checks from bank accounts and thus not reducing the reserves the banks hold on deposit with the Fed.

The Fed's solution, instead, is to double down and increase the payment of interest on bank reserves. It announced that it will begin paying interest on reserves at 0.5%. This procedure won't reduce reserves, but will give banks an incentive not to make loans at interest rates below the amount they can get from the Fed.

However, this will not totally solve the Fed's problem. Even when it was paying the banks 0.25% interest on reserves, the effective federal funds rate (the rate at which reserves at the Fed were actually being traded) was below 0.25%. This is why the Fed adopted a range for the federal funds rate of 0-0.25%.

The reason the Fed could not keep the federal funds rate at 0.25% was because financial institutions other than banks participate in the federal funds market. In particular, government-sponsored enterprises (GSEs) like Fannie Mae, Freddie Mac, and the Federal Home Loan Banks are allowed to keep funds at the Fed but are not paid interest on them. In recent years the Home Loan Banks have become the main lender in the federal funds market. (They were established during the Depression to lend to savings and loan associations to support housing, but now lend mainly to banks.)

The Home Loan Banks were able to lend federal funds at interest rates below 0.25% and still make a profit. In turn, banks were able to take the borrowed funds and deposit them with the Fed at 0.25%, making a profit as well.

So when the Fed on December 16 established a range of 0.25-0.50% for the federal funds rate, it also announced a new procedure designed to keep the federal funds rate from falling below 0.25%. The new procedure is to conduct overnight reverse repurchase agreements (ON RRP) with the Home Loan Banks (as well as with banks, other GSEs, and money market mutual funds, which are important lenders in short-term markets).

ON RRP is an imposing-sounding term, but reflects a relatively simple process: the Fed sells government securities to the financial institutions on one day and then buys them back the next. The financial institutions are essentially making an overnight loan to the Fed, with the securities as collateral.

But here's the point: the money the Fed pays to buy back the securities is not only a repayment of the original loan. It also includes an interest payment. And the Fed plans to pay interest at 0.25%, the bottom of its target for the fed funds rate, thus giving the Home Loan Banks an incentive not to lend at less than 0.25%. Although it plans to use ON RRP as a secondary tool to its main focus of paying interest on bank reserves, it anticipates that both of these tools will keep the fed funds rate within its target range of 0.25-0.5%.

It seems that the Fed has backed itself into a corner, where the only way to raise the federal funds rate is to increase its payments to financial institutions. With reserves held at the Fed equal to $2.6 trillion, even a 0.5% payment to the banks would cost $13 billion. And, of course, including the expense of the ON RRP program and increasing the fed funds rate in the future would add even more to the cost.

To add insult to injury, 25 minutes after the Fed's announcement on December 16, Wells Fargo Bank reported that it is raising its prime rate (an interest rate tied to business and consumer loans) by 0.25% but not the rates it pays to depositors. Later in the day other large banks, including JP Morgan Chase and Bank of America, made similar declarations.

Is There an Alternative?

Could the Fed, instead, choose not to pay interest to the banks and other financial institutions? This would have the effect of reducing excess reserves, but it would also mean that the Fed would have to delay raising interest rates.

That would, in fact, be a good policy decision. Although the unemployment rate is 5.0%, inflation is still below the Fed's 2% target. In the late 1990s, under then-Chair Alan Greenspan, the Fed allowed unemployment to fall below 4% without an appreciable increase in inflation. If the Fed waits, it could see how far excess reserves would fall without the payment of interest on reserves and how far the unemployment rate would fall without pushing inflation above 2%.

But what if a growing economy and a falling rate of unemployment edged the inflation rate past 2%, say, to 3 or 4%? The top 1% of the income distribution would not like inflation to eat away at their accumulated wealth. However, during times of very low unemployment the demand for workers can be strong enough to push money wages up faster than prices, so workers without a job and those who haven't seen a raise in many years would probably not be unhappy.

Under current Chair Janet Yellen, the Federal Reserve has shown a genuine concern about unemployment, but it is still trapped in its assumptions: There is a "maximum feasible" level of employment. Above that level (or below the corresponding rate of unemployment) inflation will exceed its 2% target. The conclusion from these assumptions is that the Fed should raise interest rates to prevent employment from exceeding the "maximum feasible" level.

Instead, the Fed should adopt a real full-employment target: a job for everyone who wants to work. It should adopt a "minimum feasible" target for inflation: the lowest possible rate compatible with full employment. We need a policy perspective in which economic justice for workers is a higher priority than paying the banks. ❑

Article 3.5

HOW PRIVATE EQUITY WORKS—AND WHY IT MATTERS

BY ROSEMARY BATT AND EILEEN APPLEBAUM
November/December 2015

Private equity (PE) firms are financial actors that raise billions of dollars in investment funds each year. They use these funds to buy out well-performing companies using high amounts of debt, take them private, and promise their investors outsized returns in the process. They advertise that they improve the operations of companies they buy. Sometimes they do. But more often PE firms engage in financial engineering techniques that extract wealth from companies and leave them more financially at risk than before—and sometimes bankrupt. While discredited as "leveraged buyouts" in the 1980s, these tactics have returned with a vengeance in the last fifteen years. And they are perfectly legal.

PE firms typically charge pension funds and other investors an annual management fee of 2% of capital committed to the private equity fund. Not satisfied with these payments for managing their private equity funds, PE firms also charge investors in their funds numerous other fees and expenses. This part isn't always legal: In May 2014, the Securities and Exchange Commission (SEC) revealed that its examinations of PE funds had uncovered numerous examples, some bordering on outright fraud, where PE firms had inappropriately charged fees and expenses to pension funds and other investors. In 2015, Fenway Partners, Blackstone, and KKR were the first PE firms to pay fines to the SEC to settle charges—a meager $80 million among the three.

Management fees are specified in contracts between private equity funds and the investors in these funds. But these are not the only fees that PE firms charge. They typically claim 20% of any profit the PE fund realizes on its investments as a bonus or performance fee. This performance fee—so-called "carried interest" taxed at half the rate of ordinary income—is generally not reported to investors. Private equity funds simply report returns net of these performance fees. But these fees cut deeply into the returns earned by pension funds and other private equity investors—and workers, retirees, and taxpayers have a right to know how large these payments are.

Private Equity: The Impact

Between 2000 and 2014, U.S. private equity firms invested $5.2 trillion in 32,200 leveraged buyouts that affected some 11.3 million workers in U.S. companies—considerably more than the number of workers who are currently union members. Over that period, the number of active PE firms globally grew from under 1,500 to over 3,500—a 143% rise. And, while PE investments fell sharply during the Great Recession, they have since largely recovered their pre-crisis levels. Currently, there are 3,883 U.S. private equity firms and 12,992 PE-owned companies headquartered in the United States.

In our book, *Private Equity at Work: How Wall Street Manages Main Street*, we explain how private equity firms have become such an important force in the economy and why regulators need to rein in their activities. That is because they are investors that actively manage the companies they buy, but are treated as passive investors and not held accountable for their actions. Before a company is ever purchased, the general partners of the PE fund (who make all decisions for the fund) develop a plan for how much debt can be leveraged on the company, how the company's cash flow will be used to service the debt, and how the PE firm will exit the company at a profit within a five-year window. They oversee company operations; make decisions that affect workers jobs, pay, and pensions—and then walk away. While law treats PE funds as investors, they behave as managers and employers in the companies they own.

Sometimes private equity does perform as advertised—providing access to management expertise and financial resources that help small companies grow and improve their competitiveness. Small companies have relatively few assets that can be mortgaged, but many opportunities for operational improvements in information technology, accounting, management, and distribution systems. Most PE investments, however, are in larger companies that already have modern management systems in place and also have substantial assets that can be mortgaged. Here, private equity firms use debt and financial engineering strategies to extract wealth from healthy companies, and workers, managers, and suppliers often pay the price. Job destruction outweighs job creation.

Private equity affects the lives of Americans in many ways—as workers, retirees, consumers, renters, and community members. Despite the fact that private equity ownership often leads to job and wage loss for workers, pension funds ("workers' capital") account for fully 35% of all investments in PE funds. Most workers do not know that their retirement savings are invested in these funds and may be putting other companies and their workers at risk. And despite the hype, these investments often don't yield the high returns for retirement funds that private equity firms promise. Moreover, since the Great Recession, private equity and hedge funds have bought up more than 100,000 troubled mortgages and are renting them back to people who lost their homes. In October 2015 alone, Blackstone bought up 1000 rental units in New York City as well as the City's iconic rent-controlled Stuyvesant Town-Peter Cooper Village—making the PE firm one of the city's largest landlords.

Case Study: Michael's Stores

Private Equity firms Bain and Blackstone used most of the tactics described here when they bought arts-and-crafts supplies retailer Michael's Stores in 2006 and took it private.

At the time, the company had 1,108 stores employing about 43,100 workers and $3.9 billion in sales. Its high sales revenue, healthy profits, and low debt made it an attractive takeover target. But the leveraged buyout saddled the chain with a $4 billion dollar debt. Bain and Blackstone also had Michael's sign a management services agreement through 2016 for an annual fee of $12 million—including a stipulation that if the company went public or was sold, the PE sponsors would continue to collect the fees for the remaining years of the contract even though the services would never be provided. In 2013, the PE funds did a dividend recapitalization, which yielded them $714 million, or about 70% of what the PE funds had invested. When Michael's went public in June 2014, it still carried long-term debt of $3.7 billion, and it had to pay the PE firms $30 million to cover the years remaining on the management services contract.

How Do Private Equity Firms Make Money?

Debt, or "leverage," is at the core of the private equity business model. (Hence the term "leveraged buyout.") Debt multiplies returns on investment and the interest on the debt can be deducted from taxes owed by the acquired (or "portfolio") company. Private equity partners typically finance the buyout of a Main Street company with 30% equity coming from the PE fund and 70% debt borrowed from creditors—the opposite of the 30% debt and 70% equity typical of publicly traded companies. Private equity funds use the assets of the portfolio company as collateral, and put the burden of repaying the debt on the company itself.

The private equity firm also has very little of its own money at risk. The general partners of a PE fund typically put up $1 to $2 for every $100 that pension funds and other investors contribute. PE partners invest less than 1% of the purchase price of acquired companies (2% of the 30% equity is $0.02 \times 0.30 = 0.006$, or 0.6%). Yet they claim 20% of any gains from the subsequent sale of these companies.

In other words, PE firms play with other people's money—money contributed by pension funds and other investors in its funds and borrowed from creditors. Leverage magnifies investment returns in good times—and the general partners of the PE fund collect a disproportionate share of these gains. But if the debt cannot be repaid, the company, its workers, and its creditors bear the costs. The private equity business model is a low-risk, high-reward strategy for the PE firms and their partners.

Post buyout, PE firms often engage in financial engineering that further compromises their portfolio companies.

- They may have portfolio companies take out loans at "junk bond" rates and use the proceeds to pay themselves and their investors a dividend—a so-called "dividend recapitalization."

- They may sell company assets and claim the proceeds for themselves. They may split an asset-rich company into an operating company (OpCo) and a property company (PropCo) and sell off the real estate. Proceeds of the sale are used to repay the investors, while the operating company must lease back the property, often at inflated rates. Companies in cyclical industries are especially at risk of failure as owning their property provides a buffer against market downturns. For example, the Darden Restaurants sold its struggling Red Lobster restaurant chain to the PE firm Golden Gate, which immediately sold off most of Red Lobster's property and used the proceeds to repay most of the equity investment of the PE firm and its investors. The restaurants, however, now have to pay rent, and their annual earnings are cut substantially.

- They may "waive" the management fees they charge their limited partners in exchange for a higher share in the profits, which are then taxed at the much lower capital gains tax rate, rather than as ordinary income. The IRS recently released guidance making it crystal clear that this violates tax law.

CalPERS (Finally) Releases Data on Performance Fees Paid to Private Equity

On November 24, 2015, CalPERS, the large California public employee pension fund, released long-awaited figures on the amounts it has paid private equity firms in performance fees—so-called "carried interest" that is taxed at the lower capital gains rate rather than as ordinary income. For years, the pension fund failed to ask the PE firms for this information or to report on these fees. Recently this changed under pressure from unions, media, and the tax-paying public. As widely anticipated, the number is ginormous. Over the 25 years since 1990, CalPERS acknowledges it has paid $3.4 billion in performance fees—a number it admits understates the full amount paid.

Private equity has persuaded public pension funds that its high management and performance fees are warranted by exceptionally high returns on private equity investments, but the evidence is weak. Moreover, because private equity investments are risky and require a 10-year commitment by pension fund investors, returns need to be high enough to be worth the risk and long-term investment—about three percentage points higher than stock market returns according to CalPERS benchmark. Unfortunately, half of the PE funds launched after 2005 have failed to beat this benchmark, and this is true of the PE funds in which CalPERS is invested. CalPERS's PE investments failed to beat its own benchmark in three-year, five-year and ten-year time frames.

More recently, having failed to meet their strategic objective to "maximize risk-adjusted rates of return," CalPERS staff proposed removing the requirement from the pension fund's PE policy. However, we and others concerned about the fund's risky investments urged CalPERS board members to vote it down, which they did at their December 14 meeting.

- They may require portfolio companies to pay monitoring or "consulting" fees to the PE firm for unspecified services. Payment of the fees reduces the companies' cash cushion and puts them at risk in an economic downturn. The Securities and Exchange Commission (SEC) has found that many PE firms fail to share this fee income with their investors, as legally required. Moreover, in some cases where the monitoring fee contract fails to specify the services to be provided, these payments may actually be dividends (which are not tax deductible) disguised as monitoring fees (which are)—and this tactic allows the portfolio company to reduce its tax liabilities.

- Monitoring-fee contracts typically have a term of ten years, even though the PE firms expect to re-sell portfolio companies in three to five years. As a result, at the time of the re-sale, the remaining years in the contract must be paid off, even though the PE firm will never provide any services once the company is sold.

What Happens to Companies and Workers?

The results of financial engineering are predictable. The high debt levels of highly leveraged companies make them much more likely to default on their loans or declare bankruptcy. And in cyclical industries, companies that have to pay rent rather than own their own property are more likely to go under in a recession. As we report in our book, a 2008 study by the World Economic Forum found that for the period 1980-2005, PE-owned companies were twice as likely to go bankrupt as comparable publicly owned companies. Another study of more than 2,000 highly leveraged companies found that, during the last recession (from 2007 to the first quarter of 2010), roughly a quarter of them defaulted on their debts. The financial crisis officially ended in 2009, but bankruptcies among private equity owned companies continued through 2015. Energy Future Holdings (EFH), for example, was acquired in 2007 by a PE consortium led by KKR and TPG and defaulted in 2014 with the largest debt for any leveraged buyout on record—$35.8 billion. By mid-2014, nine other private-equity owned companies defaulted on $6.5 billion in bonds and institutional loans. By 2014, defaults on the high-yield and leveraged loans that financed the 2004-2007 boom in leveraged buyouts affected a total of $120 billion (out of nearly $500 billion) in bonds and institutional loans.

In 2015, Harrah's (now known as Caesar's Entertainment) also declared bankruptcy. The company, with 30,440 unionized employees, was acquired in 2006 by Apollo Global Management and Texas Pacific Group (TPG Capital). By June of 2007, the casino chain's long-term debt had more than doubled. The gambling industry slumped in the recession and Harrah's struggled under its debt burden. The company cut staff, reduced hours, outsourced jobs, and scaled back operations, but in the end was not able to meet its debt obligations.

These examples of job loss following private equity takeovers are backed by rigorous economy-wide statistical studies by economists at Chicago, Harvard, and Maryland universities. One study, covering the period 1980-2005, found that post-buyout, private-equity-owned establishments and companies had significantly lower levels of employment and wages than their publicly traded counterparts. In the year of the PE buyouts, the target companies had higher levels of wages and employment growth than comparable public companies. Post-buyout, however, both wages and employment levels were lower in the PE-owned companies. Depending on the data and estimation techniques, PE-owned establishments registered employment levels that were, in the first two years after the buyout, 3.0 to 6.7% lower than similar establishments; after five years, 6% lower.

Bankruptcies of PE-owned companies threaten not only workers' jobs, but also their defined-benefit pensions. In typical bankruptcy proceedings, the pension plan can make its case for better treatment of workers under a court-approved Plan of Reorganization. If the bankrupt company is unable to fulfill its pension obligations, then an insurance program run by the Pension Benefit Guarantee Corporation (PBGC) provides employees with basic benefits, although not at the level they would have received had the pension remained solvent. In light of the higher rates of bankruptcy in PE-owned companies, the PGBC has disproportionately absorbed the pension liabilities of these companies.

Private equity firms have figured out a number of ways to take advantage of the bankruptcy code and more easily shift pension liabilities to the PBGC. One strategy is to use a special provision in the code—Section 363—that allows for the streamlined sale of company assets, including auctioning off the entire assets of a company without first putting in place a Plan for Reorganization for the distribution of proceeds. While the secured creditors get paid, there is no requirement to renegotiate

---

Dumping Pension Plans

A Sun Capital private equity fund bought Friendly's Ice Cream Restaurant chain in a leveraged buyout in 2007. Sun Capital immediately sold much of the company's real estate and leased the property back to Friendly's outlets. After a series of cutbacks and layoffs, it filed for bankruptcy in November 2011. Soon after, Friendly's was acquired by another Sun Capital-sponsored PE fund in a Section 363 bankruptcy sale, with its pension obligations offloaded onto the PBGC. Sun Capital was able to retain ownership of Friendly's, but neither the PE firm nor any of its funds had any responsibility for the pensions of Friendly's 6,000 employees and retirees. Oxford Automotive and Relizon, among other companies, also went bankrupt while in private equity hands and were also sold from one affiliate of a PE firm to another affiliate.

Private equity funds' strategies to avoid pension liabilities are particularly offensive given that pension funds represent over one-third of the investors in PE. These pension funds are in the contradictory position of hoping to benefit from activities that sometimes undermine the retirement security of beneficiaries in funds like their own. This raises troubling questions: are the actions of pension funds that invest in private equity consistent with the interests and values of their own members?

Finally, private equity firms have sought to avoid liability under the Workers Adjustment and Retraining Notification (WARN) Act, which requires companies that close down plants to give workers 60 days' notice and pay, whether or not they continue to work. In the recent case of PE-owned Golden Guernsey dairy, OpenGate Capital has argued that it is not liable under the WARN Act. In a surprising verdict in October 2015, the court ruled that OpenGate Capital was indeed responsible for back pay under the law.

---

pension obligations—typically the largest unsecured creditor in a bankruptcy case. As a result, pension liabilities typically get shifted to the PBGC, and employees receive only the basic guaranteed retirement benefits.

Section 363 sales were extremely rare in the 1990s (only 4% of large publicly traded companies), but they represent 21% of bankruptcies in the 2000s. According to the PBGC, employees and retirees lost more than $650 million in 363 sales of bankrupt companies owned or controlled by private equity firms from 2003 to 2012. Exploitation of the 363 loophole, in addition, has severely strained the financial stability of the PBGC in recent years.

How Should Private Equity Be Regulated?

Private equity partners act as managers and employers of the companies they take over, even though the law treats them as passive investors in the companies they own. Several legal and regulatory changes would curb the negative effects of private equity on companies and working people, while preserving the benefits of private pools of capital to stimulate growth and development in small and mid-sized companies.

A simple first step is greater transparency. With the exception of a few large publicly traded firms (including Blackstone, Apollo, and Carlyle), PE firms face far less stringent Securities and Exchange Commission (SEC) reporting requirements than public corporations, and very little of what they report can legally be made public. And privately owned PE portfolio companies have no reporting requirements at all. Even the limited partners who invest in private equity have little information about, for example, how decisions are made or how fund performance is measured.

Limiting the amount of debt that can be loaded onto portfolio companies is critical to reduce the risk of bankruptcy by PE-owned companies. Federal bank regulators took a first step in 2013 by issuing guidelines effectively reducing the willingness of banks to make loans that raise a company's debt level above six times its earnings. This has had some effect on PE firms' ability to overleverage the companies they acquire. But KKR and other large PE firms have responded by making loans available to other PE funds for leveraged buyouts. More direct steps to limit excessive use of debt include limiting the tax deductibility of interest payments or simply capping the use of debt over a certain percentage of the purchase price.

Eliminating the "carried interest" loophole in the capital gains tax would make the tax code fairer. This loophole lets private equity general partners pay the capital gains tax rate on their share of PE fund profits. Profit-sharing income of other managers, meanwhile, is taxed at the higher rate applied to ordinary income. More broadly, the carried-interest tax loophole comes at the expense of other taxpayers, who must either pay higher taxes or receive fewer or lower-quality public services. Changing the tax code to eliminate the loophole would also have the positive effect of reducing the incentive to load acquired companies with excessive levels of debt.

Reforms are also needed to hold private equity partners accountable for their actions as managers and employers in the same way as public corporations are. Private equity general partners make decisions that affect a portfolio company's debt structure, operations, human resources management, staffing levels, and plant closures. The PE firm and its funds are not passive investors and should be viewed, along with the portfolio company, as the joint employer of the portfolio company's workers. Employment laws such as the WARN Act and Employee Retirement Income Security Act (ERISA) need to be updated to explicitly reflect this new reality. Loopholes in the bankruptcy code must be closed to prevent PE firms from offloading pension liabilities onto the PBGC.

In sum, a set of legal and regulatory changes are needed to ensure that PE firms are transparent and accountable for their actions, that they pay their fair share of taxes, and that they assume the same liability as publicly traded companies for any negative effects of their actions on the jobs, incomes, and pensions of the workers in the companies they own. ❏

Sources: Eileen Appelbaum and Rosemary Batt, *Private Equity at Work: When Wall Street Manages Main Street* (Russell Sage Foundation, 2014); Steven J. Davis, John C. Haltiwanger, Ron S. Jarmin, Josh Lerner, and Javier Miranda, "Private Equity and Employment," National Bureau of Economic Research, NBER Working Paper 17399, 2011 (nber.org); Matthew Goldstein, "As Banks Retreat, Private Equity Rushes to Buy Troubled Home Mortgages," *New York Times*, Sept. 28, 2015 (nytimes.com); Andrew McIntyre, "5 Firms Steer $690M Deal for Manhattan Rental Portfolio," Law360, Sept. 11, 2015 (law360.com); Private Equity Growth Capital Council, "Private Equity by the Numbers" (pegcc.org); Eileen Appelbaum, "CalPERS Releases Data on Performance Fees Paid to Private Equity," Center for Economic Policy Research blog, November 25, 2015 (cepr.net/blogs/cepr-blog).

Chapter 4

SOCIAL POLICY

Article 4.1

THE BIG LIE ABOUT THE "ENTITLEMENT STATE"

BY ALEJANDRO REUSS
November/December 2012

> In 1960, government transfers to individuals totaled $24 billion. By 2010, that total was 100 times as large. Even after adjusting for inflation, entitlement transfers to individuals have grown by more than 700 percent over the last 50 years. ...
>
> There are sensible conclusions to be drawn from these facts. You could say that the entitlement state is growing at an unsustainable rate and will bankrupt the country.
>
> —David Brooks, "Thurston Howell Romney," *New York Times*, September 17, 2012

Is the view that "entitlements"—government programs like Social Security, Medicare, and Medicaid—"will bankrupt the country" a "sensible conclusion"? No. It's scare-mongering of the "OH MY GOD WE'RE ALL GOING TO DIE!" variety, completely unjustified by a sober look at data on government transfer payments between 1960 and 2010.

New York Times columnist David Brooks starts the passage on entitlements in his September 17 column by noting that total government transfer payments have increased by an alarming-sounding 100 times over the last half-century. In the next sentence, he acknowledges that this figure is not adjusted for inflation. (Nor for population growth.) As it turns out, the "100 times" mostly reflects the increase in the general price level (more than seven-fold between 1960 and 2010) and the growth of the U.S. resident population (not quite doubled), not the growth in transfer programs specifically. Correcting for these factors, Brooks admits, the increase is just "700 percent." One can only guess that he switched to percentage terms because he's trying to sound scary, and "700 percent" sounds far scarier than "seven times." (Brooks actually describes this figure simply as "after adjusting for inflation," but it appears that he actually adjusted for both inflation and population growth.)

That's as far as Brooks gets, so he misses another crucial adjustment. The average income in the United States is far greater today than it was in 1960.

Real GDP per capita grew by more than two-and-a-half times between 1960 and 2010. Now, looking at real entitlements spending per capita relative to real GDP per capita (or just real entitlements spending relative to real GDP), the growth over the last 50 years is down to less than three-fold. It makes perfect sense that cash benefits programs like Social Security—which send people checks and allow them to spend the money as they see fit—should grow with increasing incomes. These programs are meant to help people maintain something resembling the customary standards of living of today, after all, not those of the Eisenhower era.

With a few sensible adjustments, then, Brooks' alarming initial figure of "100 times" vanishes almost into thin air. That still leaves, however, an increase of a little less than three times. What accounts for that?

To begin with, over 70% of the increase in social benefits at all levels of government, over the half century between 1960 and 2010, is accounted for by three programs: Social Security, Medicare, and Medicaid. Two of these, Medicare and Medicaid, did not even exist in 1960. (Social Security, meanwhile, did not cover anywhere near the percentage of the labor force it covers today.) It is rather disingenuous to bemoan the "unsustainable growth" of certain government programs, over a certain period, when they did not even exist at the beginning of that period.

More generally, the growth in the Big Three social-benefits programs is the combined result of several different effects. Party, it reflects changes in the demographic composition of the population. Social Security and Medicare primarily benefit the elder population. This age group has grown as a percentage of the overall U.S. population because people are, on average, living longer and because the demographic "bump" of the baby-boom generation is beginning to reach retirement age. Partly, the increase reflects the growth in medical costs, which has been faster than the increase in the general price level. Finally, it reflects the expansion of benefits associated with these programs (Social Security retirement benefits, for example, are tied to lifetime earnings, so as earnings go up so do benefits).

Even aside from the numbers, Brooks is fundamentally wrong that transfer programs can "bankrupt the country." Transfer programs, like their name suggests, transfer income from one part of the population to another. Social Security, for example, is primarily an intergenerational transfer program. It taxes current workers to fund benefits for current retirees. (Most people pay taxes that fund other people's benefits, during one part of their lives, and then receive benefits paid for by other people's taxes, during another part.) The "losses" for those who are paying the taxes, at any given time, are not losses to society as a whole. They are balanced by the gains to those who are receiving the benefits.

In another sense, the benefits to everyone covered by these programs greatly exceed just the cash amount of the transfers. Social Security provides not only a retirement annuity (insurance against destitution during old age), but also disability benefits (insurance against being unable to work) and survivors' benefits (insurance for family members against the death of a financial provider). Medicare and Medicaid, meanwhile, pay for medical services and prescription medicines. These programs, in short, offer meaningful protection against many of life's possible calamities.

When we think of costs (of a government program or of something else) to "society as a whole," we need to think about the use of real resources—a part of society's total labor time, buildings, tools, etc.—that could have been used for some other purpose. The real costs of the Big Three transfer programs, in this sense, fall into two categories.

First, there are costs involved in administering the programs. The work hours and other resources (office buildings, desks, chairs, computers, electricity, pencils, paper clips, etc.) used to keep program records, send out benefits checks, and so on, could have been used for something else. So those represent real costs to society. In the case of the major transfer programs, however, the administrative costs are very small relative to the total benefits paid. The costs of administering Social Security, for example, are less than 1%.

Second, there are real costs for the goods and services for which government transfers pay. Medicare and Medicaid, for example, pay medical practices, hospitals, medical-supply companies, and pharmaceutical manufacturers to deliver medical care and medicines to program beneficiaries. Total transfer program costs, therefore, have increased along with rising medical costs. Part of the reason for rising medical costs has been that people now receive medical services they once could not. Magnetic resonance imaging (MRI) scans, for example, were not widely available two decades age. Now they are. Another is the rising real incomes of (some) medical professionals and the burgeoning profits of pharmaceutical manufacturers. Perhaps the most important, however, is that the U.S. health-care delivery system has enormous administrative costs, far above those of other high-income countries.

Advocates of single-payer (public) health insurance point out that such a system could 1) rein in pharmaceutical costs by using the government's purchasing power to negotiate lower prices and 2) dramatically reduce administrative costs by eliminating the crazy quilt of different private-insurance billing systems. Maybe David Brooks should start a clamor about that.

Two obvious ways to pay for growing transfer programs, from a public-finance standpoint, are: First, keep government revenue the same, but change its uses. For example, the United States could fight fewer wars, have a smaller military, and buy less military hardware. Or it could liberalize laws on recreational drug use, and reduce spending on police, courts, and prisons. (Or both!) It could use some of the savings to fund the Big Three and other social programs. Second, increase government revenue. Contrary to current mythology, the U.S. population is not being taxed to the very limits of its endurance. Of thirty high-income OECD countries, the United States ranks dead last in total tax revenue (for all levels of government) as a percentage of GDP, at less than 25%. The figure is 30% or more for 24 of the 30 countries, and over 40% for eight.

Brooks acts as if budget issues are one-sided: a matter only of how much a particular program or combination of programs costs. This one-sided view is especially evident in U.S. political discourse on deficits, which politicians and commentators often frame as a problem of excessive spending. A budget deficit, however, is the difference between expenditures and revenue—it is an inherently two-sided issue—so looking at the expenditures side alone doesn't help us understand the causes of deficits or the possible policy responses.

Could the U.S. government just raise more revenue, as a percentage of GDP, to pay for transfers that have grown as a share of GDP? Well, somehow a couple of dozen other countries seem to manage. So probably yes. ❏

Sources: Bureau of Economic Analysis, National Income and Product Accounts, Table 3.1.Government Current Receipts and Expenditures (bea.gov); Bureau of Labor Statistics, Consumer Price Index - All Urban Consumers (Series ID: CUSR0000SA0) (bls.gov); Bureau of Economic Analysis, National Income and Product Accounts, Table 1.1.3. Real Gross Domestic Product, Quantity Indexes (bea.gov); U.S. Census Bureau, Population Estimates (census.gov); Social Security Administration, Actuarial Publications, Administrative Expenditures (ssa.gov); OECD Tax Database, Table A. Total tax revenue as percentage of GDP (oecd.org/tax).

Article 4.2

THE ACA AND THE U.S. HEALTH CARE MESS

BY GERALD FRIEDMAN
January/February 2014

While it was enacted in 2010 without a single Republican vote, the Patient Protection and Affordable Care Act (ACA), a.k.a. "Obamacare," was built on a model first proposed by the conservative Heritage Foundation in the 1990s and implemented by Republican Governor Mitt Romney in Massachusetts in 2006. The ACA extends the public safety net to more of the working poor but otherwise keeps the private health insurance system intact. Rather than replacing the private system—and far from the "government takeover of health care" its critics claim—it provides subsidies for individuals to buy private health insurance through state-level "exchanges."

As social policy, the ACA is a qualified failure. The expansion of Medicaid and mandates for individuals to buy subsidized private insurance will expand health insurance to an additional 30 million people. Regulations establishing minimum standards for coverage and barring exclusions for pre-existing conditions will improve coverage for many. On the other hand, by maintaining the existing system of for-profit medicine and private insurance, the ACA does little to rein in out-of-control cost growth while leaving millions without coverage. We can hope that the ACA's strengths and its failures will soon pave the way for a rational universal system such as single payer health care.

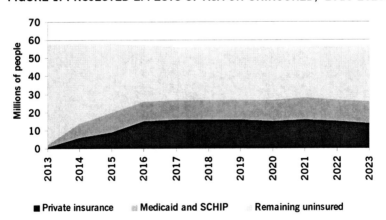

FIGURE 1: PROJECTED EFFECTS OF ACA ON UNINSURED, 2013-2023

While the ACA will provide health insurance to millions of Americans, millions of others will remain uninsured. While over 25 million will gain coverage either through the expansion of Medicaid or by buying subsidized private insurance, somewhat more will remain without coverage. Some are not covered by the act (including undocumented immigrants); others will be excused from the requirement to have insurance because of cost; and others will not comply.

FIGURE 2: COST-RELATED ACCESS PROBLEMS

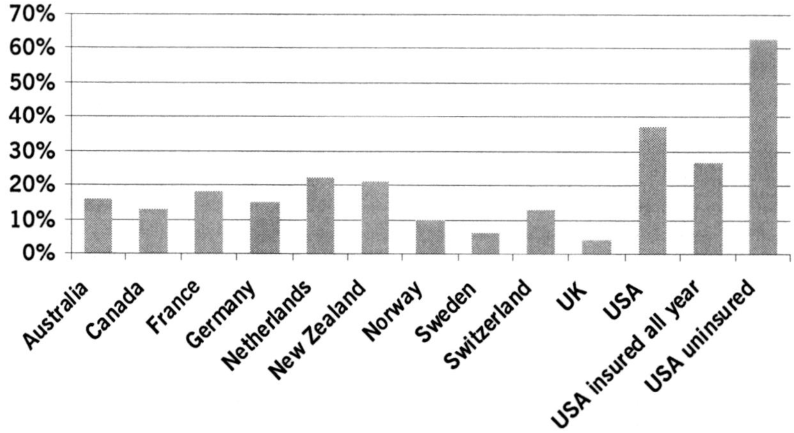

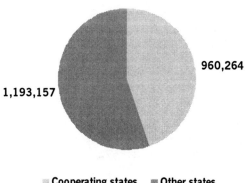

Because it builds on the existing private health-insurance system, the ACA does little to reduce access problems for people with health insurance. Those with insurance have dramatically fewer problems accessing health care (including seeing doctors and filling prescriptions) than those without. But even insured Americans are twice as likely as citizens of countries with public insurance to have trouble getting care.

The ACA's Medicaid expansion would cover everyone with incomes up to 133% of the federal poverty level. Half the states, all with Republican governors, rejected expansion, denying coverage to 7.5 million people. States can establish "health exchanges" for people to choose a health plan and sign up for federal subsidies. Republicans refused to establish exchanges in 34 states.

After a much-publicized slow start, enrollment picked up in states with their own exchanges. Problems with the federal website slowed errollment elsewhere, though it soon surged as well. Including those newly covered by the Medicaid expansion, the ACA extended coverage to about 4% of the uninsured in non-cooperating states, compared to over 15% of those in the cooperating states, by January 2014. If the proportion enrolling were the same in the non-cooperating states as in states with their own websites, an additional 4 million Americans would have had health insurance by then.

FIGURE 3: EXCHANGE ENROLLMENT, THROUGH JANUARY 14, 2014

960,264

1,193,157

■ Cooperating states   ■ Other states

FIGURE 4: PROJECTED EFFECTS OF THE ACA ON HEALTH SPENDING, BY SOURCE, 2010-2022

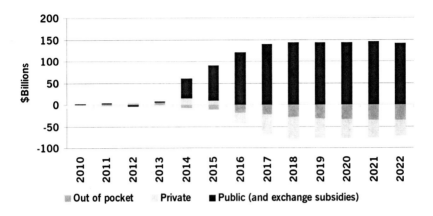

The ACA will reduce out-of-pocket spending on uncovered expenses, deductibles, and copayments. Federal subsidies will reduce premiums while coverage expansion will lower reduce hospital surcharges for the uninsured. Public spending will increase, on Medicaid and subsidies; expenditures paid for with other savings taxes on expensive insurance plans, and increases in the Medicare payroll tax for high-income individuals. Taxing the rich to provide health care for the working poor, the ACA is the largest redistributive program enacted since the 1960s.

FIGURE 5: HEALTH CARE SPENDING AS A PERCENTAGE OF GDP, ACA VS. SINGLE PAYER, 2006-2022

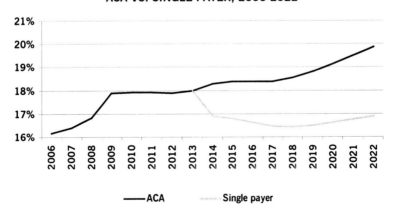

The ACA does not establish a sustainable health-care finance system in the United States. Under the ACA, health care spending will continue to increase significantly faster than the economy as a whole and the share of the economy going towards health care will rise in the next decade to nearly 20%. By controlling administrative costs and drug prices, a single-payer system can hold healthcare spending to less than 17% of the GDP. ❏

Sources: Congressional Budget Office (cbo.gov); Centers for Medicare and Medicaid Statistics (cms.gov); Gerald Friedman, "Funding HR 676: The Expanded and Improved Medicare for All Act: How we can afford a national single-payer health plan," Physicians for a National Health Program (pnhp.org); Cathy Schoen, et al., "Access, Affordability, and Insurance Complexity" Health Affairs, Nov. 18, 2013; Kaiser Family Foundation (kff.org); CNN.com, "Obamacare: Enrollment numbers and Medicaid expansion."

Article 4.3

WHY FREE HIGHER ED CAN'T WAIT
Students are rising up to demand free higher education.

BY BIOLA JEJE AND BELINDA RODRIGUEZ
March/April 2016

During the October 2015 Democratic presidential debate, Bernie Sanders offered an accurate assessment of what it will take to make free higher education a reality in the United States. "If we want free tuition at public colleges and universities," Sanders said, "millions of young people are going to have to demand it."

This is exactly what is starting to happen across the country. In recent months, we have witnessed an inspiring upsurge in mobilization around the demand, leading up to the Million Student March. On November 12, 2015, students rose up to demand free higher education, cancelation of all student debt, and a $15 minimum wage for all campus workers. The March marked the beginning of an exciting political moment that included over 100 actions carried out across the country with support from major progressive organizations and labor unions. The mobilizations coincided with a wave of protest in solidarity with students demanding racial justice at the University of Missouri. On many campuses, students combined their protests, producing stunning turnout in the hundreds and even thousands.

Why We Need It

Vermont senator and Democratic presidential hopeful Bernie Sanders has come out in support of free public higher education as part of his campaign platform. Sanders' plan calls for the elimination of tuition at four-year public colleges and universities. This would be paid for through the implementation of a financial transaction tax, which at 0.5% on Wall Street transactions could raise close to $300 billion a year.

Sanders is not alone. For years, students and advocates have been pushing for free higher education, citing many other countries where it has been free for decades. Free education could help us solve some of today's key economic problems. The bar is getting higher for well-paid jobs, with most requiring a college degree, while tuition and fees at universities are rising at staggering rates. Student debt in the United States has reached a record total of over $1.3 trillion. The average individual debt has now grown to $35,000, while wages barely keep up with inflation. The United States is clearly in need of a deep restructuring in terms of how workers are prepared to enter the labor market.

Free—totally free—higher education is key not only to solving the problem of student debt in this country, but also to responding to the demands of our changing economy and the mounting challenges ahead. By "free" we mean four years of tuition-free public higher education, and at the same time expanding financial aid to cover other costs associated with attendance (food, housing, books, etc.).

Senator Sanders summarized the predicament succinctly during the first Democratic debate: "A college degree today ... is the equivalent of what a high-school degree was 50 years ago. And what we said 50 years ago and a hundred years ago is that every kid in this country should be able to get a high-school education regardless of the income of their family. I think we have to say that is true for everybody going to college."

Education, Jobs, and Debt

Until recent years, the main story told by mainstream economists to explain unequal job prospects and growing income inequality was one of "skill-biased technological change." Technological change had reduced the demand for farming labor, manufacturing labor, and routine clerical work, with demand rising for professional and managerial roles that required specialized training. Outsourcing of low-skilled labor, they added, also contributed to this shift.

The trends in manufacturing employment seem to confirm this explanation. In 1990, the manufacturing sector was the leading employer in 37 U.S. states. By 2013, that number dropped to just seven, with health care and social services providing the most jobs in 34 states. Of over 3.85 million job openings in the U.S. in June 2015, only about 300,000 were in manufacturing. Nearly 1 million were in healthcare and education services—with many of those jobs undoubtedly requiring at least a bachelor's degree, and some requiring more advanced degrees.

But that's not the whole story. Demand for "low-skilled" workers has not vanished. "Low-skilled" jobs in retail trade, hospitality, and other sectors have represented a growing share of total employment in recent decades, and accounted for about 1.25 million job openings in June 2015. Despite growth in these sectors, wages are stagnant for middle-income workers and declining for low-wage workers. Economists like former Secretary of Labor Robert Reich, once an advocate of the skill-biased technological change theory (and a campaigner for education and job training as the main cures for economic inequality), have now abandoned the theory—emphasizing instead inequality in market and political power as the key sources of economic inequality.

Economic disparities play a huge role in determining who has access to a college education, and therefore who can compete in our changing economy. Low-income students and students of color are less likely to be able to afford the rising costs of higher education, and are getting shut out of opportunities. Enrollment rates are dropping (down by nearly 2% for the fall 2015 semester, compared to a year earlier), drop-out rates are increasing, and it is taking students longer and longer to complete their degrees due to financial obstacles.

Students who do manage to attend college increasingly rely on loans to finance their education, with students of color taking on a disproportionate debt burden. At public institutions, 63% of white students borrowed to pay for their education compared to 81% of black students. At private institutions, black and Latino students—each of your authors falls into one of these categories—borrow at higher rates than white students, with Latino students taking on the highest average debt. Higher levels of debt are also impacting students in the long term. Those saddled with substantial educational debt are less satisfied with their careers, are saving less for retirement, and are less likely to own homes.

Debt as a Barrier to Change

Debt is even shaping the jobs students pursue after they graduate. Students deeper in debt are more likely to pursue stable, high-salary positions than lower-paid public interest work, compared to their less-indebted counterparts. This finding should be concerning to all of us, considering the enormous collective challenges we face in the years ahead. If we are going to address the deep-rooted causes of racial injustice, climate change, and other social problems, we need to create incentives for students to pursue meaningful work they are passionate about, instead of making it harder and harder for them to do so.

It is particularly concerning that our debt-based system of higher education is depriving people most affected by the flaws in our current political and economic systems of opportunities to participate in reshaping them. People of color, working-class people, survivors of sexual violence, undocumented people, women, and LGBTQIA people deserve to take the lead in crafting solutions to issues that affect their communities. Higher education plays a crucial role in providing access to tools and resources to make this possible, yet people from each of these groups face pervasive barriers to pursuing a degree, graduating, and securing gainful employment. Not all deep-seated social inequalities are perfectly reflected in figures like graduation rates. Women accounted for over 57% of bachelor's degrees awarded in 2009-2010, as well as the majority of master's and doctoral degrees. Still, women face significant barriers to entering some fields, including STEM fields (science, technology, engineering, and math) known for high-paid professional jobs. Universities can and should play a role in advancing opportunities for disenfranchised groups.

Students Speak Out

Art Motta, a student at UC Santa Cruz who studies politics and Latin American & Latino studies, acknowledges that his education has helped him gain the capacity to "analyze institutionalized structures [and] power dynamics," skills critical to help him pursue his passion for advocacy and public service. "[My education] also supplies me with a wealth of background knowledge for real situations that I am bound to encounter as a student of color in a system that was not made for me."

Art represents one of many non-traditional students who had to delay pursuing a college education due to financial barriers. "I had to put my education on hold because the costs became unbearable .... I had to focus on providing for my family." Art was ultimately able to resume his studies but he is very conscious of the fact that these opportunities are not available to most of the people he grew up with. "In my community, graduating from high school was considered a major feat in itself," Art said. Pursuing a four-year degree remains further out of reach "because of the high costs associated with college." The layers upon layers of ways in which our debt-based system of higher education drives inequality are shocking and immoral. But what would things look like if higher education were free? We asked student organizers with the United States Student Association (USSA) to consider what impact free higher education would have on their lives and their communities.

Yareli Castro, a student organizer at UC Irvine who is herself undocumented, noted economic barriers that prevent undocumented students from gaining access to higher education and graduating. "One of the main reasons why my community does not go to college—or, if they do, they drop out—is [because of] financial circumstances. In many states, undocumented students do not get financial aid, loans, or any type of financial support and the burden is very heavy. Undocumented students are very often not allowed to work in this country, so this financial pressure continues mounting. Free higher education would allow my community ... to not have to worry about working many jobs [or] taking out loans, and solely work on their studies."

Filipe de Carvalho, a student organizer at UMass Amherst, reflected on the role free higher education could play in giving students opportunities they can believe in. If higher education were free, "a much larger percentage of my high school ... would see a four-year university as a real option. I believe many of my peers would have cared more about their academics in high school had they believed that they could actually go to college."

Jordan Howzell, a student organizer at UC Santa Cruz, said that free higher education would allow her to "pursue a career rooted in my passions instead of its ability to cover my student loans." If higher education were free, she would study "music and its psychiatric and rehabilitative qualities, and how music is situated in social movements and social justice issues." Several of the students interviewed expressed similar sentiments about how they would choose their majors. Some said they would opt for completely different majors, while others said they would add course work in the humanities to build a balanced worldview and skillset.

John Ashton is a student organizer at Des Moines Area Community College. "When education is expensive, only the rich can obtain it," he says. "When education is free, the disenfranchised can become the best and brightest, and after all is said and done, that is what America is all about. ... Until the cost of higher education is eliminated, [our] higher education system [will never] achieve its full potential, nor will it train enough of the next generation of workers to meet the needs of the country."

The Road Ahead

If we want to end economic inequality and build a better future, we need higher education to be free. Free higher education will not solve all of our problems, but it would be a big step in the right direction. If young people have access to debt-free, high-quality education, it will open up more opportunities for them to use their skills and strengths to build satisfying careers and serve their communities, instead of cramming themselves into thankless and soulless positions just to make ends meet.

This will inevitably take time. Students have been pushing for free higher education for years, and it has only now become a part of the mainstream lexicon. There have been some precedents in U.S. history, including the CUNY system in New York, which offered tuition-free higher education up until the 1970s. In recent years, several elected officials have introduced plans for tuition-free and debt-free college.

New York State Assembly member James Skoufis introduced a 2014 bill offering free undergraduate tuition for all students who fulfill community service and residency requirements after graduation. In Oregon last year, legislators signed off on a bill pushing tuition at community colleges down to just $50. In early 2015, President Obama announced a plan for free community college. Democratic presidential candidates Hillary Clinton and Bernie Sanders have introduced proposals for debt-free and tuition-free higher education, respectively.

It is important that we closely examine these proposals as they come out, and fight to make sure they include all groups affected by the issue. It is even more important that we craft our own narratives about why free higher education matters, and build enough power to secure the win. Young people fighting for progressive change have learned important lessons about what it takes to win over the past few years. There is a widespread understanding that we need to consistently mobilize a large base of young people and win overwhelming public support to make free higher education a reality. ❑

Sources: Dean Baker, Robert Pollin, Travis McArthur, and Matt Sherman, "The Potential Revenue from Financial Transactions Taxes," Center for Economic and Policy Research and the Political Economy Research Institute, December 2009 (cepr.net); Bureau of Labor Statistics, TED: The Economics Daily, "Largest industries by state, 1990-2013," July 28, 2014 (bls.gov); Bureau of Labor Statistics, TED: The Economics Daily, "Job openings, hires, and total separations by industry, June 2015," Aug. 14, 2015 (bls.gov); Lawrence Mishel, Elise Gould, and Josh Bivens, "Wage Stagnation in Nine Charts," Economic Policy Institute, Jan. 6, 2015 (epi.org); Douglas Belkin, "U.S. College Enrollment Has Dropped Nearly 2% Over Last Year," *Wall Street Journal*, May 14, 2015 (wsj.com); Mark Huelsman, "The Debt Divide: The Racial and Class Bias Behind the 'New Normal' of Student Borrowing," Demos, May 19, 2015 (demos.org); Jesse Rothsein and Cecilia Elena Rouse, "Constrained after college: Student loans and early-career occupational choices," *Journal of Public Economics* 95 (2011); National Center for Educational Statistics, Fast Facts, "Degrees conferred by sex and race" (nces.ed.gov); City University of New York, "When Tuition at CUNY Was Free, Sort Of," CUNY Matters, Oct. 12, 2011 (cuny.edu); James Skoufis, "Assemblyman Skoufis Introduces Bill to Provide Free Tuition at SUNY and CUNY," Jan. 27, 2014 (assembly.state.ny.us); Rob Manning. "Thousands to Benefit from Oregon Free Community College Bill," Oregon Public Broadcasting, July 17, 2015 (opb.org); Ashley A. Smith, "Obama Steps Up Push for Free Tuition," *Inside Higher Education*, Sept. 9, 2015 (insidehighered.com); Laura Meckler and Josh Mitchell, "Hillary Clinton Proposes Debt-Free Tuition at Public Colleges," *Wall Street Journal*, Aug. 10, 2015 (wsj.com); Heather Gautney and Adolph Reed Jr., "Bernie Sanders's 'College for All' Plan Is Fair, Smart and Achievable," *The Nation*, Dec. 2, 2015 (thenation.com).

Article 4.4

NO COUNTRY FOR OLD PEOPLE
U.S. market ideology is undermining human rights for elders.

BY DAVID BACON
March/April 2016

Is there a human right to age in dignity? Some countries think so. Unfortunately, ours isn't one of them.

The Organization of American States (OAS) recently adopted the first international convention on the human rights of older people (though the United States did not endorse it). The Organization of African Unity (OAU) is debating its own convention, and is expected to adopt it next year.

It is ironic that the world's poorer countries, presumably those with the fewest resources to deal with aging, are in the vanguard of establishing this set of rights. Meanwhile, the richest countries with the most resources, including the United States and members of the European Union, are arguing against applying a human-rights framework to aging. In part, their contrarian stance reflects the dominance of market ideology. In a corporate economy, people lose their social importance and position when they are not working and producing value. In the United States, the resulting set of priorities has a devastating impact on older people.

While some countries are creating a new definition of human rights to include aging, and passing conventions that incorporate it, millions of seniors in the United States live in very vulnerable and precarious conditions, which are violations of their human rights as viewed in this context.

In another 15 years, 18% of the people in the United States will be over 65 years old. Though their numbers may be increasing, however, their security is not. In fact, the future of the nation's elders is growing ever more precarious.

According to a recent study, "Senior Poverty in America," by Rebecca Vallas, director of policy in the Poverty to Prosperity Program at the Center for American Progress, 10% of seniors (4.6 million people) fall below this country's official poverty line. In 1966 it was 29%. That sounds like progress. Vallas attributes the decline mostly to Medicare, Medicaid, and other programs established during this period. But this appearance of progress, she says, doesn't account for the desperate situation of millions of seniors today. The programs have helped people, but their success at lowering poverty among some seniors masks the desperate situation of millions of others. The official poverty line is too low, has grown increasingly out of whack over the years from the real cost of living, and uses a faulty method (being originally defined as three times the basic food budget) that does not correspond to current spending patterns for low-income people.

The official poverty line defines poverty for a single person as an income less than $11,770, and for a couple, $15,930 (for Alaska and Hawaii it's slightly higher). Rent alone absorbs a huge portion of this. Even seniors at 125% of the poverty line spend more than three quarters of their income on rent, Vallas found—$11,034 for singles, and $14,934 for a couple. It's hard to imagine finding an apartment in many urban areas with rent that low.

According to Vallas, seniors across the board spend 14% of their income on medical costs. Adding that to rent, poor seniors are left with about 10% of their income for food, bus fares, and everything else. It's no wonder that so many people in line at county food banks are old.

Even an income of twice the official poverty line is hardly enough to make ends meet, and the number of seniors under this line is much greater—32% of those over 65 and 40% of those over 75.

A better criterion for poverty is the Supplemental Poverty Measure (SPM). The U.S. Census Bureau created this yardstick in response to criticism that the official poverty line grossly underestimates poverty (see Jeannette Wicks-Lim, "Undercounting the Poor," *Dollars & Sense*, May/June 2013). The SPM is based on real-life expenditures for basic necessities like food, housing, clothing and utilities. It varies from place to place and isn't meant to qualify or disqualify people for government programs. Vallas found that about 15% of seniors fall below this line, and 45% are "economically vulnerable"—below twice the SPM.

Poverty is no more evenly distributed among seniors than it is among people in general in the United States. Nearly 12% of older women (3.1 million) live below the official poverty line (vs. 7% of men), and 17% live below the SPM (vs. 12% of men), according to a 2015 Kaiser Family Foundation report. "The typical woman suffers an earnings loss of $431,000 over the course of a 40-year career due to the gender wage gap," Vallas says. "The gap is even larger for women of color." Black and Hispanic seniors are poorer in general—19% and 18% respectively are under the official poverty line, and 22% and 28% are under the SPM.

The income of seniors is overwhelmingly dependent on Social Security. The number of seniors who receive pensions from employers is declining rapidly, as corporations divest themselves of the "defined benefit" plans that, for an earlier generation, pegged payments to pre-retirement earnings for an earlier generation. Today, the average Social Security benefit is just over $16,000 per year—not far above even the official poverty line. "For nearly two-thirds of seniors, it is their main source of income, and for one-third it is their only income," Vallas notes. Without it, half of all seniors would fall below the SPM.

The official poverty statistics do not even account for people who have been left out of the Social Security system entirely. Many workers do not make contributions, including workers in the informal economy, like day laborers.

Two million seniors get Supplemental Security Income (SSI) benefits, which are based on low income rather than contributions made while they were working. But the maximum is $8,796 per year, well below the official poverty line. According to the Center for Budget and Policy Priorities (CBPP), "for nearly three-fifths of recipients, SSI is their only source of income."

Getting left out of the safety net has devastating consequences. As of 2010, roughly 45,000 adults over age 65 were homeless, according to Vallas, who projects that that this figure will increase by 33% by 2020 and more than double by 2050. The homeless population is getting older as well. The median age of single homeless adults was 35 in 1990, and 50 in 2010.

Immigration status is an even greater barrier to benefits. According to the Migration Policy Institute, about five million immigrants 65 and over make up 12%

of the total U.S. immigrant population. For those who haven't become citizens, the safety net has huge holes.

Most lawful permanent residents (LPRs) can't receive SSI or food stamps (SNAP) for their first five years in the United States, although they can collect Social Security if they've managed to accumulate any qualifying earnings. People with no legal immigration status (an estimated eleven million people) can't even apply for a Social Security card. In order to work they have to give an employer a Social Security number they've invented or that belongs to someone else. Payments are deducted from their paychecks, but these workers never become eligible for the benefits the contributions are supposed to provide.

The Social Security Administration estimated in 2010 that 3.1 million undocumented people were paying about $13 billion per year in contributions into the benefit fund. Undocumented recipients, mostly people who received Social Security numbers before the system was tightened, received only $1 billion per year in payments. Stephen Goss, the chief actuary of the Social Security Administration, told VICE News in 2014 that that surplus of payments versus benefits had totaled more than $100 billion over the previous decade.

Excluded undocumented immigrants, however, get old like everyone else. Without Social Security, they have to find some other way to survive—primarily by continuing to work or relying on family.

According to Lia Daichman, president of the Argentina chapter of the International Longevity Alliance, and the ILA's representative at the United Nations, "governments should guarantee that all people have a non-contributory pension, to be able to live without the support of younger people." Her own country, Argentina, began paying nearly every old person a pension in 2003, with medical and social benefits, even those who made no contributions. "This is good for women," she emphasizes, "because we often work in the home and weren't able to contribute, or because we worked in the informal economy." Even Nepal, one of the world's poorest countries, has instituted a non-contributory pension of 700 rupees a month.

Daichman doesn't view elders as needy people asking for charity. "People have a right to income and a dignified life," she asserts. "They worked all their lives for it." This perspective underlies her work trying to convince the international community to codify this right. The convention adopted by the OAS is a step towards the goal, she believes, in part because it will cover such a large area. In Latin America and the Caribbean, nearly 71 million people were older than 60 in 2015; by 2030 that figure will increase by over 70%, to 121 million people, according to a 2015 United Nations study of the aging of the world population.

Adopting new definitions and conventions on human rights (especially economic ones), even if they are not immediately implemented, helps to set a goal—a vision of how we want the world to work. Passing human rights treaties is also an important step in establishing rights in international law.

The OAS convention enumerates 27 specific rights, with many sub-categories, from the right to independence, political participation, and freedom from violence to the right to a healthy environment. Some of the key rights it asserts are economic. Older people, it says, "have the right to social security to protect them so that they can live in dignity," and governments should provide income "to ensure a dignified life for older persons." Seniors also have the right to "dignified and decent work" with benefits, labor and union rights, and pay equal to all other workers. Older people have the right to healthcare, housing, education and to "participate in the cultural and artistic life of the community, and to enjoy the benefits of scientific and technological progress."

The U.S. government does not recognize many of these rights, however—to housing, income, education, and healthcare, for instance. In this country these are all commodities, bought and sold on the market. Yet Social Security itself is a product of an earlier era in U.S. political life, in which President Franklin Roosevelt postulated that all people had the right to "freedom from want." Today a "cost/benefit analysis" is the more likely framework—weighing the need to ensure a dignified life for seniors against the cost of providing it.

Social welfare programs in the United States are the product of popular struggle against the inherent dynamic of a market economy to demand as high a rate of profit as possible. Old people, children, the disabled, and others who don't immediately produce profit are a social cost, and vulnerable in a system like this. Popular struggle is necessary to demand their needs be met. When popular movements weaken, the safety net then starts getting pulled apart. U.S. opposition to a human rights treaty for the aged is based not on a lack of morality, uncaring politics, or bad intentions, but on the way the system functions.

In declining to endorse the OAS convention on aging, the U.S. government inserted a note declaring: "The United States has consistently objected to the negotiation of new legally binding instruments on the rights of older persons. ... We do not believe a convention is necessary to ensure that the human rights of older persons are protected. ... The resources of the OAS and of its member states should be used to identify practical steps that governments in the Americas might adopt to combat discrimination against older persons." In other words, instead of having to abide by a binding agreement, each country should be free to do as it chooses.

As radical as they might sound to U.S. ears, these economic rights don't even test the limits of the ways a globalized economy now affects the aged. Enormous movements of people, for instance, fleeing war and poverty, have led to the separation of families. UN conventions, and almost all countries, recognize the right to migrate because of war and persecution. Should this be expanded to recognize a right of old people to reunite with their families, if they're separated by war or previous migration? Should the United States recognize the right of a migrant in California's Central Valley, for instance, after a lifetime working in the fields, to travel home to Mexico, and then return to their family putting down roots in Fresno?

"Of course it should," says Susan Somers, president of the International Network for the Prevention of Elder Abuse. "All we need is a little political will. But get it into a convention? That's a hard road, because of every nation's immigration laws. We're not trying to force countries to change their culture or ways of life. But when they come into conflict with harm, culture and tradition are no excuse."

A proposed U.N. convention has been stalled over these disagreements, and Daichman and Somers say opposition is coming from the United States, Australia, Israel, and the European Union. "They are really trying to push us back," Somers fumes. "They think it's going to cost them something, and that older people aren't deserving. Yet the budget item for treaties is so small compared to peace keeping and the Security Council—almost nothing."

A growing and vocal constituency is not simply waiting for wealthy nations to come around, however. Among Asian countries, Malaysia, Indonesia, Thailand, Bangladesh, and even Myanmar have made statements about the human rights of older people. "Human rights are at the core of everything," Daichman says. "The rights of people getting old should be considered human rights because they're human beings." ❑

Sources: Draft Resolution—Inter-American Convention on Protecting the Human Rights of Older Persons; Organization of American States, "The Americas Becomes First Region in the World to Have an Instrument for the Promotion and Protection of the Rights of Older Persons," press release, June 15, 2015 (oas.org); Rebecca Vallas, "Senior Poverty in America: The Looming Crisis No One's Talking About," Center for American Progress (americanprogress.org); Interview with Rebecca Vallas, November 2015; Juliette Cubanski, Giselle Casillas, and Anthony Damico, "Poverty Among Seniors: An Updated Analysis of National and State Level Poverty Rates Under the Official and Supplemental Poverty Measures," Kaiser Family Foundation, June 10, 2015 (kff.org); Social Security Administration, "Effects of Unauthorized Immigration on the Actuarial Status of the Social Security Trust Funds" (ssa.gov); Roy Germano, "Unauthorized Immigrants Paid $100 Billion Into Social Security Over Last Decade," VICE News, Aug. 4, 2014 (news.vice.com); National Immigration Law Center, "Overview of Immigrant Eligibility for Federal Programs" (nilc.org); National Immigration Law Center, "A Quick Guide to Immigrant Eligibility for ACA and Key Federal Means-tested Programs" (nilc.org); Interview with Susan Somers, November 2015; Interview with Lia Daichman, November 2015; Center on Budget and Policy Priorities, "Policy Basics: Introduction to Supplemental Security Income"(cbpp.org); United Nations Department of Social and Economic Affairs, "World Population Ageing 2015" (un.org/en/development/desa).

Article 4.5

DO TRADE AGREEMENTS FORECLOSE PROGRESSIVE POLICY?

BY ARTHUR MacEWAN
May/June 2016

> Dear Dr. Dollar:
> Doesn't the increasing liberalization of U.S. international economic poli-
> cies foreclose the possibilities for progressive policies in this country? Don't
> these policies undercut the effectiveness of fiscal policy efforts to stim-
> ulate employment and output? And don't they virtually rule out many
> progressive reforms, such as a single payer health care system or new envi-
> ronmental regulations?   —*Anonymous, by voicemail*

The simple answer to this set of questions is: yes and no. But let's step back for a minute.

From the North American Free Trade Agreement (NAFTA), adopted in the early 1990s, to the Trans-Pacific Partnership (TPP) and the Transatlantic Trade and Investment Partnership (TTIP) being advanced today, criticism has focused on the negative impacts of these agreements on employment in many U.S. industries. These negative impacts are real and are one factor contributing to the decline of manufacturing in the United States, to the stagnation of wages, and to the hollow-ing out of the "middle class."

Yet, another impact of these agreements generally gets ignored—namely their negative impacts on progressive economic and social policies. Here too the impacts are real, but they are not absolute.

Take the issue of fiscal stimulus—that is, when the government runs a budget deficit, spending more to increase output and create jobs than it is taking in as taxes. In 1970, imports of goods and services were only 6.3% as large as GDP, but in 2014, imports were equal to 18.2% of GDP. This implies that in the earlier era, of a dollar spent on goods and services in general, only 6.3% would go towards imports. Today, as liberalization of trade has brought about the larger role for imports in GDP, a much larger share would go for the stimulation of jobs and output abroad. That is, the impact would in part "leak" out of the U.S. economy.

However, stimulus spending need not be spending "in general." If the gov-ernment focused its spending on physical infrastructure (roads, bridges, public transport systems) and early childhood education, for example, less of the impact would "leak" out of the country. And certainly there are great needs for spending on infrastructure and early childhood education. (There would still be "leakage" in the later rounds of spending, as those who received the government funds—for example, construction companies and workers, preschools and early-childhood teachers—spent what they had received.)

NAFTA, UPS, and Canada: It's All about Money

In 2000, under provisions in NAFTA, the U.S. courier company UPS sued Canada Post (Canada's public postal service), claiming $230 million in lost profits. UPS argued that Canada Post had an unfair advantage because it used the public postal system to support its own courier business. In 2007, UPS finally lost its suit, leading the president of Canada Post to comment: "This dispute was all about money. The United Parcel Service of America is attempting to force postal administrations around the world out of the parcel and courier business in order to increase their market share."

Source: "Canada Post claims victory at NAFTA over UPS," CBC News, Jan. 13, 2007 (cbc.ca).

To an extent, the American Recovery and Reinvestment Act of 2009 (ARRA) did focus spending on infrastructure investment. And, while there is controversy regarding its impact, it did seem to have a positive, though limited impact (it wasn't big enough) in contributing to the recovery from the severe recession of 2007–2008.

The constraints that the decades of liberalization of U.S. international economic activity places on social programs is related to investment, not trade. Various agreements—like NAFTA, TPP, and TTIP—incorporate provisions that derive from the General Agreement on Trade in Services (GATS), a treaty of the World Trade Organization (WTO) that came into force in 1995. These agreements allow firms from outside a country to sue the government of that country if it imposes "over-burdensome" regulations or policies that undermine the firm's profits.

For example, a mining firm based in one country could sue the government of another county in which it is operating if environmental protection regulations are put in place that harm the firm's profits. Or, for a second example, a private health care firm based abroad could sue if the establishment of a single-payer health care system were established in the United States, harming the firm's profits. The threat of such suits could deter the government form implementing these sorts of programs. It might seem, then, that the government's hands would be tied, preventing the enactment of progressive programs.

But let's not forget what government we are talking about here. These profit-protecting provisions of the WTO and particular international economic agreements have been largely the creation of the world's most powerful government—i.e., the U.S. government. If the U.S. government wanted to change those provisions—that is, if it wanted to clear the way for progressive programs—it would not have great problems in doing so. If it is not unrealistic to believe that a U.S. government would want to create a single-payer health care system or a strong set of environmental protection regulations, it is not unrealistic to believe that it could also abrogate or get around those profit-protecting provisions.

The example described in the box shows the real threat to public services that is created by the provisions in trade agreements. It also shows how in a relatively rich country—Canada in this case—with the resources and expertise to fight such a threat, a government can prevail. The situation of less-powerful, low-income countries is very different.

So, yes, the liberalization of U.S. international commerce does create constraints on progressive economic policies and social programs. But, no, these constraints are by no means absolute. Ultimately, the constraints are political, not technical constraints of economic agreements. ❑

Sources: "The Trans-Pacific Partnership clause everyone should oppose," Elizabeth Warren, Washington Post, February 25, 2015 (washingtonpost.com); "The Economic Impact of the American Recovery and Reinvestment Act Five Years Later," Final Report to Congress, Executive Office of the President, Council of Economic Advisers, February 2014 (whitehouse.gov).

Chapter 5

THE ENVIRONMENT

Article 5.1

GREEN-STATE AMERICA

BY FRANK ACKERMAN
November 2016

In January, Donald Trump will endorse climate denial, renouncing the Clean Power Plan and climate targets in general. This will damage the fragile global momentum toward emission reduction, established in last year's Paris agreement. If the United States refuses to cooperate, why should much poorer, reluctant participants such as India do anything to cut back on carbon?

But among many things that this dreadful election did not represent, it was not a statement of (dis)belief about climate change. Large parts of the country recognize the validity of modern science, understand the urgency of the problem, and remain committed to ambitious carbon reduction targets.

Suppose that many of our state governments got together and told the rest of the world about our continuing commitment to action: we are still abiding by the U.S. pledges under the Paris agreement, or even planning to do more. Not just NGO reports, blog posts, or individual signatures, but an official, coordinated announcement from government bodies with decision-making power over emissions—primarily states, perhaps joined by Indian tribes and major city governments.

The participating states could in theory be on either side of the partisan divide, but of course one side is more likely to sign on at present. Think of Green-State America, initially, as the states that voted for Clinton, and have either a Democratic governor or both houses of the legislature controlled by Democrats. (As it happens, that's all the states that voted for Clinton except Maine and New Hampshire.) Those 18 states plus the District of Columbia account for 30% of U.S. greenhouse gas emissions. The governor or the legislative leadership of each state could sign the Green-State Climate Agreement, pledging their state to continued dialogue, cooperation, and rapid reduction in emissions. Tribal leaders and city mayors could do the same for their jurisdictions.

Green-State America is the world's fifth-largest emitter, behind only China, the rest of America, India and Russia. We emit more greenhouse gases than Japan, Brazil, or Germany. If we were a separate country, our participation would be essential to international climate agreements. Even though we are states rather than a nation, we might be able to help reduce the international damage, by letting the world know that much of America still cares about the global climate.

Why should we address global plans at the state level? The United States is a federation of states, governed by archaic eighteenth-century interstate agreements—aka "the wisdom of the Founding Fathers"—such as the electoral college. (If we were a one-person, one-vote democracy, Hillary Clinton would be our next president, just as Al Gore would have been 16 years ago.) The expected assault on environmental and other regulations is likely to include efforts to give more power back to the states, reducing the role of federal rule-making in favor of state-level pollution control. State-level international climate policy is just one step further down that road.

Green-State America is less carbon-intensive than our neighbors; with 30% of national emissions, we have 43% of the U.S. population and 49% of GDP. Our emissions amount to 12 tons of CO_2-equivalent per capita, compared to 21 tons in the rest of the country. There is more to be done to control carbon emissions in America—but it will be easy for other states to join us, one at a time.

And this could be a model for other issues. Green-State America might also want to support international treaties on the rights of women, the treatment of migrants, the rights of indigenous peoples, and more.

For now, it's time to act to protect the climate. It's time to tell the world that Green-State America keeps its promises, because climate change trumps the election returns. ❏

Article 5.2

HOW GROWTH CAN BE GREEN
Economic Growth, Clean Energy, and the Challenge of Climate Change

AN INTERVIEW WITH ROBERT POLLIN
November/December 2016

In a Gallup poll earlier this year, almost two-thirds of those polled said that global warming worried them "a great deal" or "a fair amount." Yet many are also worried that serious climate policy will require deep sacrifices—including big declines in production, incomes, and employment. In August, Robert Pollin, professor of economics and co-director of the Political Economy Research Institute (PERI) at UMass-Amherst, spoke with Dollars & Sense *co-editor Alejandro Reuss about these issues: Why "negative growth" is not a solution to climate change, why "green growth" is the best way to reduce greenhouse emissions, and how it can work in both high-income and low-income countries. —Eds.*

Dollars & Sense: You've argued in favor of "green growth" as a pathway for climate stabilization. That cuts against a conventional wisdom—both among advocates of serious action on climate policy and critics of such action—that greenhouse gas emissions reductions require a reduction in growth, no growth, or even negative growth. What's the basic case you make for green growth?

Robert Pollin: The argument for green growth is premised on the notion that, while an economy is growing, a given percentage of economic activity is devoted to the transformation of the energy sector—from fossil-fuel based energy to clean energy. According to my research, roughly speaking, if we look at about 1½% of GDP per year—and I've done it for different countries, so it could be the United States, it could be Spain, it could be Brazil, it could be South Africa, or it could be the world as a whole—1½% of GDP invested in clean energy—that is, clean renewable energy sources and energy efficiency—that I've costed this out and you could get to a global reduction in absolute CO_2 emissions on the order of 40% within twenty years, which is along the lines of the Intergovernmental Panel on Climate Change goals. That means that what you're doing is, as the economy is growing, you're taking part of economic activity and moving it from dirty activities to clean energy activity. So growth therefore becomes supportive of emissions and climate stabilization.

D&S: If the fruits of growth were heavily invested in projects to increase energy efficiency or develop sources of alternative "clean" energy (wind, water, solar), could a green growth approach actually achieve greater GHG emissions reductions than a hypothetical no-growth or de-growth alternative?

RP: If we're talking about a no-growth scenario, unless you're transforming the energy system you get no reduction in emissions. If you're at a flat level of economic activity, you get exactly the same level of emissions. If we cut GDP by 10%, and you keep the energy system the same, then emissions will go down by 10%, period. And a 10% emissions reduction is nowhere near what's required. On the other hand, reducing GDP by 10% would be the worst depression the world had ever experienced. GDP didn't go down by 10% during the 1930s. During the Great Recession of 2007-2008, global GDP went down by 2½%. So there's no way to get to a climate stabilization path just on the basis of cutting growth. If we want to go to zero growth, or we want to go to negative growth, we still have to transform the energy system, and the best way to transform the energy system is in a framework in which the economy is growing, because then you have a lot of opportunities and a lot of investment. You're creating more jobs. If you're trying to transform the energy system in a phase of no growth, you're imposing a depression, and who's going to be for that? Nobody, except the most fanatical environmentalists. But working people are going to see massive job loss, on a scale much greater than 2007-2009, greater than the 1930s. That has no political support and doesn't solve the problem anyway.

D&S: Is "green growth" a viable course of action for the developing world today? The high-income countries, including some that are now moving in the direction of greener energy, have mostly achieved high incomes through a carbon-intensive path. Can developing countries dramatically raise standards of living on the basis of a low-carbon-intensity path?

RP: Yeah, well the key is that the costs of delivering energy through clean renewable sources plus high efficiency are basically at parity now in developing countries, under average conditions. "Under average conditions" means that there is wide dispersion. It doesn't mean that in every single site if you put up a wind farm or install solar panels that the costs are going to be at parity with, say, the rich countries. But on average, if we believe the research that's out there, they are. And this also depends a lot on investments in high efficiency, because in developing countries the energy systems are very wasteful, so it's easy to get high returns from investing in raising efficiency standards. So actually the green growth path is even more effective in developing countries. I myself have written about it for India, for Brazil, for South Africa, for Indonesia. In a country like Indonesia or India—they expect to be high-growth countries, growing at 6, 7, or 8%—they can actually do that if they keep putting 1½% of GDP so that their growth dividend moves into clean energy, and you start to see their emissions going down as a feature of economic growth itself.

D&S: What about the means of promoting investment in energy efficiency and alternative energy that you're talking about? You've written about the importance of a leading government role in promoting investment in those sectors. Are you skeptical that governments can just re-set the incentives to private actors— through a carbon tax or emissions permits system—and have that bring about the necessary investments?

RP: Well, we have to be skeptical, because it hasn't happened. And we have to be skeptical because there are obviously extremely powerful interests that are quite pleased with the profits that they're receiving from burning fossil fuels. That's a political question. On the other hand, as I said, on average the costs of renewable energy are close to parity or on parity with fossil fuel energy. Energy efficiency pays for itself, by definition. In fact, in the United States in 2007, under President George W. Bush, a law was passed that required the federal government to raise efficiency standards in all federal buildings by 30% as of the year 2015. Now, we didn't do it, but in the buildings that were retrofitted—there's a website and it shows it was saving the taxpayers hundreds of millions of dollars. So why isn't it happening? One, there's inertia. You do have to do the up-front investment. Two, there's opposition from the fossil fuel industry. So we have to struggle around those things, at the same time recognizing that achieving these kinds of growth projections for clean energy are quite feasible economically and are good for jobs. That's the other big barrier, this notion that you're going to hurt jobs if you're going to protect the environment. Well, you know, the thing that I've been focusing on for several years is that it's actually beneficial for employment to pursue the green growth path as opposed to maintaining the fossil fuel infrastructure. ❑

Article 5.3

RENT IN A WARMING WORLD
What's rent got to do with climate change? More than you might think.

BY JAMES K. BOYCE
March 2014

R ent isn't just the monthly check that tenants write to landlords. Economists use the term "rent-seeking" to mean "using political and economic power to get a larger share of the national pie, rather than to grow the national pie," in the words of Nobel laureate Joseph Stiglitz, who maintains that such dysfunctional activity has metastasized in the United States alongside deepening inequality.

When rent inspires investment in useful things like housing, it's productive. The economic pie grows, and the people who pay rent get something in return. When rent leads to investment in unproductive activities, like lobbying to capture wealth without creating it, it's parasitic. Those who pay get nothing in return.

Two other types of rent originate in nature rather than in human investment. Extractive rent comes from nature as a source of raw materials. The difference between the selling price of crude oil and the cost of pumping it from the ground is an example.

Protective rent comes from nature as a sink for our wastes. In the northeastern states of the U.S., for example, the Regional Greenhouse Gas Initiative requires power plants to buy carbon permits at quarterly auctions. In this way, power companies pay rent to park CO_2 emissions in the atmosphere. Similarly, green taxes on pollution now account for more than 5% of government revenue in a number of European countries. When polluters pay to use nature's sinks, they use them less than when they're free.

FOUR TYPES OF RENT

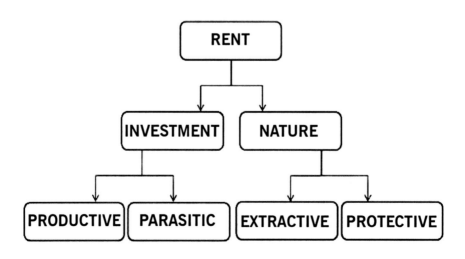

Extractive and protective rents both originate in nature, but one promotes resource depletion, the other conservation. The resulting tension between these two types of rent from nature is becoming more visible in a warming world.

A daunting obstacle to climate policy arises from the vested interests of fossil fuel corporations in continuing to reap extractive rent. The current value of the world's oil, coal and natural gas reserves is estimated at $27 trillion. Much of this will have to be written off if we phase out fossil fuels. "You can have a healthy fossil-fuel balance sheet, or a relatively healthy planet," Bill McKibben observes. "You can't have both."

Creating protective rent by capping or taxing carbon emissions will shrink extractive rent. Fossil fuel corporations have shown themselves willing to fight hard to defend extractive rent. But the question of who will receive climate protective rent– and who will fight for it — remains up in the air.

One possibility is to return climate protective rent to the people via equal per capita dividends— a policy known as "cap and dividend" in the case of permits or "fee and dividend" in the case of taxes. Another is to give free permits to polluters and let them pocket the rent as windfall profits— a policy known as "cap and trade" but more accurately termed "cap and giveaway." A third option is to let the government keep the money, as in the case of Europe's green taxes.

Dividend proponents argue that recycling rent to the people is necessary to secure durable public support for climate policy as fossil fuel prices rise during the decades-long clean energy transition. Cap-and-giveaway proponents argue that surrendering the rent to fossil fuel corporations is necessary to neutralize their opposition to climate policy.

Underlying these strategies are very different beliefs about who owns nature's sinks, and about politics. Dividends are based on the principle that the gifts of nature belong to everyone equally. Cap-and-giveaway is based on the premise that the same corporations that profit from extracting nature's wealth ought to be paid to leave it in the ground.

Dividends make sense if we believe that it's possible to enact a policy that benefits the majority of people financially as well as environmentally. Cap-and-giveaway makes sense if we believe that might makes right, and that the power of the people can never match the power of the corporations.

The serial defeats suffered by cap-and-trade bills in Washington have cast doubt on the political realism of "realpolitik" environmentalism. When the chips were down, the fossil fuel industry proved unwilling to buy into the new-rent-for-old deal.

The only way we'll see a switch from extractive rents for corporations to protective rents for the public will be if ordinary people join together to make this happen. The small-d democratic politics that this will demand may seem like a quaint idea in the political climate of the early 21st century. But nothing less is required. To change the rent we get from nature, we must change who gets it. ❏

Article 5.4

NOT JUST FOR FUTURE GENERATIONS

How climate policy can benefit most people in the here and now

AN INTERVIEW WITH JAMES K. BOYCE

March/April 2016

*A*s the United Nations Climate Conference began in Paris on November 30, 2015, economist James K. Boyce joined D&S co-editor Alejandro Reuss for an interview on the future of climate policy. Boyce, professor of economics at UMass-Amherst and director of the Program on Development, Peacebuilding, and the Environment at the Political Economy Research Institute (PERI), has written extensively on a wide variety of environmental issues. (See, for example, "Mapping Environmental Injustice," co-authored by Klara Zwickl, Michael Ash, and Boyce, in this chapter.) In this interview, he emphasized how the dominant narrative about climate policy—the current generation's pain for future generations' gain—is both incorrect and politically damaging. —Eds.

Dollars & Sense: With the Paris Climate Change Conference now underway, climate policy is undoubtedly at the forefront of many people's minds. We often hear climate policy debates framed by the question of whether the current generation will be willing to sacrifice our standards of living, by reducing energy use and achieving emissions reductions, for the benefit of future generations. You've criticized that sort of framing of climate issues.

James K. Boyce: That's right. I mean that framing is almost ubiquitous. One of the reasons why these international negotiations have proven so difficult is that if everybody believes that this is going to be a painful thing to cut our carbon emissions, then they all want somebody else to go first. It's like a global free-rider problem—no one wants to be the one who cuts emissions more than someone else because they'll bear the pain and everybody else shares in the gain. I think that framing of the problem has been a huge obstacle to progress, and it's not true. In fact, it is, on the contrary, true that we can design climate policies that benefit the majority of people here and now, in the present generation. So instead of always wanting somebody else to go first, if we designed the policies right, everyone will want to go first and I think that's a critical piece of the conversation that needs to be lifted up.

D&S: One of those benefits that you've talked about and written about is called "air quality co-benefits of climate policy." So what are air quality co-benefits, and why are those important?

JB: When we burn coal, oil, and natural gas—the fossil fuels—we not only release carbon dioxide into the atmosphere, which is the most important of the greenhouse gases propelling climate change, but we also release a lot of other really nasty stuff: particulate matter, sulfur dioxide, nitrogen oxide, a host of air toxics—things that are hazardous to people here and now when we breathe them. By cutting down on our use of fossil fuels, we will not only help to protect the climate for future generations by reducing CO_2 emissions, but we'll also help to improve air quality for the present generation. Those improvements can be really substantial. In fact, people who've tried to calculate how much, in terms of dollars, the public-health benefits of cutting carbon emissions would be find magnitudes of benefits that are as big, or even in some cases bigger, than the dollar values that have been put on reducing greenhouse gas emissions. So we're talking about big benefits here, even in a country like the United States which has relatively good air-quality regulation.

My grad student Brandon Taylor and I, for example, recently did some calculations on the clean-air benefits, the public-health benefits that would come from implementing one of the climate bills that's been introduced in the current session of Congress, the Healthy Climate and Family Security Act, introduced by Congressman Chris Van Hollen from Maryland. Van Hollen's bill would put a cap on carbon emissions, auction off the permits, give the money back to the people, and reduce the use of fossil fuels by 80% by the year 2050. We estimated that over that period, implementation of that bill would save about 700,000 lives in the United States. That is to say it would avert 700,000 premature deaths; that's about—what?—250 times the number of people who died in 9/11? We're talking about a lot of preventable mortality that could be averted by moving forward in the clean-energy transition.

When you then look at countries like China or India, where the air-quality problems are even worse, the public health co-benefits of a clean-energy transition are that much greater. So I think this is something that really needs to be part of the conversation. When we're talking about cutting back on the use of fossil fuels, we're really talking about making cleaner air for everybody on the planet today, and improving public health, preventing premature deaths, preventing respiratory diseases, cancers, heart problems, asthma, and a host of other illnesses that are related to air pollution from fossil-fuel combustion.

D&S: Just to follow up on that point, probably a lot of our readers will have thought about the so-called "export of pollution"—the relocation of high-polluting industries from high-income countries like the United States to elsewhere in the world, and the insulation of people in high-income countries, especially affluent people, from the effects of that pollution. And yet, the argument that you make really says, well that may be true, but still there's a lot of benefit to be gained in countries like the United States from an air-quality and public-health standpoint.

JB: Yes, that's absolutely right. I mean, you can't export burning gasoline in your automobile. You can't export emissions from burning coal, oil, and natural gas to generate electricity. Those things are going to be in your own country, and we've still got a lot of that here in the United States. Despite having relatively strong air-quality legislation under the Clean Air Act, we've still got thousands of premature deaths every year that are attributable to burning fuels. So, the only way to really drive down those public-health costs is to transition away from, what really, when you think about it, is an awfully primitive technology. It's digging up poisonous stuff that's been buried under the ground for millions of years and burning it to generate heat and power. Really, I think people are going to look back on that in a hundred years and say, "Boy, people were sure primitive back in the 19th and 20th, and early 21st century if that's the way they were generating their power," where we now know that in fact it's possible to generate energy very cleanly, at very low cost, by tapping the sun, the wind, geothermal sources of power, and so on. So I think we're not only talking here about trying to improve the environment for people yet to be born, we're talking about improving the environment for ourselves.

D&S: You've also written a lot about climate policies like a carbon tax, or auctioned carbon permit system, and argued that those could be designed in a way that would yield net income benefits to most people. Now, again, in the current discourse, the idea is that a carbon tax or some other price on carbon would hurt most people in the pocketbook, in particular lower-income people who tend to spend larger percentages of their incomes on fuel and the like. So how is it that most people would end up benefitting from such policies, properly designed?

JB: Well, this is another really important part of the conversation. The fact that a carbon price is one of the most important instruments to achieve reductions in emissions by making fossil fuels more expensive, is again part of the reason why people think, "Oh, it's going to be painful for us to reduce our use of fossil fuels because we're going to have to pay more for these things." It's true we are going to have to pay more, but the important thing to realize is that money doesn't disappear from our economy. When consumers pay more for oil, coal, natural gas, and everything that's produced and distributed using them, for electricity, for gasoline for their cars, etc.—that money doesn't get shipped to Saudi Arabia, it doesn't get buried in a tin can in your backyard, it doesn't get shot to the moon. It gets distributed somewhere, and the question is: Who gets the money?

In effect, by putting a limit on the amount of carbon we're burning, we're converting the atmosphere from something that was free, that you didn't have to pay to use, into something that's limited and that we have to pay to use—to park carbon in that limited atmospheric space. The question then is: Well if we're going to pay, who should get the money? Who does that space belong to? Who owns the parking lot, so to speak, the atmospheric parking lot for carbon emissions? I would submit that it's not owned by the corporations, it's not owned by the government, it's owned by all of us in common and equal measure. And consistent with that principle, then, the money that's collected by auctioning permits, or by charging a carbon tax, ought to go back to the people as the rightful owners of the resource we're paying to use.

If you did that, people who have smaller carbon footprints, who don't burn as much fossil fuel, will receive more in dividends than they pay in higher fuel bills. This includes mostt low-income people because they can't afford to burn as much fossil fuel—a lot of low income people in this country can't even afford to drive a car, they certainly don't have 4,000 or 8,000 foot houses that they're heating, they certainly don't fly off in airplanes to take vacations in sunny places in the middle of the winter, right? They don't burn as much carbon, and so their carbon footprints are relatively small compared to the more affluent people who have bigger houses, bigger cars, fly around in airplanes, etc. By putting a price on carbon, everybody pays in proportion to their use of the scarce resource—that limited ability of the atmosphere to absorb emissions—and by recycling that money to the people as equal per person dividends, everybody gets paid back the same amount regardless of the size of their carbon footprint. So what that means is that people who have smaller carbon footprints come out ahead, and people who have bigger ones come out behind.

When you do the math, what you learn is that the majority of the American people would actually benefit through a recycling of the money: Low-income households would come out ahead, middle-income households would be kept whole—so their real incomes wouldn't suffer by virtue of the rising prices of fossil fuels—and the wealthier households would end up paying more than they get back. But—you know what?—they can afford it.

D&S: I think that, when they hear a description of that policy, most people have a favorable reaction to the clarity and the simplicity of it: You pay in proportion to the carbon emissions that are embedded in what you consume, and then you get back an equal share of what everyone pays into that pool. Some people, however, may live in an area where the electrical utilities are all using coal-fired plants, and this is a kind of emissions that's very difficult for them to avoid individually. Is there an argument in favor of, say, adjusting the policy so that, if you're stuck in that kind of area paying for high-carbon-intensity electricity, you're not penalized for that?

JB: Well you're raising an important point, Alejandro, which is that there are some regional and interstate differences in carbon footprints based, above all, on the composition of the electricity supply. In states like Oregon or Vermont, that don't use much fossil fuel for electricity, people have lower carbon footprints at a given level of income than people in, say, Indiana or a number of other midwestern states that use more coal for their electricity supply. So that's an important issue. Now, on the other hand, there's a lot to be said for keeping the policy simple, and even in a state like Indiana, which has the most carbon-intensive electricity mix, when you

What to Make of the Paris Agreement?

The agreement that came out of the Paris conference was a lot better than nothing, but a lot less than what's needed. So you could call the glass half-full or half-empty. The negotiators gave up on crafting an agreement on the allocation of carbon emissions across countries, since this was seen as an insurmountable stumbling block due to the pervasive (but wrong-headed) belief that cutting emissions has to mean present pain for future gain. Instead, each country was asked to propose its own "intended nationally determined contribution." This strategy had the virtue that for the first time the newly industrializing countries—including major emitters like China, India, and Brazil—offered to curtail their emissions. But the sum total of the proposed reductions is inadequate to stabilize the climate, and moreover the agreement has no teeth, no real enforcement mechanism, apart from naming and shaming countries if in practice they don't live up to their commitments.

What we can hope is that the Paris agreement will be a stepping stone. If and when people throughout the world start seeing the present-day benefits from reduced burning of fossil fuels—cleaner air, more jobs, and more money in their pockets if the revenue from carbon pricing is returned to them as dividends—they can be expected to demand more ambitious targets and more rapid progress. When people try something new and discover it tastes good, they usually want more. With the right policies, the world's transition to a clean and renewable energy future could really taste great.

—*James K. Boyce*

calculate how carbon pricing would affect the households, the majority of households would come out ahead if the money's recycled as a dividend. But it would be a slimmer majority in Indiana than it would be in, say, Oregon.

For that reason, I think, it's desirable to think about other elements of the policy that could specifically try to channel resources to states like Indiana, to the most coal-intensive states—partly to assist those states in driving forward the clean energy transition and to cushion the impact on consumers in those states, and partly because in some of the coal-heavy states you've actually got jobs which are linked to the present energy infrastructure. We need to make sure that, as we transition to a clean-energy economy, we don't penalize the people who have been working in the old energy economy, but instead we make sure that they're able to take advantage of the expanded employment opportunities that come with the building-out of our clean-energy infrastructure.

One way to do that would be to channel 75%, let's say, of the carbon revenue back to the public as dividends, and to have 25% of it held as money for public investment—because overall in our economy, about 25% of the investment is by federal, state, and local governments. This is what Senators Maria Cantwell, Democrat of Washington State, and Susan Collins, Republican of Maine, actually proposed in an act they introduced back in 2009 called the CLEAR Act. If you do this—they proposed to channel 75% back to the public as dividends, 25% for public investment in clean and renewable energy—what you can do then is allocate that public investment in ways that takes these regional differences into account. And I think that's not a bad idea.

D&S: To bring this back around full circle to where you started: You talked at the beginning of this interview about this narrative of present-day sacrifice as something that has politically hamstrung serious action on climate change. What do you see as the potential for a real, significant impact of reframing the way that people think about this, away from present sacrifice and toward the potential for present benefits?

JB: I think we already see rising awareness around the world and within this country—really, across the nation and across the political spectrum—of the fact that climate change is real, that burning fossil fuels is a major contributor to the problem, and that we need to do something about it. So, the political will to do something about it has been building. What I think has been holding it in check has been in no small measure the idea that, "Ah gee, but even though we ought to do something, it's really going to hurt and should we really do it? Should we do it if the Chinese aren't doing it? Should we do it if we don't know for sure how much the planet's really going to warm up, etc.?" All these reservations about doing something have held progress back. I think bringing out the ways in which we can design climate policy to achieve clean-air benefits—which means not just having carbon reductions happen regardless of where they're emitted, but also to target the reductions to the places, the industrial sectors, the most heavily impacted communities, to make sure that we get significant reductions in emissions in those places where the air quality and public health co-benefits are likely to be greatest—that's one way to try to break through that resistance. The other way is to design the policy so that the revenue generated by pricing carbon actually comes back to the people, so people end up, in most cases, financially better off in pocketbook terms than they would have been without the policy.

Once the public grasps that not only is this a good thing to do for future generations—for our children and grandchildren and those that will come after them—but it's actually a good thing for us too, I think at that point we have a foundation for really moving forward on a policy, and a policy that can command bipartisan support. Because it's not really a matter of red states vs. blue states or Republicans vs. Democrats. It's not a matter of bigger government vs. smaller government. It's a matter of getting the price on carbon to reflect the fact that burning this stuff comes at an environmental cost to the present and future generations, and making sure that that policy is implemented in a way that, far from hurting the public today, is going to benefit us. ❑

Article 5.5

REDUCING GREENHOUSE GASSES

BY ARTHUR MACEWAN
March/April 2016

Dear Dr. Dollar:
We require certain standards on automobiles to improve their energy effi-
ciency. What about users of electric power? What measures can we take there?
A carbon tax? But wouldn't that place the burden on low-income people?
—Anonymous, via email

Prices matter. When the price of a good goes up, people tend to buy less of that
good. This is the basis for the argument for a carbon tax. By raising the price
that users of fossil fuels would pay (for coal, oil, natural gas), the carbon tax would
lead households and business to use less, reducing the emission of greenhouse gases.

A carbon tax could be a useful step in bringing about less pollution by power
plants as well (as by other carbon fuel users). But it has problems. First of all,
higher fuel prices place the burden of change disproportionately on people with
low incomes. A rich person and a poor person may both have to cool their homes
during increasingly hot summers, but the higher electricity costs brought about by
the carbon tax would be a larger share of the income of the poor person than of the
rich person. Similarly, both the rich and poor may have to drive their cars to work,
but the cost burden on the poor (again, as a percentage of their incomes) would
be greater. And public transportation, alas, is often a very limited option. Or consider the cost of heating a home—again, a larger share of the income of the poor.
And the poor seldom have the funds for energy-saving investments (e.g.,
insulation).

Furthermore, adjustments due to higher prices can be slow. To have their full
impact, the higher prices must alter the investment decisions of businesses and
households, leading them to organize their activities in more fuel-efficient ways.
But those decisions—e.g., building a new power plant or factory, or buying a new
car—may not take place until years after the tax is adopted. Even when power
plants pass the tax on to consumers in the form of higher prices, our dependence
on a plethora of electrical appliances will not shift rapidly. Over time, a higher
price (due to a carbon tax or other causes) will lead to adjustments. (The experience in British Columbia (see box) is encouraging.) But it is unlikely that we have
enough time to wait for these price-induced adjustments.

There are, however, both ways to speed up changes and ways to prevent the
impact from falling heavily on low-income people. One way to speed things up,
an important one, is regulation. If we can require auto makers to produce cars
that are less polluting—which we already do—there is no good reason why we
cannot have regulations that force more rapid change in the electric power industry. Indeed, some such regulations already exist. For example, regulations require
coal-burning power plants to use "scrubbers," an apparatus that cleans the toxic

gases passing through the smokestack of the power plants (though not CO_2, the principal greenhouse gas). Yet, as with the auto industry, regulations could push changes in the power plants more rapidly. The restraint on the implementation (and enforcement) of regulations is the political power of the carbon-fuel industry, not economic or technical factors.

Another important change would be to offset the price increase of carbon-based energy production by reductions in the cost of green-energy pro-duction—reductions relative to the price of carbon-based energy. Currently, the U.S. government and many other governments provide substantial subsidies to carbon-based energy. These subsidies come, for example, as tax breaks, leasing arrangements, support for exploration, and several other forms. While there are subsidies to green energy production, these are small by comparison.

Subsidy estimates vary widely, but according to a 2014 statement by Oil Change International (which is dedicated to exposing the true cost of fossil fuels): "In the United States, credible estimates of annual fossil fuel subsidies range from $10 billion to $52 billion annually, yet these don't even include costs borne by taxpayers related to the climate, local environmental, and health impacts of the fossil fuel industry." And according to the International Energy Agency, in its World Energy Outlook (2014), "Fossil fuels are reaping $550 bil-lion a year in subsidies [globally] and holding back investment in cleaner forms of energy ... Oil, coal and gas received more than four times the $120 billion paid out in incentives for renewables including wind, solar and biofuels ...."

Altering these subsidies and providing firms and households with lower-cost green energy is one important part of an additional step in energy change, namely providing options to the heavy use of carbon-based fuels. One other important option is noted above: more public transportation. Still another is programs that would support energy conservation, of which an example is sub-sidies for residential and commercial building insulation. Further, tax incentives can be used to lead firms and households to pursue both green-energy-use and energy-conservation options. Each of these actions would reduce the cost of alternatives relative to the cost of relying on carbon-based fuels.

Finally, one of the ways that that the impact of higher energy prices on the poor can be eliminated would be to provide tax rebates to the poor that would balance the higher energy costs. Not politically easy, but certainly possible.

A carbon tax and some of the other steps noted here—e.g., tax incentives—are perhaps relatively acceptable politically because they are "market solutions." However, they are not sufficient solutions. Imposing effective regulation, chang-ing the structure of government subsidies, and creating convenient and affordable options are important parts of any serious effort to abate global warming. ❏

Sources: Oil Change International, "Fossil Fuel Subsidies: Overview" (priceofoil.org); Bloomberg Business, "Fossil Fuels With $550 Billion Subsidies Hurt Renewables," November 11, 2014 (bloomberg.com).

Article 5.6

JOBS, JUSTICE, AND THE CLEAN-ENERGY FUTURE

BY JEREMY BRECHER
September/October 2016

Today, there are 400 parts per million (PPM) of carbon dioxide in the atmosphere, far above the 350 ppm climate scientists regard as the safe upper limit. Even in the unlikely event that all nations fulfill the greenhouse gas (GHG) reduction pledges they made at the Paris climate summit at the end of 2015, carbon in the atmosphere is predicted to increase to 670 ppm by the end of this century. The global temperature will rise an estimated 3.5 degrees Celsius (6.3 degrees Fahrenheit) above pre-industrial levels. For comparison, a one-degree increase was enough to cause all the effects of climate change we have seen so far, from Arctic melting to intensified hurricanes to desertification.

Limiting climate catastrophe will require drastic cuts in the burning of the fossil fuels that cause climate change. But many workers and their unions fear that such cuts will lead to drastic loss in jobs and economic well-being for working people—aggravating the shortage of good jobs and the burgeoning inequality we already face. Is there a way to escape the apparent lose-lose choice between saving the climate and saving jobs?

A Possible Clean Energy Future

A series of reports by the Labor Network for Sustainability (LNS), and partners provides good news: The U.S. can meet the targets for greenhouse gas (GHG) reduction that climate scientists say are necessary while also creating half-a-million jobs annually and reducing the cost of energy to consumers. The reports, gathered in the LNS Climate, Jobs, and Justice Project, also show that protecting the climate in a way that maximizes the benefit for working people and discriminated-against groups will take deliberate public policies and action by unions and their social movement allies.

In 2015, LNS asked Frank Ackerman of Synapse Energy Economics to assess the employment effects of meeting the Intergovernmental Panel on Climate Change (IPCC) target of reducing GHG emissions by 80% by 2050 (or "80x50"). Ackerman developed a Clean Energy Future model based on Synapse's many years of analysis of energy systems. [Disclosure: Ackerman is a longtime associate of *Dollars & Sense* and a former *D&S* collective member. —Eds.]

Ackerman and his coworkers set themselves the task of meeting three challenges simultaneously. The Clean Energy Future scenario should meet the IPCC target of reducing GHG emissions 80% by 2050. It should provide more good jobs than the business-as-usual scenario (what would happen if no changes are made to address climate change). And it should not place higher costs on American consumers.

The resulting report, "The Clean Energy Future: Protecting the Climate, Creating Jobs and Saving Money," shows that the United States can reduce GHG emissions 80% by 2050—while adding half-a-million jobs annually and saving Americans billions of dollars on their electrical, heating, and transportation costs.

The Clean Energy Future constructs a baseline "business as usual" reference case based primarily on projections from the federal Energy Information Administration's Annual Energy Outlook. It compares that reference case to a clean energy alternative based primarily on scenarios developed by the National Renewable Energy Laboratory (NREL) and original research by Synapse. It uses IMPLAN, a widely used model of employment impacts, to evaluate the jobs impacts of each of the two scenarios.

In the Clean Energy Future model, energy efficiency programs match the performance of today's most effective state programs. A national Renewable Portfolio Standard requires 70% renewable electricity by 2040. The cost of solar photovoltaic cells that convert sunlight into electricity drops 75% from 2010 to 2020. (The reference case already projects a 40% reduction.) Coal is entirely phased out. No new nuclear plants are built and existing plants are retired at the end of their 60-year life expectancy. By 2050, gas cars and light trucks are replaced by electric vehicles, and 80% of gas- and oil-fired space-heating and water-heating is replaced by electric heat. Wind and solar power grow enough to provide electricity for the new vehicles and heating. The Synapse team has prepared detailed analyses showing these projections are realistic, even conservative.

The Clean Energy Future plan covers electricity generation, cars and light trucks, space and water heating, fossil fuel supply, and waste management. It reduces GHG emissions across these sectors by 86% by 2050, compared to emissions in 1990.

If these reductions are made, meeting the "80x50" target (at least 80% reduction in emissions by 2050) for the entire economy will require far less stringent reductions in the remaining sectors. If non-electric industry, mass transit, freight transport, and agriculture reduce their emissions by 42%, the entire economy can meet the 80% reduction target. The report discusses a variety of studies indicating how those reductions could be achieved or indeed exceeded.

Creating New Jobs

The Clean Energy Future will create a substantial number of new jobs. The increase in jobs created, compared to the business-as-usual scenario, will start around 200,000 per year in 2016–2020 and rise to 800,000 a year in 2046–2050. The average job gain compared to business-as-usual scenario is 550,000 per year for the entire period. There are several reasons for this advantage. The Clean Energy scenario spends less on imported oil and less money ends up in the pockets of the owners of gas pipelines, coal mines, and oil wells and refineries, many of them overseas. Much of that money is spent instead paying workers to produce more labor-intensive forms of renewable energy and energy efficiency.

Nearly 80% of the new jobs provided by the Clean Energy Future will be concentrated in manufacturing and construction. The scenario will immediately start to create hundreds of thousands of new jobs in energy efficiency, ranging from insulation to high-efficiency heating and cooling, to fuel cells and combined heat and power (CHP) installations, to use of tree planting to cool urban areas. In the 2020s, a second

Jobs and Climate Policy In the States

The Climate, Jobs, and Justice Project includes three reports that take a closer look at what the Clean Energy Future will mean in three states, Illinois, Maryland, and Connecticut. These states were selected both because they present very different problems and potentials for climate policy and because they all have active organizing around climate and jobs that can test the relevance and usefulness of the Clean Energy Future.

If Illinois were an independent country, it would be the 20th largest economy in the world and the 34th largest emitter of GHGs. It is also a state with enormous potential for wind and solar energy. As a result, the state can phase out its coal and nuclear production while adding enough renewable energy capacity not only to replace it but also to run a new electric-vehicle fleet and export energy to other states.

The "Illinois Jobs and Clean Energy: Protecting the Climate and the State Economy" report lays out a climate protection strategy that will produce more than 28,000 net new jobs per year over business-as-usual projections through 2050. That represents almost 0.5% of total employment in the state, so it should reduce the unemployment rate by one-half percentage point. Three-quarters of the jobs created will be in the relatively high-wage construction and manufacturing sectors. The report indicates that even more jobs could be created if Illinois accelerated its climate timetable and made itself a center for export of renewable energy and renewable-energy-related manufactured goods such as wind-turbine components and solar-energy equipment.

"Maryland's Clean Energy Future: Climate Goals and Employment Benefits" presents a plan to reduce Maryland's net emissions of greenhouse gases (GHGs) to 80% less than the 2006 level by 2050—while adding more than ten thousand jobs per year. It identifies the state's major industrial emitters of GHGs and lays out strategies for reducing their emissions. The report also indicates that Maryland can use the burgeoning state and national demand for clean energy to create good, stable jobs in a growing climate-protection sector: manufacturing jobs, jobs for those who have been marginalized in the current labor market, and jobs for skilled union workers in the construction trades. It argues that Maryland needs a robust job-creation and clean-industry development strategy to realize that potential.

"The Connecticut Clean Energy Future: Climate Goals and Employment Benefits" shows how a largely non-industrial state with extreme economic inequality can create a rapidly growing climate-protection sector that creates stable jobs for unionized workers, effective job ladders for those previously excluded from good jobs, and expansion of energy efficiency, renewable energy, and other sectors. It presents a plan that meets the state's official goal of reducing GHG emissions 80% below the 2001 level by 2050 while adding more than 6000 jobs, most of them in construction and manufacturing.

Connecticut can achieve many of its other goals, such as reducing poverty and inequality, improving air quality, raising workforce skill levels, and reducing unemployment while implementing an aggressive climate-protection plan, but to realize these "co-benefits" it will need policies designed to do so. Public policy must assure that Clean Energy Future jobs are good, secure, permanent jobs with education, training, and advancement. New, high-quality jobs and/or dignified retirement must be provided for approximately 600 workers who may lose jobs in the Clean Energy Future—less than one-tenth of the jobs that will be gained. Existing inequality and racial, gender, and other injustices must be counteracted through job pathways, strong affirmative action provisions, and local hiring requirements. And a more local and less top-down energy system can be created through a rising Renewable Portfolio Standard requiring in-state electricity generation; shared solar generation; electric grid modernization; and encouragement for local clean-energy initiatives.

wave of jobs will develop producing, installing, and maintaining wind turbines, solar panels, and other forms of renewable energy. In the 2030s, new jobs will develop in the auto industry due to the increasing production of electric cars and trucks. Starting in the 2040s, the clean energy scenario will save so much money that a significant number of jobs will be created by the money saved on fossil fuels that will be spent instead on job-creating expenditures. Over the 35-year period, the average of 550,000 extra jobs per year will include 187,000 jobs in manufacturing and 240,000 in construction.

The Clean Energy Future will provide many new jobs for each that is lost. There will, however, be fewer jobs in coal, oil, and gas extraction and burning and in nuclear energy. For example, there will be about 100,000 fewer jobs each year in mining and extraction compared to the business-as-usual scenario. The report calls for a "just transition" for the workers who hold those jobs, including "assistance in training and placement in new jobs, or retirement with dignity."

Some studies have projected a far higher number of jobs created by climate protection policies, sometimes running in the millions. There are several reasons the numbers in the Clean Energy Future scenario are lower. It is based on the large and continuing reduction in the cost of renewable energy, which makes it possible to meet GHG reduction targets at far lower cost—but therefore also with considerably less labor. Unlike some studies, it is not based on extensive expansion of biofuel production, which creates large numbers of low-paid agricultural jobs. The program is designed to keep the cost of transition to a minimum, which also holds down the number of jobs created. Finally, the projections are based on conservative assumptions derived from a detailed knowledge of the electrical system. The report emphasizes that if society is prepared to spend more money, a far more rapid and job-intensive program could result.

The Costs Will Be Less

Over the 35-year period, the Clean Energy Future will actually cost slightly less than the business-as-usual case. It will actually save $7 per person annually in electricity, transportation, and heating costs—while meeting climate goals and creating jobs.

Why are the costs so modest? One reason is that the costs of solar, wind, and other forms of renewable energy have been getting dramatically lower and, according to Synapse's projections extrapolated from those of the federal Energy Information Administration and the National Renewable Energy Laboratory, they are likely to continue to do so.

"The Clean Energy Future" points out that there is another reason as well. Economists often assume that the status quo already represents the greatest possible efficiency; if it were possible to do things more efficiently, people would already be doing so in order to maximize their gains in the market. This is often put in the form of such adages as "there is no such thing as a free lunch" and "if there were pennies lying around on the ground someone would have already picked them up."

But in the case of energy in particular, the evidence indicates that there is so much waste in the current energy system that major cost savings can be realized by such available means as insulating buildings and co-generating heat and electricity.

Investment in such measures will be highly cost-effective and provide a high return. There are various reasons these "pennies" are not currently being picked up, including the market power of large energy corporations, the monopolies held by energy utilities, counterproductive government regulations, and incomplete knowledge. But those pennies can be picked up and utilized as part of the transition to the Clean Energy Future.

A Floor, Not a Ceiling

The Clean Energy Future plan provides a floor, not a ceiling, for what can be accomplished. It shows how we can meet climate goals with no net cost, and that doing so will create more jobs. But we can, and indeed should, do more. For example, mass transit can be expanded far faster. GHG reduction targets can be met earlier. GHG emissions can be reduced to near zero. We can achieve such goals just by accelerating the same basic plan.

We can also achieve other goals besides climate protection as part of the same process. To achieve maximum benefit from the Clean Energy Future, the project advocates four basic policies:

Pacific Northwest: Fossil Fuel vs. Clean Energy Jobs

Whenever there is opposition to a pipeline, fossil-fuel power plant, oil well, or other fossil-fuel project, it raises a legitimate question: Where are the people who would have built and operated the project going to find jobs? An LNS Climate, Jobs, and Justice project report, "The Economic Impact of Clean Energy Investments in the Pacific Northwest: Alternatives to Fossil Fuel Exports" by Noah Enelow of Ecotrust Knowledge Systems, examines job prospects for such an area, Grays Harbor County in western Washington State.

The report compares a recently defeated oil-export terminal to possible clean-energy projects. The Grays Harbor Westway and Imperium crude-oil storage-and-export terminal would have received oil brought by train from Utah and shipped it to Asia. The project would have created an estimated 231 construction jobs during its year of building and 148 operations jobs thereafter.

Enelow developed plans for two complementary clean-energy initiatives as an alternative. The first is a utility-scale solar photovoltaic array, with electrical components manufactured in-state. It would produce 478 construction jobs—more than twice as many jobs as the coal export terminal. But once built, the solar facility would produce only seven direct operations jobs compared with 148 direct operations jobs for the export terminal.

The report proposes a complementary investment in energy efficiency for commercial buildings, such as those financed by Property Assessed Clean Energy (PACE) programs. This would create 262 direct jobs in Grays Harbor County—exceeding the Westway/Imperium proposal by 114 jobs. In short, the combined utility-scale solar and energy-efficiency proposal would create far more jobs both in construction and in permanent operations than the oil-export terminal.

Source: Noah Enelow, Labor Network for Sustainability, "The Economic Impact of Clean Energy Investments in the Pacific Northwest: Alternatives to Fossil Fuel Exports," March 2016 (labor4sustainability.org).

Climate protection will require the creation of tens of thousands of new jobs. But there is no guarantee that they will be good jobs. Indeed, depending on other economic trends, spending on climate protection could increase inequality and provide increasingly insecure, contingent work. Climate protection strategy should be designed to provide the maximum number possible of good, secure, permanent jobs with opportunities for education, training, and advancement. The deterioration in the quality of jobs is directly related to the reduction in the size and bargaining power of labor unions; reinforcing the right of workers to organize and bargain collectively should be an explicit part of public policy for climate protection.

Because some jobs will be lost in fossil fuel-related industries, we need a vigorous program to provide new, high-quality jobs and/or dignified retirement for workers in those industries. A Superfund to protect workers and communities from negative side effects of climate policies should be a central part of any climate program. Anything less will be unjust to workers and will undermine political support for climate protection programs.

The Clean Energy Future plan opens up new opportunities to counter the growing inequality and rampant racial, gender, and other injustices of our society. But many of those opportunities will be lost unless we have deliberate policies to realize them. Climate protection programs should include job pathways and strong affirmative action provisions for those groups that have been most excluded from good jobs in the past.

The Clean Energy Future also opens up a wide range of opportunities for creating a more democratic economy and society. It allows for a less top-down and more distributed energy system, potentially reducing control by centralized utilities and increasing that of local and grassroots entities. It provides many opportunities for local economic initiatives, ranging from energy coops to local and community-based enterprises of many kinds. It will reduce the wealth and power of the fossil fuel corporations that have such a dominant role within our political system. These opportunities should not be squandered.

A Worker-Friendly Approach to Climate Protection

The Clean Energy Future laid out in the Climate, Jobs, and Justice Project represents a practical plan to reduce GHG emissions 80% by 2050. It shows that climate protection is not only affordable, but that it can actually save Americans money. The plan will create half a million more jobs than continuing on a fossil-fuel pathway, most of them in manufacturing and construction. It shows that—should we choose to do so—we can reduce carbon emissions enough to stabilize the climate, create growing numbers of good jobs, and at the same time avoid imposing new costs on consumers and taxpayers.

For unions, the Clean Energy Future presents a worker-friendly approach to climate protection. It overcomes the false assumption that workers must make a choice between climate protection on the one hand, and jobs and economic well-being on the other. It can form a key element in a workers' program for climate protection—one that can unify trade unionists, environmentalists, and the growing majority of Americans who are deeply concerned about climate change.

More and more unions are making climate protection a central part of their program. Unions and federations ranging from SEIU to the California Labor Federation have passed resolutions on climate change in the past few months. Climate caucuses have been formed in central labor councils up and down the West Coast. In January 2016, LNS organized the first Labor Convergence on Climate which brought together 75 labor leaders to forge a common strategy to change organized labor's approach to climate protection; the Convergence included invited representatives of state AFL-CIOs, city central labor councils, and individual unions, including building trades, manufacturing, public employee, and service unions, including elected officers. Such efforts open the way for organized labor to become a significant participant in the climate protection movement.

As the devastation caused by climate change grows the consciousness of the need to halt it is likely to grow as well—not only in the labor movement but throughout society. Whether it will grow strong enough fast enough to limit climate disaster is today an open question. (For discussion of the obstacles to climate protection and strategies for overcoming them, see my book, *Climate Insurgency: A Strategy for Survival* (2016) and my forthcoming books *Climate Solidarity: Workers vs. Warming* and *Against Doom: A Climate Insurgency Manual* (PM Press: 2017).)

The Clean Energy Future represents a pathway away from climate destruction that is also far better for workers and consumers than our current pathway based on fossil fuels. Should we let greed and inertia prevent us from taking it? ❏

Sources: "Clean Energy Future, 2016-2050," Climate, Jobs, and Justice Project, Labor Network for Sustainability, Sept. 21, 2015 (labor4sustainability.org); Brian Kahn, "A Global Milestone: CO2 Passes 400 PPM," Climate Central, May 6, 2015 (climatecentral.org); "Scoreboard Science and Data," Climate Interactive (climateinteractive.org); Andrew Jones, John Sterman, Ellie Johnston, and Lori Siegel, "With Improved Pledges Every Five Years, Paris Agreement Could Limit Warming Below 2C," Dec. 14, 2015 (climateinteractive.org).

Chapter 6

CORPORATIONS

Article 6.1

IF CORPORATIONS ARE PEOPLE,
WHAT KIND OF PEOPLE ARE THEY?

BY GEOFF SCHNEIDER
June 2016

In 1886, the U.S. Supreme Court ruled, in *Santa Clara County v. Southern Pacific Railroad*, that corporations have the same legal status as persons. The legal rights of corporations gradually have been expanded in the United States since that time to include the right to free speech and to contribute unlimited amounts to political campaigns (a product of the Supreme Court's 2010 *Citizens United* ruling). A key question that emerges from U.S. corporate personhood is: If corporations are people, what kind of people are they?

One of the key characteristics of a corporation is that, by its very legal structure, it is an amoral entity. It exists for the sole purpose of making profits, and it will do whatever is necessary to increase profits, without considering ethical issues except insofar as they impinge on the bottom line. A crucial reason for this behavior is that chief executive officers (CEOs) and other executives have a legal "fiduciary duty" to act in the best financial interests of stockholders. As conservative economist Milton Friedman stated in his book *Capitalism and Freedom*, "there is one and only one social responsibility of business—to use its resources and engage in activities designed to increase its profits so long as it stays within the rules of the game, which is to say, engages in open and free competition without deception or fraud." Thus, those who control corporations are obligated to do whatever they can within the law to make as much money as possible.

This can lead to behavior that some have called psychopathic. In the provocative 2003 film, "The Corporation," the filmmakers argue that corporations meet the diagnostic criteria used by psychiatrists to determine if a person is psychopathic. Those criteria are:

- Callous disregard for the feelings of others;
- Reckless disregard for the safety of others;
- Incapacity to maintain enduring relationships;
- Deceitfulness: repeated lying and conniving others for profit;
- Incapacity to experience guilt; and
- Failure to conform to social norms with respect to lawful behaviors.

Although at first blush the claim that corporations are psychopaths seems incredible, if we consider the worst behaviors of corporations over the last few decades, and the disturbing frequency with which such behaviors seem to recur, it is possible to see why so many people hold corporations in such low esteem. Below, we describe briefly some of the most horrific behaviors of large corporations in recent years.

Rana Plaza Building Collapse, 2013:

An Example of Corporate Abuses of Subcontracting and Sweatshops

For decades, U.S. and European clothing manufacturers have been moving their operations overseas to countries with extremely low wages and with few safety or environmental regulations. One of their favorite destinations in recent years has been Bangladesh, where wages for clothing workers are the lowest in the world (only $0.24 per hour until the minimum wage was raised to $0.40 per hour in 2014), and where few safety standards are enforced. Bangladesh now has more than 5,000 garment factories handling orders for most of the world's top brands and retailers, and is second in garment manufacturing output behind China.

In 2013, the Rana Plaza building that housed several clothing factories collapsed, killing 1,134 people in the worst disaster in garment-industry history. It was later discovered that the building was constructed with substandard materials in violation of building codes. Even more disturbing was the fact that the owners of the factories insisted that employees return to work even after an engineer inspected the building the day before the collapse and deemed it unsafe due to cracks in the walls and clear structural deficiencies. The factories were making clothes for Walmart, Benetton, and many other large, multinational companies.

Disasters like this one, along with the torture and killing of a Bangladeshi labor activist in 2012, are a product of the subcontracting system used by large clothing manufacturers. The corporations issue specifications for the garments that they want to have manufactured, and contractors around the world bid for the right to make the garments. The lowest bidder wins. But what kind of factory is likely to have the lowest bid? Given the regular occurrence of disasters and labor abuses in garment factories, it appears that the contractors who win bids are those who are the most likely to pay workers the least under the most unsafe conditions. Huge multinational clothing companies are only too eager to participate, while at the same time claiming that they are not responsible for the deaths and abuses because they themselves were not the factory owners. The factory owners in Bangladesh were charged with murder, but there were no major consequences for the clothing companies. The callous disregard for the feelings and safety of others and incapacity to experience guilt that many clothing manufacturers display is certainly consistent with the definition of a psychopath.

BP Oil Spill in the Gulf of Mexico, 2010:

Taking Chances with People's Lives and the Environment

The 2010 BP oil spill in the Gulf of Mexico was the worst in U.S. history. The Deepwater Horizon oil rig exploded on April 20, 2010, killing 11 people and spilling 210 million gallons of oil into the Gulf. Investigations into the causes of the spill indicated significant negligence.

- Deepwater drilling procedures were adapted from shallow-water techniques, without adequate consideration of the differences of the deep-water environment.
- Federal regulators relaxed requirements for environmental reviews, tests, and safety plans at the request of BP, and encouraged but did not require key backup systems.
- BP used well casings, cement, and other equipment that violated company safety guidelines and industry best practices, despite concerns raised by BP engineers.
- Warning signs were ignored, and safety tests delayed despite the warning signs.

The human and environmental costs of the spill were devastating. In addition to the human deaths, millions of birds, turtles, dolphins, and fish were killed. The Gulf tourism industry was devastated for several years, costing businesses $23 billion in lost revenue. And the Gulf still has not recovered, with ongoing problems cropping up related to the environment and wildlife.

The primary culprit here was BP's relentless pursuit of lower costs. Poor quality materials plus skimping on safety measures created conditions for the explosion and meant that BP was unable to deal with the disaster once it happened. Although BP was found guilty of negligence and fined a record $18.7 billion, that amount was only about 8% of their annual revenue, and no BP official went to prison.

ExxonMobil and Climate Change Denial, 1981-2008:

Lying to People for Profit

In 1981, a team of researchers at Exxon conclusively established the connection between the burning of fossil fuels, the spewing of greenhouse gases into the air (especially carbon), and climate change. Their research was supported by dozens of other studies by climate scientists. These studies have been so convincing that over 97% of climate scientists agree that climate change is occurring and that human activity is a significant cause. As anyone who studies scientific research will know, it is rare to have near-universal agreement on something as complex as climate change, which helps us to understand that the evidence for climate change is overwhelming.

Despite this evidence, Exxon, which merged with Mobil in 1999, spent millions of dollars on a public-relations effort to deny the existence of climate change so that they could continue to sell as much of their oil as possible. As documented in the book *Merchants of Doubt* (later adapted as a film of the same name), Exxon funded foundations who paid a small group of scientists and public-relations professionals to cast doubt on the idea of climate change in order to prevent action from being taken. And their impact in the United States was dramatic. While much of the world was taking climate change seriously and enacting policies to begin reducing greenhouse gas emissions, the United States was increasing its use of fossil fuels and its emissions.

ExxonMobil now states publicly that it accepts the idea that climate change is occurring, and the company has stopped formally funding climate change denialism. However, ExxonMobil's reduction in public funding of denialism has coincided with a dramatic increase in untraceable "dark money" being used to fund climate change denialism. One cannot help but wonder who is funding such efforts.

Thanks to ExxonMobil and others who have prevented progress on climate change, we are now faced with the prospect of dramatic climate events that will cost many people their lives. We are likely to see increasing droughts, food shortages, heat waves, sea-level rise, floods, and other disasters that threaten our very existence. All so that ExxonMobil and other giant companies could sell more barrels of oil. As is so often the case, there have been no criminal prosecutions related to these incidents.

Enron's Fraudulent Use of Derivatives and Shell Companies, 1990-2002:

Financial Deregulation Plus Executive Stock Options are a Toxic Mix
One of the arguments in favor of corporations is that, thanks to the profit motive, they tend to innovate in order to make money. But, what kind of innovations might result from the profit motive? Enron executives Kenneth Lay and Jeffrey Skilling used the deregulated environment in financial markets in the 1990s and early 2000s (the same environment that also produced the financial crisis) to create an innovative financial model build on fraud and subterfuge.

Enron was the world's largest energy trading company, with a market value of $68 billion. But its real innovation was in shady accounting practices. Enron would start by undertaking a legitimate investment, such as building a power plant. They would then immediately claim all of the expected profit from the power plant on their books, even though they had yet to make any money on the investment, making them appear to be an incredibly profitable company. If the power-plant profits ever came in below expectations, Enron would transfer the unprofitable assets to a shell company—a company that did not really exist formally, other than as a vehicle for Enron to dispose of losses—thereby hiding Enron's losses from its investors. Shell-company investors were given shares of Enron common stock to compensate them for the shell-company losses. Thus, Enron appeared to be incredibly profitable even while it was incurring losses, which caused its stock price to soar.

Much of the reason for this behavior was the incentive system created by financial markets. At the time, most CEOs and highly placed executives were paid most of their salaries in stock options. This meant that they could make more money if they could get the company's stock price to increase, which would allow them to cash in their stock options at a higher value. In theory, paying CEOs in stock options gave them an incentive to run the company in the most profitable way possible, which would then cause the stock price to go up. But stock options also gave executives an incentive to artificially prop up stock prices in order to cash in, which is what the Enron executives did. Meanwhile, the accounting auditors who were supposed to flag questionable and illegal financial transactions looked the other way in order to keep Enron's business.

As Enron's losses mounted, the executives cashed in all of their stock options and left the company bankrupt. More than 5,000 employees lost their jobs and millions of investors lost their savings. Lay, Skilling and 15 other Enron executives were found guilty of fraud. But these sordid events didn't stop an even bigger financial market manipulation from dragging down the entire global economy less than a decade later.

Goldman Sachs, CMOs, and the Financial Crisis of 2007-2008:

Betting Against Your Own Clients

The global financial crisis of 2007-2008 was a product of a number of corporate misdeeds, fueled by greed and the deregulation of financial markets. To increase their profits in the early 2000s, banks started loaning money to extremely risky, subprime borrowers with very poor credit scores to purchase houses. The banks then bundled large groups of these subprime mortgage loans into securities called collateralized mortgage obligations (CMOs). The banks did not care about the credit-worthiness of borrowers because they immediately sold these securities to investors.

As more and more subprime borrowers took out mortgage loans, the real-estate market boomed, forming a huge bubble. At the peak of the bubble in 2006-2007, default rates on mortgages started to increase rapidly. Realizing that subprime loans were likely to fail, Goldman Sachs and several other big investment banks began to do something highly unethical: they sold bundles of subprime mortgages (as CMOs) to investors, and they used financial instruments called credit default swaps to bet that the mortgages in the CMOs they sold were going to default and that the CMOs would become worthless. In other words, they sold investors CMO securities that they believed were going to fail, and they even made bets in financial markets that the CMOs they sold would fail. Goldman Sachs was not the only investment bank to do this. Deutsche Bank and Morgan Stanley also engaged in similar transactions to profit at the expense of their own investors.

As in so many other cases of corporate malfeasance, the consequences amounted to little more than a slap on the wrist. Goldman Sachs paid a $550 million fine in 2010 to settle the fraud case brought by the Securities and Exchange Commission (SEC), an amount that was just 4% of the $13.4 billion in profits Goldman Sachs made in the previous year. In 2016, Goldman Sachs agreed to an additional $5.1 billion fine for misleading investors about the quality of the CMOs they sold them. However, not a single Goldman Sachs official went to jail.

VW Programs Cars to Cheat on Emissions Tests, 2009-2015:

The Things a Company Will Do to Become #1

Martin Winterkorn, Volkswagen's chief executive officer from 2007 to 2015, established the goal of making VW the largest car company in the world, and he embarked on an ambitious plan to achieve that goal. Much of his plan hinged on developing fuel-efficient, clean diesel cars as an alternative to hybrids. But, when VW discovered that it could not develop an inexpensive technology to remove pollution without compromising the car's gas mileage and overall performance, they turned to a fraudulent approach. VW programmed 10.5 million cars so that the cars would detect when they were being tested for emissions, and during testing the cars' engines would run in a way that they would meet emissions standards. But when the cars were driven normally, they would spew pollutants at a rate much higher than allowed by law.

A nonprofit group, the International Council on Clean Transportation, discovered the problem when they tested numerous diesel cars in 2013. They alerted the Environmental Protection Agency (EPA), which launched an investigation in 2014. As is so often the case, VW responded to the investigation aggressively, accusing regulators and testers of being incompetent. But additional testing established conclusively that VW cars had been programmed to reduce emissions when tested, and to spew large amounts of pollutants when driven normally. The EPA told VW that it would no longer allow the company to sell diesel cars in the United States in 2015, and accused them of violating the Clean Air Act. Particularly problematic was the fact that VW diesels spewed large amounts of nitrogen oxide, in amounts up to 40 times the legal limit. Nitrogen oxide is a pollutant that causes emphysema, bronchitis, and contributes to many other respiratory diseases. The EPA estimates that the additional pollution from VW diesel cars will cause as many as 34 deaths and sicken thousands of people in the United States. Other studies predicted up to 200 premature deaths.

VW did briefly become the largest car company in the world in July of 2015 when they surpassed Toyota, but since the scandal became public the company has fallen back. On June 27, 2016, VW agreed to pay $14.7 billion in fines to the government and compensation for VW diesel car owners. A criminal inquiry is also underway.

General Motors' Faulty Ignition Switches, 2005-2007:

Why Would Anyone Sell a Product That They Knew Could Kill People?

Imagine yourself as a CEO or vice president of a major corporation. An engineering report comes across your desk, noting that a part in one of your products is faulty, and that the consequences of that part failing could be the injury or even deaths of some of your customers. Would you still sell the faulty product, even knowing that it might kill people? This is what General Motors (GM) did with its faulty ignition switch.

This particular sordid story starts in 2010, when a 29-year-old nurse named Brooke Melton died in a car crash after losing control of her car. Her parents, who knew that she was a safe driver and that her car had been behaving oddly, sued GM and hired engineering experts to try to determine the cause of the crash. They discovered that the problem was the ignition switch that had been installed on over 22 million GM cars manufactured from 2001 to 2007. The ignition switch could turn from "On" to "Acc" just by being bumped lightly or if the key was on a particularly heavy keychain. The shift from "On" to "Acc" could disable the power steering, anti-lock braking, and airbags and cause the car to stall.

As the investigation progressed, the full scale of GM's deceit became apparent. In 2001, GM engineers initially detected the defective part, labelling it the "switch from hell." Problems with the switch cropped up repeatedly over the next several years. In 2005, internal documents show that GM acknowledged the problem but chose not to fix it because it would be too costly. Instead, they sent a note to GM dealerships telling them to urge customers to use lighter key chains. Each year, people died as ignition switches failed and air bags failed to deploy, but GM continued to hide the problem and refused to recall cars and repair the problem.

Finally, thanks to the Melton lawsuit and government investigations that followed, GM recalled the vehicles and repaired the faulty switch. But not before at least 124 people died in crashes related to the faulty part. GM paid a $900 million fine in 2015, and other settlements with victims brought the total cost of the debacle to $2 billion. While this put a dent in the company's 2015 profits of $9.7 billion, no individuals faced criminal charges for their actions.

Are Corporations Psychopaths?

Above, we highlighted seven examples of horrific corporate behavior. In each case, corporations exhibited many of the behaviors characteristic of psychopaths, especially a callous disregard for the feelings and safety of others, deceitfulness, avoidance of admitting guilt and taking responsibility for their actions, and failure to respect social and ethical norms and the law. But, are these behaviors typical of powerful, profit-hungry corporations, or are they exceptions?

As we all know, many corporations behave ethically, and many invent useful and innovative products that improve our lives. Yet, every year a certain number of corporations cast ethics and morality to the side and engage in unscrupulous behavior, resulting in economic harm, injury, and even deaths. There appear to be aspects of the corporate structure that encourage such behavior, including the relentless quest for maximum profits, the lack of personal responsibility for any illegal actions taken by the corporation, and the power corporations have to manipulate the legal system and government regulators.

Regarding the last point, one of the elements to every story above was the inadequate efforts of government regulators. The push for deregulation by various politicians directly facilitated many of the above corporate misdeeds. And government regulators are often overmatched by corporate legal teams with almost unlimited resources, which allows many corporations to avoid serious consequences even in cases where they have done something horrible. Even when corporations have been caught red handed in clear violation of the law, the penalties are usually little more than a slap on the wrist and are often far less than the profits from the offense in question. Corporate wealth and power appear to allow them to avoid significant checks on their behavior. Thus, instead of engaging in "open and free competition without deception or fraud," as Milton Friedman hoped that they would, some corporations use deception and fraud with near impunity in order to outdo the competition.

Such problems could be fixed. We need a regulatory system with teeth, where corporate lobbyists don't have undue influence over how they are regulated. And we need real consequences for corporate crime. When corporations find out that their actions or products may harm people, if they refuse to take action and to inform the public and regulators of the problem, the people who make those decisions should go to prison.

Finally, like real people, corporations should face real consequences when they break the law. A corporation that engages in particularly egregious behavior, especially a corporation that does so repeatedly, should face sanctions that have a real impact on executives and stockholders. For cases in which a corporation causes deaths, the corporation should face the "death penalty": having its charter revoked and its assets seized by the public. If stockholders could potentially lose all of their investment in a company that behaved illegally, they would begin checking up on companies and we would see much less illegal and unethical behavior.

Of course, all of these solutions require us to get corporate money out of politics. As long as corporations can buy off politicians, they can continue to act as psychopaths and face very little in the way of consequences. ❑

Article 6.2

THE CORPORATE P.R.OPAGANDA MACHINE

BY ROB LARSON
July/August 2016

Gawker, the media startup pioneer that strattled the line between tabloid gossip and legit news breaking, has declared bankruptcy. The filing largely owes to the huge judgement against the company in the lawsuit brought against it by the former pro wrestler Hulk Hogan, upheld at the amount of $140 million. Gawker had uploaded an excerpt of the wrestler's sex tape, leading to Hogan body-slamming the company with invasion-of-privacy litigation.

However, Hogan likely could not have afforded the representation to bring and win such massive damages—and in May it was revealed that Hogan's legal team was underwritten by the billionaire PayPal co-founder and noted libertarian Peter Thiel, who subsidized Hogan's team to the tune of $10 million. This tag-team subsidy arises from Gawker's alleged outing of Thiel as gay in 2007, leading to Thiel becoming the pay pal of a number of plaintiffs bringing litigation against the company. Notably, Thiel's legal staff made the unusual move of avoiding claims that would have been partially payable with Gawker's insurance—suggesting the goal was indeed to bankrupt the company rather than recovering maximum damages.

While Gawker's bankruptcy filing will let its management maintain control of the company as it looks for a buyer, we are left to confront the ramifications of the power of extremely rich people to destroy media entities that, for whatever reason, have displeased them. This sets up a cage match between the freedom of media to disseminate information and the power of money, in various forms, to suppress or warp our information landscape.

The left should feel positive about the broad subject of freedom of information, after victories on U.S. net neutrality in 2015 and the rejection by the U.S. Appeals Court of the industry's legal appeal in June. The Title II net neutrality rules are very valuable in limiting what telecom firms, like cable and phone companies, can do in tampering with the actual flow of information we rely on. But the control by market actors over the information that's prevalent in the first place is quite another story. While conservative economists celebrate the market as an open and valuable information-aggregating system, the business world has been very self-consciously learning how to manipulate and mislead us, from the supermarket to Wall Street. But educated, information-hungry readers and activists, demanding transparency and neutrality, aren't tapping out yet.

Putting Their Money Where Your Mind Is

The broad power of capitalism to shape our information landscape is most easily seen in the relentless character of modern marketing. Advertising professionals estimate that urban consumers see a staggering 5,000 ads per day, compared to about 2,000 in 1970. This absurd number speaks to the crucial role of advertising in media, as recounted in James Curran and Jean Seaton's classic UK media analysis, *Power Without Responsibility*, considered to be one of the most influential books on media history in the UK. They observe that as circulation numbers rose, advertising became an essential new revenue stream for newspapers, making them (and later other media) more profitable and successful. But Curran and Seaton show that this new business model came with a cost: "Even non-socialist newspapers found that controversial editorial policies led to the loss of commercial advertising. ... Yet publications which conformed to the marketing requirements of advertisers obtained what were, in effect, large external subsidies which they could spend on increased editorial outlay and promotion in order to attract new readers." Thus free-market forces narrowed the diversity of opinion in the media, and contributed to the galaxy of marketing material we encounter daily. But a more cutting-edge aspect of information control is what image-conscious corporations like McDonald's call "brand work." In the face of spreading consumer demand for healthier food, the company has pioneered newer, sneakier means to distort the (obviously accurate) perception that its processed food is unhealthy. "In exchange for perks like free trips, access to important people and sometimes financial compensation, bloggers are encouraged or even contractually bound to write about a company. ... Some bloggers ... get paid as much as $20,000 for the work, which by McDonald's ad-campaign standards isn't much money," the *New York Times* reports.

The brand work is designed for "reaching an audience that has become wary of slick ad campaigns," since the ad comes not from the company itself but "from somebody they trust," as Harvard Business School marketing professor Thales Teixeira puts it. For today's often budget-stressed blue- and white-collar mothers, receiving a five-figure payment for a lowly blog post, or being flown to meet high-ranking corporate officials, is a major event, even if invisibly cheap for McDonald's colossal marketing budget. A "mom blogger" describes how after meeting company president Jan Fields, "Now I relate to her ... and in turn I relate to McDonald's." These sponsored trips and conversations often center on parents' fears about the health ramifications of fast-food diets, which meetings with execs and their paid nutritionist staff are meant to assuage. This undercover promotion of favorable perceptions is a small but notable new wrinkle in the big effect of capitalist institutions on what information is prominent.

Big Brother, Inc.

But the effort to shape our perceptions of firms is only one side of the coin. The other side has to do with how firms collect data to fine-tune promotions, which means large-scale information gathering. The large U.S. retailers have come to lead the wave of private collection of personal data in order to tailor sales pitches—and without the consumer's awareness that this is happening. Profiling the retail giant Target as a leader in modern data-driven marketing, the *New York Times* reports that firms can "buy data" about virtually any aspect of your work history, consumption profile, or even social and political views.

In fact, the only drawback so far for retailers is how well their data collection works, fearing that customers might be "queasy" or "uncomfortable" if they realized retailers were able to infer they were moving or expecting a child just from scouring their previous purchasing choices. Target ultimately developed a poker face, where the company "camouflaged how much it knew," in order to encourage new shopping habits in customers going through life changes. An executive confides that "we started mixing in all these ads for things we knew pregnant women would never buy, so the baby ads looked random." Target even told their statistician to stop communicating with the press, perhaps concerned they had tipped the industry's hand.

While brick-and-mortar retail may have been the pioneer, the online environments of today have redefined the practice. We're all familiar with the creepy feeling of looking at goods on Amazon.com or searching for a product on Google, and then seeing ads for those very products stick with you as you browse the broader Internet. This more nakedly obvious consumer profiling and pitch-tailoring has brought the issue closer to popular attention. This creates an opportunity for activism that is fueled by unease with the lopsided commercial information landscape.

The Price Is Righteous

It's important to consider the ideological foundation for all these information market shenanigans, since every power system needs a plausible-sounding justification. Here, the hoary conservative economic ideology has been dusted off and built around figures like Frederich von Hayek, the Austrian economist and great "libertarian" figure. Hayek famously claimed that government regulation, like today's net neutrality requirements or product labeling laws, would stifle the rich freedom of the market and create a *Road to Serfdom*. Railing against government interference, Hayek feared that public efforts to police commercial media would lead to state control and totalitarian propaganda. He claimed that "the effect of propaganda in totalitarian countries is different not only in magnitude but in kind from that of the propaganda made for different ends by independent and competing agencies. If all the sources of current information are effectively under one single control, it is no longer a question of merely persuading the people of this or that." Hayek's argument was that while particular PR operations from corporate or other sources might mislead, any government attempt to fix this is a Faustian bargain. This claim was relevant for the proto-fascist European conditions he wrote in, but commercial media now thoroughly dominate the world system, and the problems of private media are largely ignored by economists of Hayek's conservative stripe.

More broadly, Hayek held that markets overall were efficient systems for communicating crucial economic information, through prices. "It is more than metaphor," he wrote in the *American Economic Review*, "to describe the price system as a kind of machinery for registering change, or a system of telecommunications which enables individual producers to watch merely the movement of a few points." Without needing access to all economic information, we can simply rely on price points to let us know if particular commodities are more or less valuable. Hayek conceived of the market as a neutral machine summarizing and transmitting information, with limited propaganda, coming from relatively harmless competing groups. This does not address the reality that market-based media are under major constraints to secure advertising revenue, creating a strong incentive to maintain the existing system.

P.R.opaganda

For this reason, Hayek's blissful lack of concern about propaganda in such a setting runs head-on into the work of figures like Edward Bernays, a pioneer of propaganda and public relations for both the state and private capital. Bernays' long career among today's various power centers makes it difficult to accept this view that business has little propaganda power. He wrote, "It was, of course, the astounding success of propaganda during [World War I] that opened the eyes of the intelligent few in all departments of life to the possibilities of regimenting the public mind .... Business offers graphic examples of the effect that may be produced upon the public by interested groups." And certainly the PR world brags about having "The Power to Change the Debate," to quote the webpage of the major D.C. PR firm Berman and Company.

Hayek's insistence that state propaganda is "different not only in magnitude but in kind" from the widespread corporate use of similar tools is also disputed by Bernays' view of things: "New activities call for new nomenclature. The propagandist ... has come to be known by the name of 'public relations counsel.'" His point, clearly, was that these are fancy names for essentially the same job, just on behalf of another power center in society. He further claimed:

Public opinion is no longer inclined to be unfavorable to the large business merger. It resents the censorship of business by the Federal Trade Commission. It has broken down the anti-trust laws where it thinks they hinder economic development. It backs great trusts and mergers which it excoriated a decade ago .... This result has been, to a great extent, obtained by a deliberate use of propaganda in its broadest sense .... But it would be rash and unreasonable to take it for granted that because public opinion has come over to the side of big business, it will always remain there.

Bernays was surely correct on this last point, for as the Occupy movement and the Sanders campaign have demonstrated, the grip of corporate PR is firm but far from unbreakable. The reader is free to identify with the stance of either Bernays and Hayek, although the latter position requires explaining why corporate America pays for 5,000 ads per person per day if their effect is so dissimilar to repetition-based propaganda.

Original Spin

The power of market institutions makes itself felt elsewhere, even in market segments that seem to be based on delivering very objective information. Consider rating services—firms that measure some process or trend and produce reports summarizing them. Recently, Volkswagen has dominated headlines for its faked emission readings, but in fact the issue is systemic. The *Wall Street Journal* describes "a system in which car makers pay the very firms that test and certify their vehicles.

That system relies on the use of so-called 'golden vehicles,' stripped down prototypes that car makers send to testing firms for inspection." This "widespread" and "cozy" relationship "allows car models to undergo tests before they are fitted with everything from back seats to wheels with heavier tread, boosting fuel efficiency and lowering emissions." The article cites European critics suggesting "the commercial ties between car makers and testing firms allow them to wield too much influence over test results," with an environmental group in Brussels adding "There is no incentive to be tough on car makers."

An especially striking example of market rating systems actually comes from the *Journal* itself. The prominent conservative business paper has for years reported excellently on the problems caused by market deregulation, while calling for even more of it on the editorial pages. In February 2008, the paper ran an editorial about the then-emerging financial crisis, focusing on the credit-rating companies Standard & Poor's, Moody's, and Fitch, whose job is to rate financial products, like bonds, in terms of their expected yields and risk. These "Big Three" agencies became notorious for granting very safe "AAA" ratings to the highly risky subprime mortgage securities issued during the housing bubble of the 2000s. The *Journal* editors claimed this was because SEC regulators had prevented other agencies from entering the market (until 2006), which would have encouraged more competition and rating honesty. However, the bigger issue is that the rating agencies make far more money if they grant high ratings to junky "subprime" assets, because the large investment banks and financial firms selling them are willing to pay for these favorable ratings, called an "issuer pays" model.

The *Journal* leaves the blame on the government, but apparently has no problem with the issue of an information provider being paid by the companies whose products it's supposed to evaluate. The paper does acknowledge the issue: "But every business has potential conflicts. In the newspaper industry, we sell ads to the same people we cover. The question is how firms manage these conflicts—and whether the marketplace is allowed to discipline companies that fail investors." Indeed, in an official corporate reply on the editorial page a week later, an S&P official said, "Reputable news outlets like the *Journal* keep a strict 'church and state' separation between their editorial and business operations. Similarly at S&P, we have rigorous policies to support the independence of our ratings, including separating our analytical and commercial activities, and structuring analysts' compensation so that it is not dependent upon fees related to the ratings they assign." This debate is interesting and revealing, since both business media like the *Journal* and credit-rating agencies like S&P are important parts of modern information markets.

The first relevant point is that the marketplace has disciplined S&P, but not quite how the *Journal* editors expected. They would probably agree with Hayek, that the information relevant to financial securities would be most accurate if aggregated through market firms in competition with each other. This competition would force them to improve the accuracy of creditworthiness, providing valuable risk information much as the market produces prices for other goods and services. And indeed, after the cataclysmic 2008 crisis, the Big Three were chastened for their embarrassing rating biases and tightened up their criteria. S&P stiffened its rating criteria the most, but then found it was losing market share—since in the marketplace, making money means being hired by the firms whose securities they are supposed to judge impartially.

But this meant S&P's business suffered relative to the other firms as it assigned lower ratings to financial products, and eventually the firm announced it was "introducing modified business standards that made it easier to give bonds higher ratings," as the *New York Times* business section described.

The changes seemed to work. More banks began choosing S.& P. to rate the new bonds backed by residential mortgages …. Since S.& P. eased its standards last year, its market share has risen to 69 percent from the 18 percent it had in the first years after the crisis …. On nearly every deal since it changed its standards, S.& P. has been willing to make more optimistic predictions about the bonds it was rating than the other agencies rating the deals …. Bankers want more optimistic predictions because they make the bonds easier to sell to investors.

So the "market discipline" is not to accurately share *correct* information, as Hayek and the *Journal*'s editors insisted would happen, but to supply the *right* information—that which is most convenient for immediate profit-making.

Secondly, this "church and state separation" between newspaper ad departments and editorial offices isn't very impressive. Besides the examples described above, the *Journal* itself has let its own ad-driven business model trample its alleged integrity. The advertising industry's trade magazine, *Advertising Age*, has reported on the huge growth of "sponsored content," which is material paid for and supplied by outside companies but set up to *look* like regular news coverage:

By wrapping ad messages in a format that looks like editorial content—and calling them something else, such as 'sponsored' or 'partner' content—they hope to trade on the trust and goodwill editorial has built up with the audience …. The *Wall Street Journal* publishes three special sections underwritten by Deloitte [the financial services giant] … where editorial stories by *Journal* reporters run alongside a box of content marked as sponsored. Deloitte has no influence over which editorial stories appear, a *Wall Street Journal* spokeswoman said.

These same principles definitely also apply to the *Journal*'s corporate parent, News Corporation. In 1998, journalists for a Fox-owned Florida TV station prepared a story on a synthetic hormone designed to increase milk production in cows, produced by Monsanto, the enormous manufacturer of Roundup weed killer and other commercial chemicals. The journalists found that the hormone caused serious health problems in the cows and was likely to affect milk drinkers hormonally. Monsanto threatened Fox with "dire consequences," presumably in the form of withdrawn advertising and legal suits. The network's legal staff dragged the journalists through dozens of revisions removing any mention of cancer, and attempted bribes and bullying, including an episode where the journalists claimed the station manager said, "We paid $3 billion for these television stations. We will decide what the news is. The news is what we tell you it is." The story never did run, so while Hayek claimed the market is an "efficient mechanism for digesting dispersed information," what you may end up digesting is synthetic cow hormones.

Other cases are more obvious, like right-wing billionaire Sheldon Adelson's 2016 purchase of a modest-circulation Las Vegas newspaper, the *Review-Journal*. Adelson paid $140 million for a paper with under 200,000 readers, an insane level of overpaying relative to the paper's modest ad revenue, strongly suggesting the buyer and sellers saw power and influence in owning it. Indeed, the *Review-Journal*'s journalists were told to monitor Adelson's local political enemies, and the publisher began requiring staff to get written permission before covering his purchase of the paper. The transaction itself was done through an obscure proxy, presumably to hide Adelson's role, further raising a stink. Indeed, the *New York Times*, itself owned by wealthy and powerful figures, described this purchase as a "Power Play."

But left outside of the coverage of this and other billionaire media purchases (like libertarian Amazon CEO Jeff Bezos' 2013 purchase of the *Washington Post* for $250 million dollars) is the more basic institutional reality: Personal agendas aside, these media will continue to operate as profit-making enterprises whose main day-to-day goal will be to deliver attractive commercial opportunities to advertisers, not to deliver the truth.

There are still limits to the ability of corporate control over media to suppress major stories, much as state propaganda has to acknowledge basic developments that can't be hidden from the public. The necessity of covering major, unignorable disasters like the BP Deepwater Horizon spill or the 2008 financial crisis indicates that cowtowing to advertisers is also not absolute, and especially business media must report major trends to remain relevant. But these giant, conspicuous cases are the exceptions, and learning the embarrassing details will still require turning to alternative media, including publications that focus on omissions by the commercial media like the Fairness and Accuracy in Reporting (FAIR) newsletter *Extra!*. Independent media focused on the economy like *Dollars & Sense* lack major ad revenue, however, and require sustained support from their readership to persist and grow—not everyone can count on a billionaire with a grudge!

Staying in business in media means not biting the invisible hand that feeds you. ❑

Sources: Lukas Alpert, "Gawker Files for Bankruptcy, Will Be Put Up for Auction," *Wall Street Journal*, June 10, 2016; Nick Madigan and Ravi Somaiya, "Hulk Hogan Awarded $115 Million in Privacy Suit Against Gawker," *New York Times*, March 18, 2016; Andrew Ross Sorkin, "Peter Thiel, Tech Billionaire, Reveals Secret War With Gawker," *New York Times*, May 25 2016; Louise Story, "Anywhere the Eye Can See, It's Likely to See an Ad," *New York Times*, Jan. 15, 2007; Keith O'Brien, "How McDonald's Came Back Bigger Than Ever," *New York Times*, May 4, 2012; Charles Duhigg, "How Companies Learn Your Secrets," *New York Times*, Feb. 16, 2012; Friedrich Hayek, *The Road to Serfdom* (University of Chicago Press, 2007); Friedrich Hayek, "The Use of Knowledge in Society," *American Economic Review*, Vol. 35, No. 4, Sept. 1945; Edward Bernays, *Propaganda* (Ig Publishing, 2005); Jason Chow, Ruth Bender and David Gauthier-Villars, "Europe's Cozy Car Testing," *Wall Street Journal*, Oct. 1 2015; "AAA Oligopoly," *Wall Street Journal*, Feb. 26, 2008; Vickie Tillman, "Standard & Poor's Gives Its Side of the Story," *Wall Street Journal*, March 8, 2008; Nathanial Popper, "S.&P. Bond Deals Are on the Rise Since It Relaxed Rating Criteria," *New York Times* Dealbook, Sept. 17, 2003; "News Organizations Face Tricky Trade-Off With 'Sponsored Content,'" *Advertising Age*, Sept. 23, 2013; "Monsanto and Fox: Partners in Censorship," *PR Watch*, April-June 1998; Friedrich Hayek, Nobel Prize Lecture, "The Pretence of Knowledge," Dec. 11, 1974; Ravi Somaiya, Ian Lovett and Barry Meier, "Sheldon Adelson's Purchase of Las Vegas Paper Seen as a Power Play," *New York Times*, Jan. 2, 2016.

Article 6.3

CLASS WAR BY OTHER MEANS
Tennessee, Volkswagen, and the Future of Labor

BY CHRIS BROOKS
September/October 2016

In 2008, the governments of the city of Chattanooga, Hamilton County, the state of Tennessee, and the United States all collaborated to provide Volkswagen (VW) with a $577 million subsidy package, the largest taxpayer handout ever given to a foreign-headquartered automaker in U.S. history. The bulk of the subsidy package, $554 million, came from local and state sources. The federal government also threw in $23 million in subsidies, bringing the grand total of taxpayer money that VW received in 2008 to $577 million. According to the Subsidy Tracker at the website of watchdog group Good Jobs First, the package provided to VW included "$229 million from the state for training costs and infrastructure; $86 million in land and site improvements from the city and the county; state tax credits worth $106 million over 30 years; and local tax abatements worth $133 million over the same period." In exchange for this massive infusion of public wealth onto Volkswagen's corporate balance sheets, the company promised to create 2,000 jobs in Chattanooga, bringing the price tag for each promised job to $288,500.

When asked to respond to concerns about VW's record-shattering subsidy package, then-Tennessee Governor Phil Bredesen, a Democrat, unabashedly replied, "I don't know whether it's fair that a Mercedes Benz costs $90,000, I just know if I want one that's what I've got to pay." Tennessee's U.S. Senator Lamar Alexander, a Republican, applauded the deal as another significant mile marker on the way towards "Tennessee's future" of becoming the "the No. 1 auto state in the country." The political logic is pretty clear: massive subsidies are just the price that the public is expected to pay in exchange for the limited number of jobs made available to them within the "free enterprise" system.

The VW subsidy deal is just one example of how large corporations leveraged the widespread suffering caused by the Great Recession, the longest and deepest economic crisis since the 1930s, to bleed the funds of state governments in exchange for jobs. In a 2013 report studying the rise of "megadeals"—subsidy deals with a local and state subsidy cost of $75 million or more—Good Jobs First found that "since 2008, the average number of megadeals per year has doubled (compared to the previous decade) and their annual cost has roughly doubled as well, averaging around $5 billion." This was certainly the trend in Tennessee, where VW was the first of three separate megadeals negotiated in the state from 2008 to 2009. The same year that the VW deal was announced, Hemlock Semiconductor received over $340 million in government giveaways to develop a $1.2 billion polycrystalline silicon manufacturing plant in Clarksville, Tenn. By 2014, the plant was shuttered and all 500 promised jobs evaporated. Wacker Chemie received over $200 million in subsidies to build a billion-dollar plant in Bradley County, just outside of Chattanooga, to produce materials used in solar panels and semiconductors. Another megadeal was brokered with Amazon, which received over $100 million in local and state subsidies to build a distribution center in Chattanooga's industrial development park, which is shared with the Volkswagen plant.

The Bipartisan Consensus

The subsidy deals with Volkswagen, Hemlock, Wacker, and Amazon were all originally negotiated by Tennessee Governor Phil Bredesen, a Democrat, and U. S. Senators Lamar Alexander and Bob Corker, both Republicans, and was approved by the Tennessee General Assembly, which in 2008 came under Republican control for the first time since Reconstruction. These deals were drafted in collaboration between state politicians (both Democratic and Republican) and business elites in total secrecy. Tom Rowland, mayor of Cleveland City in Bradley County, the location for the Wacker plant just outside of Chattanooga, revealed the frequency of such secret meetings: "You don't know how many times we have slipped Gov. Bredesen, Sen. [Bob] Corker and [Tennessee Economic and Community Development commissioner] Matt Kisber into the Chamber office."

By 2010, the state was firmly under the control of a Republican governor, Bill Haslam, and a Republican super-majority in the General Assembly. By 2012, the Republicans held over two-thirds of all state government offices in what they called a "super duper majority." The parties might have changed, but the love for corporate welfare did not, as the Republicans continued to build upon and extend all of the agreements from the previous governor's administration.

In fact, President Obama came to Chattanooga to join in on Tennessee's bipartisan economic consensus. During his 2013 jobs tour, the President delivered a speech at the Chattanooga Amazon distribution facility, praising the company for doing its part to restore the middle class through "good jobs with good wages." The starting wage at the Chattanooga warehouse is $11.25 an hour.

"Good Jobs" and Concessionary Unionism

According to a 2015 study by the Center for Automotive Research, auto workers at VW in Chattanooga had the lowest hourly pay and benefits of any employees in a U.S. car factory. The starting hourly wage rate for an assembly line worker at Volkswagen is about $15 an hour, or approximately $31,000 a year. A full-time production employee can top out their pay in seven years at a wage rate of $23 an hour, or about $48,000 a year. That makes the top pay at Volkswagen less than 80% of the estimated annual median income for Hamilton County. Third-party contractors hired by Volkswagen to work on the line in the plant and the network of auto suppliers servicing the factory pay even lower hourly wage rates. Yet U.S. Senator Corker describes production jobs at VW as "good paying," Hamilton County Mayor Jim Coppinger prefers the term "family-wage jobs," and Chattanooga Mayor Andy Berke describes VW as providing "living-wage jobs" that are helping to "build our middle class."

Tennessee's billionaire governor, Bill Haslam, who happens to be the richest politician in the country, has expressed little concern over whether or not the jobs brought to the state were high paying. In fact, it appears that he is proud that they are not. In official material directed to foreign companies by the Haslam administration, the governor touted a pro-business environment in which companies can exploit a "low-cost labor force" thanks to the state's "very low unionization rates." (That's alongside the boon of state and local taxes that are "some of the lowest in the region.") Since the Great Recession, the United Auto Workers (UAW) has been overseeing the erosion of gains made by auto workers in previous decades. The union has been able to maintain higher wages and benefits for the auto workers they represent when compared to manufacturing overall, but the difference has shrunk dramatically in recent years. According to the *Detroit Free Press*, "Back in 1960, a Detroit Three UAW autoworker was paid 16% more than the average U.S. manufacturing worker. By the early 2000s, that wage gap had grown to nearly 70% in favor of the UAW worker, but shrank back to 33% by this year."

Shouldering the Subsidy: Tennessee's Regressive Tax System

Tennessee has one of the most regressive tax systems in the country. Currently, Tennessee has no state income tax and a constitutional amendment, passed by referendum in 2014, prevents the state government from ever establishing an income or payroll tax. Moreover, earlier this year the state legislature passed a bill to phase out the state's tax on dividends and income from bonds by 2022, resulting in millions of dollars in tax revenue being stripped from city budgets. This will likely result in city governments raising revenue by hiking property taxes, further shifting the burden of raising revenues for the state onto the working and middle classes.

The lack of an income tax means that the Tennessee state government relies to a large degree on sales taxes to raise revenue. The sales tax is especially regressive due to the state's refusal to exempt essentials like groceries (though groceries are at least taxed at a lower rate than the overall sales tax), while completely exempting luxury goods such as "attorneys' fees, services such as haircuts and massages, and goods for horses and airplanes." Additionally, the state fails to offer any tax credits to low-income taxpayers to offset either sales or property taxes. This means that the primary form of wealth for the working and middle classes—a family home—is taxed to provide the vast majority of revenue for local governments. Meanwhile, major forms of wealth for the ruling class—corporate stocks and bonds—are not. Tennessee's working and middle classes are being squeezed under the highest average combined state-local sales tax rate in the country, while the owners of capital skirt any responsibility for paying their share.

This regressive system is compounded with every tax abatement given to a large multinational corporation, such as Volkswagen. When the state increases its reliance on sales taxes to offset the holes punched into the budget by corporate tax breaks, this increases the overall tax burden on the poor and working class. The only other option to raising revenue through regressive taxes is for the state to cut services. Cuts to services, such as healthcare, public education, infrastructure, and transportation, are just another way to shift the burden onto the working class. While public services diminish, highly profitable multinational corporations, such as Volkswagen, benefit from direct state supports, like state-financed job training and capital-improvement grants, which improve their bottom-line and further entrench wealth inequality.

The federal tax system, on the whole, is progressive, according to a 2016 Tax Policy Center report. Economists with the Federal Reserve Bank studied the impact of state taxes on income inequality and found that Tennessee's regressive tax system "reverses around one-third of the compression [in the income spread] caused by federal taxes"—the most of any state in the country.

The union, to be sure, is operating under difficult conditions in the auto indus-try: trade deficits in manufacturing that were growing even prior to the Great Recession, the relative increase of jobs in parts plants that pay less than assembly plants, the growth in auto employment at nonunion "transplants" (belonging to non-U.S. headquartered companies like Volkswagen and Toyota), and the rise of temp agencies and "just in time" production as part of the overall lean production management processes in the industry. All of these changes, however, have taken place in the context of the UAW's top-down brand of business unionism, which has led to its deeply concessionary approach to collective bargaining and new organiz-ing. For example, an Economic Policy Institute (EPI) report jointly authored by a former UAW leader, a former vice president from Ford, and an academic expert on "workplace innovation," lauded the UAW for being "a full partner for more than a decade in experimenting with innovations in work organization" and working with corporate management at the Big Three to reduce a "major portion" in the "cost dif-ferential" with non-union foreign-headquartered auto makers:

> In 2005, there was a gap of $3.62 between the average hourly wage of $27.41 at Ford and $23.79 for the transplants. When fringe benefits, legally required payments, pension benefits, retiree health care, and other post-employment labor costs are added in, the gap grew to $20.55 ($64.88 versus $44.33) …. In 2010, following the 2007 introduction of the entry wage and concessions made during the 2009 government bailout, the wage gap stood at $4 ($28 for Ford versus $24 for the transplants), and the gap when including fringe benefits and post-employment costs stood at $6 ($58 for Ford versus $52 for the transplants).

Incredibly, the UAW leadership has continued to proudly highlight how contract concessions have induced an ever-closer wage convergence between transplants—located largely in low-wage, Republican-dominated states in the southeastern United States—and U.S.-headquartered automakers in historically union-dense strongholds, like Michigan. They hold this up as proof of their labor-management partnership credentials while simultaneously championing the auto industry as lift-ing up "good jobs" and "the middle class." Despite the reality of declining wages, benefits, and jobs, the public appears to believe the same. According to an analysis of several polls by the National Employment Law Project (NELP), a majority of the general public believes that "manufacturing is the most important job sector, in terms of strengthening the economy."

At the Chattanooga VW plant, workers also face a brutal lean-production man-agement model on the assembly-line floor that works to squeeze higher productivity from a scant and beleaguered workforce. The working conditions on the assembly line are so physically demanding that many production workers cannot see work-ing at VW as a long-term career. Yet in 2013, when the UAW announced that they were seeking to organize the Chattanooga plant, the union decided against organizing around the salient issues in the plant and instead chose to frame their entire organizing campaign around collaboration with the company to form the first German-style "works council" in the history of the United States. The UAW's strategy was exclusively predicated on advancing what the union championed as an innovative form of labor-management partnership. The UAW even went so far as to sign a neutrality agreement with Volkswagen which committed the union to "maintaining and where possible enhancing the cost advantages and other competitive advantages that [Volkswagen] enjoys relative to its competitors." When pressed to account for why the union would make such a shocking concession, then-UAW president Bob King issued this reply:

> Our philosophy is, we want to work in partnership with companies to succeed. Nobody has more at stake in the long-term success of the company than the workers on the shop floor, both blue collar and white collar. With every company that we work with, we're concerned about competitiveness. We work together with companies to have the highest quality, the highest productivity, the best health and safety, the best ergonomics, and we are showing that companies that succeed by this cooperation can have higher wages and benefits because of the joint success.

Continued Investments, Too-Big-To-Fail, and Too-Big-To-Jail

In July 2014, Volkswagen announced that it was planning to invest $600 million into expanding the Chattanooga plant, adding additional assembly lines for the production of an SUV for the North American market. According to local news reports:

> More than a third of that investment will initially come from state and local governments who agreed to pump more than $230 million of upfront tax dollars into the project to woo VW into expanding in Chattanooga rather than at its other major North American plant in Puebla, Mexico, where labor costs are far lower. Combined with other property tax breaks, TVA incentives, road projects and other potential tax credits, Volkswagen could qualify for more than $300 million of grants, credits and other government assistance over the next decade....

The expansion of the Chattanooga plant brings the total subsidy package provided to Volkswagen up to about $877 million dollars. Following the official announcement of the expanded subsidy deal, Tennessee House Majority Leader Gerald McCormick, whose district includes Chattanooga, told the press, "I think it is a good investment and we will convince the Legislature of that because there are just so many ripple effects from this investment that will help so much of our state." The ripple effects of such an enormous single investment took on a completely different character with the announcement, in September 2015, that the EPA was fining Volkswagen for installing "defeat devices" on their automobiles, allowing the diesel cars produced at the Chattanooga plant to temporarily hide the emissions they produce.

Since the EPA's announcement, VW has acknowledged that it produced over 11 million diesel vehicles worldwide that contained software allowing them to cheat nitrogen oxide tests. This software, installed on 2009–2015 diesel VWs, reduced

---

Inequality's Racial Disparities

According to the 2015 report "State of Black Chattanooga," by the Ochs Center for Metropolitan Studies, the median wealth of white households in Tennessee bounced back in the years after the Great Recession, increasing by 2.4% between 2010 and 2013, to $141,900. Contrast that with the median wealth of Black households in the state, which continued to spiral down in the same time period, falling more than 33% to $11,000.

The arrival of Volkswagen, Wacker, and Amazon has failed to fundamentally alter the overall low-wage economy in Chattanooga and Hamilton County. When these "mega-deals" combine with the further subsidies provided to land developers for luxury condos and apartments in Chattanooga's urban core and the expanding priority placed by local governments on police and jails, the results are gentrification, displacement, and incarceration. Currently, 27% of Chattanoogans overall live in poverty, almost double the national average, and that number jumps to 36% in the city's Black community. In the eleven lowest-income neighborhoods in the city, in which about three-quarters of residents identify as Black, the poverty rate is 64%. Only 17% of the Tennessee population is Black, yet Black people are 44% of our state's prison population.

Concerned Citizens for Justice, a grassroots organization dedicated to Black liberation in Chattanooga, describes this underlying systemic approach by politicians and business leaders as "an arrangement that is good for rich financiers and developers and bad for Chattanooga's working class and oppressed majority." The numbers certainly bear out their analysis.

---

emissions while the cars were hooked up to testing devices, only to let pollution "spill out of the tail pipe at up to 40 times the allowable level" when cars were on the road. An analysis performed by the Associated Press (AP) estimates that about 100 people in the United States have likely died as a result of the pollution produced by VW's diesel Passat over the last few years. AP's analysis estimates that the death toll in Europe is substantially higher, likely resulting in hundreds of deaths for every year the cars were on the road.

After the EPA's announcement in September 2015; VW's stock price plummeted and VW Group CEO Martin Winterkorn resigned. Volkswagen Group of America President and CEO Michael Horn admitted, during his official testimony before Congress in October, that the defeat devices were installed for the express purpose of beating emissions tests. In November 2015, the Chattanooga VW plant stopped the production of the diesel Passat. More recently, VW has agreed to a partial settlement with federal and state authorities of over $15 billion as new lawsuits and government investigations from around the world continue to make headlines.

How have the local and state government responded to the news of VW's rampant criminality and corruption? Speaking to reporters about VW and the scandal, Governor Haslam said, "We're married to them. We want this plant to be a success." Hamilton County Mayor Jim Coppinger, meanwhile, told reporters, "We need for the plant to be successful. It's important to our economy." The state is too invested in VW—politically and financially—to be in any position to truly hold the company accountable for its actions.

A New Road Forward

Put it all together and we have a formula for maximizing corporate profits that mixes equal parts political opportunism with class collaboration. Following the Great Recession, voters were desperate for jobs. Politicians, campaigning on bringing jobs to voters, are willing to provide massive subsidies to companies willing to locate in their voting districts. The union, desperate to organize new bargaining units from which to collect dues *and* to be seen as a legitimate partner with corporate and political elites, actually agrees to "maintain" and "enhance" the competitive advantages corporations gain by pushing private business costs off onto the public while providing jobs with lower wages, reduced benefits, and deteriorating working conditions. Meanwhile, the public believes they are getting "good jobs," while the actual quality of those jobs continues to decline. The companies laugh all the way to the bank.

With their backs to the wall, unions like the UAW can no longer put off organizing auto makers and suppliers that choose to locate their plants in the South, but they will not succeed by promising to "work in partnership" with the companies. Labor organizers in the South will usually be working in an environment in which both business and government are hostile to unions. When the UAW narrowly lost the VW vote in 2014, the union should have learned a valuable lesson. The company might have formally committed to being "neutral," but the business and political elites in the South made no such agreement. If unions fail to win over the broader working class, they have no chance of winning representation elections—especially in states like Tennessee, where only 6% of all workers belong to a union, and in cities like Chattanooga, where the unionization rate is even lower, at an abysmal 3.4% of all workers.

To win, unions will not only have to jettison the pipedream of courting management with promises of maximizing worker productivity and containing costs. Rather, they will have to return to their militant roots: connecting shop-floor fights with community organizing. This approach has been successfully exemplified by the Chicago Teachers Union (CTU) and the Grassroots Collaborative, a labor-community alliance that has become a permanent fixture in Chicago politics and generated immense public support for CTU's militant fights with the city's investor class and mayor. CTU's combination of bottom-up work-site organizing and authentic, non-transactional support for community organizations and their struggles were critical preludes to the union's relatively successful 2012 strike. A long-term strategy focused on this kind of organizing would go a long way towards building the kind of movement infrastructure that labor needs to win in the South.

All of this is easier said than done. But we are currently faced with the atrocious working conditions and ever-diminishing wages and benefits of manufacturing jobs, the spread of poverty throughout our communities, the deep underfunding of public services, and the rising tide of anger and resentment (especially among young people) towards the economic and political elite. The time is ripe for organizers to begin harvesting the fruits of our exploited labor.

Sources: Frank Ahrens and Sholnn Freeman 2007. "GM, Union Agree on Contract to End Strike," *Washington Post*, Sept. 27, 2015 (washingtonpost.com); Associated Press, "TN touts 'low-cost labor force' to lure foreign business," Sept. 2, 2015 (tennessean.com); Associated Press, "Volkswagen now under investigation for tax evasion," Nov. 24, 2015 (timesfreepress.com); Associated Press, "Haslam visits VW Chattanooga plant to encourage workers," Oct. 7, 2015 (tennessean.com); Josh Bivens, "Worst economic crisis since the Great Depression? By a long shot," Economic Policy Institute, Jan. 27, 2010 (epi.org); Seth Borenstein, "AP analysis: Dozens of deaths likely from VW pollution dodge," Associated Press, Oct. 5 2015 (freep.com); Jessica Bruder, "With 6,000 new warehouse jobs, what is Amazon really delivering?" Reuters blog, June 17, 2015 (blogs.reuters.com); Bill Chappell, "'It Was Installed for This Purpose,' VW's U.S. CEO Tells Congress About Defeat Device," National Public Radio, Oct. 8, 2015 (npr.org); Concerned Citizens for Justice, "Chattanooga's Perfect Storm: A Tornado of Inquality," 2015 (concernedcitizensforjustice.org); Daniel Cooper, Byron Lutz, and Michael Palumbo, "The Role of Taxes in Mitigating Income Inequality Across the U.S. States," Division of Research and Statistics, Federal Reserve Board, June 17, 2015 (byron.marginalq.com); Joel Cutcher-Gershenfeld, Dan Brooks, and Martin Mulloy, "The Decline and Resurgence of the U.S. Auto Industry," Economic Policy Institute, May 6, 2015 (epi.org); Carl Davis, et al., "Who Pays? A Distributional Analysis of the Tax Systems in All 50 States," The Institute on Taxation and Economic Policy, January 2015 (itep.org); Lydia DePillis, "Auto union loses historic election at Volkswagen plant in Tennessee," *Washington Post*, Feb. 14, 2014 (washingtonpost.com); Scott Drenkard and Jared Walczak,. "State and Local Sales Tax Rates in 2015," The Tax Foundation, April 8, 2015 (taxfoundation.org); Dave Flessner, "State, local governments boost incentives to lure VW Chattanooga plant expansion." *Chattanooga Times Free Press* July 15, 2014 (timesfreepress.com); Dave Flessner, "Volkswagen union could signal change for Tennessee," *Chattanooga Times Free Press*, Sept. 1, 2014 (timesfreepress.com); Justin Fox, "Farewell to the Blue-Collar Elite." Bloomberg News, April 6, 2015 (Bloomberg.com); Greg Gardner, "UAW deal to slow, not reverse manufacturing wage slump," *Detroit Free Press*, Oct. 10, 2015 (freep.com); Good Jobs First, AccountableUSA— Tennessee (goodjobsfirst.org); Good Jobs First, VW subsidy tracker (subsidytracker.goodjobsfirst. org); Christopher Goodman and Steven Mance, "Employment loss and the 2007-2009 recession: an overview," *Monthly Labor Review*, April 2011 (bls.gov); Josh Goodman, "In Legislative Elections, Majorities and Supermajorities at Stake," The Pew Charitable Trust, Nov. 2, 2012 (pewstrusts. org); Steven Greenhouse, "Low-Wage Workers Are Finding Poverty Harder to Escape," *New York Times*, March 16, 2014 (nytimes.com); Randall Higgins, "Tennessee: 1, 2, 3 – billion," *Chattanooga Times Free Press* Feb. 27, 2009 (timesfreepress.com); Sarah Leberstein and Catherine Ruckelshaus, "Manufacturing Low Pay: Declining Wages in the Jobs That Built America's Middle Class," National Employment Law Project, 2014 (nelp.org); Philip Mattera, Kasia Tarczynska, and Greg LeRoy, "Megadeals: The Largest Economic Development Subsidy Packages Ever Awarded by State and Local Governments in the United States," June 2013 (goodjobsfirst.org); Alexandra Martellaro, "All 4 Tenn. constitutional amendments pass," WBIR Nov. 4, 2014 (legacy.wbir.com); Mike Pare, "VW plant stops production of diesel Passats while awaiting emissions fix," *Chattanooga Times Free Press*, Nov. 11, 2015 (timesfreepress.com); Mike Pare, "Haslam: Volkswagen still 'solid investment,'" *Chattanooga Times Free Press*, Oct. 8 , 2015 (timesfreepress.com); Mike Pare, "VW reviewing future investments, but local officials remain upbeat Chattanooga plant," *Chattanooga Times Free Press*, Dec. 7, 2015 (timesfreepress.com); Mike Pare, "Wacker eyes another factory even as it marks opening of new Bradley County plant," *Chattanooga Times Free Press*, April 19, 2016 (timesfreepress.com); Charlie Post and Jane Slaughter, "Lean Production: Why Work is Worse Than Ever and What's the Alternative?" *A Solidarity Working Paper*, 2000 (solidarity-us.org); Yolanda Putnam, "State of blacks in

Chattanooga: 'Inequality is the new normal,' professor says," *Chattanooga Times Free Press*, Jan. 13, 2015 (timesfreepress.com); Alana Semuels, "Congratulations Tennessee: You've Got the Most Regressive Tax System in America," *The Atlantic*, Oct. 21, 2015 (theatlantic.com); Jimmy Settle, "Hemlock closing Clarksville plant permanently," *The Leaf-Chronicle*, Dec. 17, 2014 (theleafchronicle.com); Andy Sher, "Chattanooga: VW incentives largest in state," *Chattanooga Times Free Press,* July 24, 2008; Andy Sher, "Tennessee legislative politics veer right," *Chattanooga Times Free Press*, June 13, 2010 (timesfreepress. com); Andy Sher, "Sen. Bo Watson slams VW over labor policies, UAW recognition," *Chattanooga Times Free Press*, March 18, 2015 (timesfreepress.com); Andy Sher, "Chattanooga to lose roughly $5 million annually after state lawmakers repeal Hall Income Tax," *Chattanooga Times Free Press*, April 23, 2016; Benjamin Snyder and Stacy Jones. 2015. "Here's a timeline of Volkswagen's tanking stock price," *Fortune*, Sept. 23, 2015 (fortune.com); "The List: The lowest paying cities in the U.S.," *Chattanooga Times Free Press*, August 19, 2014 (timesfreepress.com); Tax Policy Center, "Are federal taxes progressive?" (taxpolicycenter.org); Kasia Tarczynska, "Tennessee Officials Ponder the Future of VW's Subsidies," Good Jobs First blog, Oct. 6, 2015 (goodjobsfirst.org); *The City Paper* (Nashville), "Phil the Dealmaker: Volkswagen announcement is latest deal," July 21, 2008 (nashvillecitypaper); "Governor Haslam Announces Volkswagen Group of America to Expand Chattanooga Manufacturing Operations, Produce New Midsize SUV Line," Tennessee Department of Economic and Community Development, press release, July 14, 2014 (tnecd.com); Scott G. Thomas, "Income inequality is a problem everywhere, but especially in the South," *The Business Journals*, Jan. 31, 2014 (bizjournals. com); Judy Walton, "Chattanooga's poverty spikes in, around city core," *Chattanooga Times Free Press*, May 21, 2013 (timesfreepress.com); "Forbes: Tenn. Gov Haslam is richest politician in U.S.," WBIR, Jan. 21, 2015 (legacy.wbir.com); Reid Wilson, "After huge tax incentive package, Boeing still ships jobs out of Washington," *Washington Post*, Oct. 8, 2014 (washingtonpost.com); Bernie Woodall, "U.S. auto labor cost study shows impact of two-tier wage system," Reuters, March 23, 2015 (reuters.com); David Welch, "How new autoworkers became second-class employees," Bloomberg News, March 7, 2015 (crainsdetroit.com); Jeff Woods, "Ramsey Mocks Media, Hails 'Super Duper' Majority," *Nashville Scene* Dec. 2, 2014 (nashvillescene.com); Jordan Yadoo, "How Higher Wages for U.S. Autoworkers Could Help You Get a Raise, Too," Bloomberg News, Nov. 23, 2015 (bloomberg.com).

Article 6.4

HOPSOPOLY
Global beer mergers reach a new level.

BY ROB LARSON
January/February 2017

When major beer label Budweiser announced that they would rename their product "America" through the 2016 U.S. election, it raised droll hackles from a variety of observers. George Will suggested in the conservative *National Review* that the beer was less than fully American because it was produced by a foreign-owned firm, an irony also observed in the more liberal *Washington Post*. John Oliver's HBO staff did what most US media did in 2016, and took the opportunity to give more TV time to the Trump campaign, in this case to mock Trump's taking credit for the name change. Most commenters counted themselves clever for being aware the Bud label is foreign-owned, but all of them missed the real point: It's not that "America" is foreign-owned, but that it's owned by a brand-new global semi-monopoly that perfectly represents the power-mongering of neoliberal capitalism.

Macrobrew

There are indeed American men and women who will tell you it broke their hearts when in 2008 Anheuser-Busch was bought by the InBev transnational. InBev is itself a product of the merged Belgian InterBrew giant and the Brazilian conglomerate AmBev, as Barry Lynn reviews in his book on market concentration, *Cornered*. Lynn observes that this merger, along with 2007's union of Miller and Coors under South African Breweries' control, meant that beer-loving America was subject to corporate decisions made further and further away, and thus "basically reduced to reliance on a world-bestriding beer duopoly, run not out of Milwaukee or St. Louis but out of Leuven, Belgium, and Johannesburg, South Africa."

And now, just Belgium! Unmentioned in any of the recent rash of commentary was that "America's" owner AB InBev itself announced this year a $108 billion purchase of SAB Miller, which together would sell about 30% of the world's beer, including 45% of total beer sales in the United States. The merger would create a "New World of Beer" in which AB InBev will have "operations across multiple continents and a host of countries," as the business press described it. The *Financial Times* projected that the combined global giant is expected "to control almost half the industry's total profits." SAB Miller will also benefit from bringing its operations under AB InBev's umbrella, since the latter pays an incredibly low effective tax rate in its Belgian corporate home, paying well under 1% on its nearly $2 billion profit in 2015.

Of course, regulators have to approve large-scale mergers in each of the many, many countries in which the merged empires do business. The European Union's competition laws, and antitrust law in the United States, are meant to bring legal action against monopolists, or firms planning to merge into something close to one. But in the neoliberal era, a capital fact is the steep drop-off of anti-monopoly suits—the business press has reported that, from Reagan to Obama, the repeated promise to aggressively enforce limits to market concentration "hasn't worked out that way." And indeed, for the proposed hopsopoly the news is so far, so good. In addition to Australia and South Africa, the European Union is set to allow the consolidation, China's Ministry of Commerce okayed the plan and the U.S. Justice Department approved the $100 billion deal, with reservations (see below).

These approvals require certain divestments—sales of pieces of the corporate empires before, or just after, they merge. Such sales can keep market concentration numbers just low enough for regulators to sign off. Yet these deals are so big that the divestments are *themselves* concentrating the market—Molson Coors is buying AB InBev's share of their currently joint-owned MillerCoors for $12 billion. These spun-off assets mean Molson Coors will itself have a 25% share of the U.S. beer market, second only to the new SAB-AB InBev combination. In the same way, Constellation Brands became the third-largest American brewer by buying several beer labels from the Mexican firm Grupo Modelo back in 2013, when InBev was buying it and needed to divest a few brands to appease regulators.

Tapping the Craft Keg

Smaller-batch craft beers produced by independent microbrewers provides limited escape from monopolized beer. Constellation paid a full $1 billion for the California craft brewer Ballast Point, in a move the *Wall Street Journal* suggested "signals that the craft-beer industry, which has a roughly 10% market share in the U.S., has crossed a threshold and become a big business that large brewers expect to continue to grow in the years to come." The growth potential of microbrews is a valuable opportunity for the majors, especially considering that beer's share of total U.S. alcoholic-beverage spending fell in 2015 for the sixth straight year, and not just to its perennial foe—wine—but also to liquor as the craft cocktail trend flourishes. And this is in spite of the industry spending over a billion (yes, billion) dollars annually just on TV ads.

This all means that the future growth center of microbrews is increasingly essential to the industry majors, as are export markets. But the growth hopes for microbrews are dimming. The industry must look fearfully at the slowing growth of craft labels, with a mid-single digit growth rate in 2015-16, down from double digits in previous years. What growth there is, is concentrated in the labels held by the industry giants. Market observers notice that while niche labels are still taking market share from the majors, albeit more slowly, "AB InBev's own U.S. craft portfolio … increased sales 36% in the first half [of 2016]. After a spate of acquisitions, most notably that of Goose Island, AB InBev is the third-largest craft brewer in the country," although that reflects the fragmented contours of that market segment. In the less concentrated craft market, few beers have a large market share, unlike in large-scale commercial brewing. The *Journal* notes, "Craft beer accounts for just 1% of the company's total volume," still an important future growth center for what they call "big beer."

That slowing craft growth is having big effects on the markets for beer ingredients, especially hops, the flowering body of the *Humulus lupulus* plant used to give beers their bitter or sweet flavors. Hops suppliers haven't been able to keep up with spiking demand from craft brews for a wide array of obscure varieties, despite a growing proportion of U.S. hops growers producing for small labels since the global brands' hops are now mostly grown in Germany. The slow-growing plant, and the fast-changing demand for particular varieties have limited the ability of hops growers to keep pace, and with the market's own growth now slowing, the fear is rising of an oversupply in the industry if crops are only harvested as demand fades. The very small size of the many craft labels, and their uncertain prospects, means farmers are often resistant to committing their production to obscure microbrewers.

Growth-seeking is also driving the major brewers toward foreign markets, as the *New York Times'* DealBook feature observes that "in China, Anheuser-Busch InBev and SABMiller are betting on premium products," with "the two beer behemoths" buying up large stakes in China's top-selling brands. "Together, the international brewers account for about one-third of the overall beer market in China. As they pursue a merger, given their dominance, Anheuser-Busch InBev and SABMiller are expected to prune their portfolio in China to keep regulators happy," and indeed the popular Snow brand was ultimately sold off to a Chinese state-owned company.

These different growth prospects are all threatened by a gradual worldwide reconsideration of health benefits of modest alcohol consumption. While public health agencies had for years considered small amounts of alcohol to have some health upsides (mostly heart-related), the emerging view is that these benefits are outweighed by health risks, leading to a growing number of health agencies amending their guidance to recommend lower levels of consumption.

Economies of Ale

Scale economies occur when a firm's per-unit costs decrease as the scale of production increases. Typically observed in industries, like manufacturing, that have high up-front costs, economies of scale arise from "spreading" a large starting investment over a growing amount of output. A brewery that cost $10 million to build, and which produces one million cans or bottles in a year, would have a per-unit fixed cost of $10. Producing ten million cans, the per-unit fixed cost is just a dollar per can. The big costs of brewing tanks, sturdy equipment for mixing the ground grains and the flavorful hops, the cost of the actual brewery structure itself—all add to a brewery's starting investment and create the potential for scale economies.

Economies of scale are usually observed at the plant or factory level, but can also arise at higher levels of operation, including in administration. For example, two large companies may merge and then lay off one of their human resources departments, if one computerized HR office can handle all the employees at the new, merged firm. But these returns to scale, associated with a higher level of market concentration, are often counterbalanced by increasing layers of corporate bureaucracy and the challenges of managing large commercial empires.

So returns to scale constitute strong incentives for firms to grow, both in dollar terms and in market share, gaining scale and profitability. They do have limits, but once firms have reached large and cost-efficient sizes they are often happy to go on growing or merging, in order to gain more market power. The result is that in many industries, from the manufacturing sector to telecommunications to financial services, rich competitive markets give way over time to other market structures, including the few large companies of an oligopoly or the single colossal monopolist.

As with other industries, from tobacco to chemicals, the industry is pushing back in significant part by getting directly involved in the research process. A former cigarette-industry executive now working for booze giant Diageo claimed in the press that a study critical of alcohol advertising was "junk science" and said, "We push back when there are dumb studies." This raises again the prospect of "science capture," the growing phenomenon of private entities with a material interest attempting to influence the scientific process. Indeed, some are funding their own research, the findings of which unsurprisingly support the economic activity of the industry doing the funding.

High-Proof Political Economy

The corporate beer empires aren't shy about using their newly enlarged market power, either. *Cornered* author Barry Lynn recounts a classic episode in which Anheuser-Busch targeted Boston Beer, the owner of Sam Adams:

For reasons still not entirely clear, the giant firm unleashed a devastating, multifront assault by armies of lawyers, lobbyists, and marketers who accused Boston Beer (to the government and to the public through the media) of deceptive packaging. Anheuser-Busch then followed up with an even more devastating second assault, in which it locked Boston Beer products out of the immensely powerful distribution networks that it controls. Ultimately, an arbitrator rejected all of the megafirm's contentions, and Boston Beer survived to brew another day, but the company, less than 1% the size of Anheuser-Busch, was left on the verge of bankruptcy.

Boston Beer remains the second-largest U.S. craft brewer, but the industry has not forgotten this power play.

And today's even-bigger corporations are brewing up new retail-level strategies. The *Journal* reports that AB InBev had planned to "offer some independent distributors in the U.S. annual reimbursements of as much as $1.5 million if 98% of the beers they sell are AB InBev brands." The money would come in the form of the conglomerate footing the bill for distributors' share of marketing costs, like displays at the retail level. The move has craft brewers crying foul, and understandably, since it leaves independents with a pitifully small fraction of store display space and promotion dollars left for them to fight over. The incentive plan also requires that distributors only carry craft brewers that operate below certain low thresholds of annual production, which most do.

The importance of this corporate proposal lies in the middle-man layer of the industry, created by state laws at the end of Prohibition. Beer brewers must sell their output to distributors, who then sell it on to the retailers where you pick up a six-pack. While there are hundreds of distributors in the United States, most are under agreement to sell exclusively either product from AB InBev or MillerCoors. But in addition to deals like these, the beer manufacturers are also able to buy and operate their own distributors—the state of California is investigating AB InBev after it bought two distributors in the state, with concerns about the giant declining to carry independent micros. The company presently owns 21 distributors in the United States and has further used its gigantic revenues to continue buying up independent brewers like Goose Island—now part of the global company and thus available to AB InBev's distributors—on its terms.

Raise a Glass

Popular opposition to the megamerger has been scattered, in a year punctuated by billion-dollar mergers in agriculture, chemicals, insurance, and drugs. In South Africa, a market important enough to require merger clearance as a condition of the deal (and the "SA" in "SABMiller"), a labor union objected to the deal's terms. Among those terms are rules covering a 2010 issue of SAB shares to workers and retailers, which would have matured in 2020. The union membership prefers to "cash out" earlier, or be granted an up-front payment in addition to the existing shares. Labor opposition to market concentration is always notable, although this case revolves more around the treatment of the workforce on a quite specific compensation issue, rather than an objection to capital accumulation in general.

The ultimate approval of the merger by the South Africa's Competition Tribunal was significantly a foregone conclusion. As *Bloomberg* observes, South Africa's bond rating has been downgraded, reflecting world investor fear of policy changes not to their advantage. This meant that the country's leader, President Jacob Zuma of the African National Congress (ANC), was especially eager to approve the megadeal, all the more after recent poor showings for the ANC in local races. This led to unusually prompt action by Zuma—*Bloomberg* noted in March 2016 that "SABMiller itself is still waiting for approval to merge its African soft-drink bottling assets, 15 months after it filed the request," while the AB InBev-SAB merger took just half that time.

A number of other unions represent organized brewery workers in the United States, including the Machinists, the Operating Engineers, the Auto Workers, and the International Brotherhood of Teamsters (IBT). The IBT lodged an objection to a particular feature of the deal, writing a letter to the Attorney General requesting antitrust scrutiny of the related closure of the "megabrewery" operated by MillerCoors in Eden, N.C. While MillerCoors is to be sold to Molson as part of the deal, the closure does affect the market significantly, particularly since the huge facility produces 4% of all U.S. beer output, making the reduction more than can be compensated for at other facilities. This significant tightening of supply raised the question of antitrust violation to the IBT, due both to the further concentration of the market but also to the fact that the facility was essential for rival brewer Pabst, which for years has not brewed its own hipster swill but has had it produced by Miller under contract at the Eden brewery. Miller had previously indicated it has no interest in maintaining the deal past its expiration. The U.S. legal settlement appears to make no mention of this issue, but Pabst is now suing Miller over the terms of their brewing agreement, and the IBT lawsuit against Miller continues. For their part, unions from the acquiring company have also been skeptical, noting that the giant corporation has cut its Belgian workforce in half, to just 2,700 over ten years. The *Times* reports, "They also predict that the company will load up on debt to buy SABMiller, leading to pressure for further cutbacks."

Beyond labor, the large and still-growing craft sector of the marketplace has looked with suspicion on industry consolidation for some time and had a clear eye of the stakes, if not typically engaging in action beyond contacting legislators or regulators. The press in brewery-heavy St. Louis describes how craft independents view the deal "warily," as "smaller breweries remain worried a larger A-B InBev will have more influence on what beers retailers stock on their shelves and hamper access to supplies such as hops." They also see influence-building intent behind legislation the corporations have supported, like a bill passed by the Missouri state legislature allowing brewers to lease large commercial coolers to retailers. Craft brewers oppose the governor signing the bill, "arguing only large brewers such as A-B InBev can afford to buy the coolers, which will likely be filled by retailers with A-B brands."

Likewise, industry rag *All About Beer Magazine* has expressed enormous skepticism of not just the new megadeal but the whole history of consolidation in the industry, in the United States and the UK. In a beautiful expression of widespread market-skepticism, Lisa Brown wrote, "This is about a company that has historically used the strategy of controlling and purchasing the wholesale tier of the industry now getting much more influence and potential control of that sector, while also gaining a lot more spending money for lawyers and lobbying."

Reflecting these popular sentiments, the Brewers Association—the industry group representing the many small craft brewers and independent labels—requested significant safeguards from the Department of Justice should the deal clear. It wanted an end to AB InBev's preferential distribution and limits to its "self-distribution" plans, since influence over distributors gives big brewers an additional potential lever of power over retailers. Evidently the DoJ heard the complaints, because happily for today's craft drinkers the department's allowance of the merger

---

Opiate of the Masses

Fittingly, the first great scholar of capital concentration, Karl Marx, was a product of the beer-loving German people. Marx pioneered the study of capitalism's near-universal gravitational tendency, and for today's economy we have an analytical vocabulary to help understand the growth of capital.

- Concentration of capital, the growth of market share by a few big firms within a market.
- Consolidation, the growth of corporate capital by buying firms in separate industries.
- Capital accumulation, the overall growth in the capital stock of an economy.

Marx wrote in his giant classic study, *Capital*, that "The laws of this centralization of capitals, or of the attraction of capital by capital," depended ultimately on "the scale of production. Therefore, the larger capitals beat the smaller. It will further be remembered that, with the development of the capitalist mode of production, there is an increase in the minimum amount of individual capital necessary to carry on a business under its normal conditions." In other words, fancier technology and more expensive investments make it harder for small brewers to operate at the low costs of established firms.

Many more conservative economists have resisted this conclusion, and insisted that free markets have an enduringly competitive character, even in older industries. Friedrich Hayek, the Austrian economist and one of the conservative world's most revered thinkers, derided the argument that "technological changes have made competition impossible in a constantly increasing number of fields ... This belief derives mainly from the Marxist doctrine of the 'concentration of industry.'"

Marx might reply by raising a glass in toast, filled with amber-hued global corporate beer.

came with numerous conditions on top of the planned divestments, with some directed at these kinds of maneuvers. The department limited AB InBev from enforcing distributor incentive deals (like the one above), and crucially imposed a cap of 10% on the proportion of AB InBev's sales that can be sold through wholly-owned distributors. This is intended to limit the giant's influence over distribution and hopefully reserve shelf space for independent labels.

The agency further put the Big Beer giant under a new requirement to submit for approval all acquisitions of craft beers for the next ten years, benefiting consumers desiring a wider range of brews, and preserving more successful independents from corporate concentration. These requirements, resulting from demands for redress from retailers and craft brewers, do sound satisfyingly stringent. However, the firm retains enormous market power, is strategically positioned to grow in developing markets (especially in Africa), and can be expected to work to undermine or evade these rules in the future. As always, antitrust rules keep oligopoly form maturing into full monopoly, and impose meaningful limits on anticompetitive practices, at least when enforced aggressively. That enforcement tends to ebb and flow however, and it's unclear how the Trump administration will prioritize breaking up giant mergers with its emerging neoliberal shape.

With the worldwide trend for tighter corporate ownership and global oligopoly, it's the investor class that's getting fat off our beer. A more aggressive labor movement of organized malters and brewers, reinforced by irate craft consumers, could resist further job cuts and demand bolder regulatory roadblocks to this consolidation. Or better yet, rather than choosing your poison between super-concentrated markets or moderately concentrated ones, an incensed and tipsy anticapitalist movement could take over these global giants' facilities and brew the beers themselves.

There are few consumers who enjoy shop-talk about their personal favorites more than beer drinkers, providing a natural opportunity for sharing this and other episodes of capitalist globalization. Raising consciousness about capitalism's predations, even in beer, could encourage a movement to socialize brewing. In a democratically managed economic system, the freewheeling ethos of the microbrew movement would be free to flourish without being blackballed out of the market by the majors, or bought out if they manage to succeed.

Now *that* would be a happy hour! ❏

Sources: Tripp Mickle, "Budweiser to Rebrand Beer to America Through Elections," *Wall Street Journal*, May 11, 2016 (wsj.com); George Will, "This Bud's for You, America," *National Review*, May 18, 2016; Travis M. Andrews, "Budweiser seeks approval to be called 'America' this summer," *Washington Post*, May 10, 2015 (washingtonpost.com); Tripp Mickle and Saabira Chaudhuriab, "InBev's SABMiller Deal Still Faces Hurdles," *Wall Street Journal*, Nov. 11, 2015; Barry Lynn, *Cornered: The New Monopoly Capitalism and the Economics of Destruction* (John Wiley & Sons, 2009); James Fontanella-Khan and Patti Waldmeir, "China brewer sale clears path to AB InBev's £71bn SABMiller deal," *Financial Times*, March 2, 2016 (ft.com); James Kanter, "Anheuser-Musch InBev Aims Its Tax-Trimming Skills at SABMiller," *New York Times*, Oct. 19, 2015 (nytimes.com); Leonard Silk, "Economic Scene; Antitrust Issues Facing Reagan," *New York Times*, Feb. 13, 1981; Brent Kendall, "Justice Department Doesn't Deliver on Promise to Attack Monopolies," *Wall Street Journal*, Nov. 7, 2015; Foo Yun Chee and Martinne Geller, "EU regulators to conditionally clear AB Inbev, SABMiller deal," Reuters, May 20, 2016; Tripp Mickle and Saabira Chaudhuriab, "SABMiller Board Backs AB InBev's Higher Offer," *Wall Street Journal*, July 29, 2016; Tripp Mickle and Brent Kendall, "Justice Department Clears AB InBev's Takeover of SABMiller," *Wall Street Journal*, July 20, 2016; Gina Chon and Scheherazade Daneshkhu, "AB InBev-SABMiller merger critics in US seek concessions," *Financial Times*, Dec. 8, 2015; Tripp Mickle, "Constellation Brands to Buy Craft-Beer Maker for $1 Billion," *Wall Street Journal*, Nov. 16, 2015; Tripp Mickle, "Cocktails Sip Away at Beer's Market Share," *Wall Street Journal*, Feb. 15, 2016; Nathalie Tadena, "Bud Light is a Heavier TV Ad Spender than its Peers," *Wall Street Journal* CMO TOday blog, May 22, 2014; Trefis Team, "Does The Declining U.S. Beer Trend Spell Doom For Brewers?," *Forbes*, June 29, 2015 (forbes.com); Stephen Wilmot, "Why Craft Brewing Slowdown Won't Benefit Big Beer," *Wall Street Journal*, Aug. 26, 2016; Tripp Mickle, "Trouble Brewing in the Craft Beer Industry," *Wall Street Journal*, Sept. 27, 2016; Amie Tsang and Cao Li, "China embraces Craft Beers, and Brewing Giants Take Notice," Dealbook, *New York Times*, Jan. 15, 2016; Justin Scheck and Tripp Mickle, "With Moderate Drinking Under Fire, Alcohol Companies Go on Offensive," *Wall Street Journal*, Aug. 22, 2016; Tripp Mickle, "Craft Brewers Take Issue With AB InBev Distribution Plan," *Wall Street Journal*, Dec. 7, 2015; Tripp Mickle, "Anheuser Says Regulators Have Questioned Pending Distributor Buyouts," *Wall Street Journal*, Oct. 12, 2015; Tripp Mickle, "AB InBev Defends SABMiller Buy to Senate," *Wall Street Journal*, Dec. 8, 2015; Tripp Mickle, "AB InBev Facing Union Opposition to SABMiller Acquisition," *Wall Street Journal*, June 3, 2016; Janice Kew, "Zuma Appeal to Business Bodes Well for AB InBev-SAB Beer Merger," Bloomberg News, March 15, 2016; James P. Hoffa, president, International Brotherhood of Teamsters, letter to U.S. Attorney General Loretta Lynch, June 6, 2016 (teamster.org); Bruce Vielmetti, "Historic brewing names Pabst, MillerCoors locked in legal battle," *Milwaukee Journal Sentinal*, May 5, 2016 (jsonline.com); Lisa Brown, "Craft brewers eye merger of A-B InBev and SABMiller warily," *St. Louis Post-Dispatch*, June 26, 2016 (stltoday.com); Lew Bryson, "Mega-Merger? How About No?," *All About Beer Magazine*, May 17, 2016; Brewers Association press release, "Brewers Association Statement on AB InBev Acquisition of SABMiller," July 20, 2016; U.S. District Court for the District of Columbia, United States of America v. Anheuser-Busch InBev SA/NV, and SABMiller plc, July 20, 2016; Karl Marx, *Capital*, vol. 1, ch. 25 (1867); Friedrich Hayek, *The Road to Serfdom* (1944).

Article 6.5

THE FAILURE OF MODERN INDUSTRIAL AGRICULTURE

BY JOHN IKERD
March/April 2015

Americans are being subjected to an ongoing multimillion-dollar propaganda campaign designed to "increase confidence and trust in today's agriculture." Food Dialogues, just one example of this broader trend, is a campaign sponsored by the U.S. Farmers and Ranchers Alliance—an industry organization whose funders and board members include Monsanto, DuPont, and John Deere. The campaign features the "faces of farming and ranching"—articulate, attractive young farmers, obviously chosen to put the best possible face on the increasingly ugly business of industrial agriculture, which dominates our food- production system.

Genetically engineered crops, inhumane treatment of farm animals, and routine feeding of antibiotics to confined animals—among many other problems—have eroded public trust in American agriculture. In response, the defenders of so-called modern agriculture have employed top public relations firms to try to clean up their tarnished public image. Their campaigns emphasize such issues as water quality, food safety, animal welfare, and "food prices and choices."

Mounting public concerns in each of these areas are supported by a growing body of scientific evidence. For example, a 1998 EPA study found 35,000 miles of streams in 22 states polluted with biological wastes from concentrated animal feeding operations. The number of "impaired waters" in Iowa has tripled since the late 1980s, as industrial farming systems, such as factory farms, have replaced traditional family farms.

On food safety, a recent U.S. Centers for Disease Control and Prevention study reviewed dozens of studies linking routine feeding of antibiotics in concentrated livestock operations to people being infected with antibiotic-resistant bacteria, such as MRSA. "Use of antibiotics in food-producing animals allows antibiotic-resistant bacteria to thrive," they concluded. "Resistant bacteria can be transmitted from food-producing animals to humans through the food supply." The big agricultural corporations claim that they are committed to the humane treatment of animals—while advocating legislation to criminalize unauthorized photography in concentrated animal feeding operations. Numerous scientific studies over the past 50 years have documented inhumane treatment in these "animal factories." The mistreatment is not only a result of inevitable overcrowding in confinement operations, but also results from routine management practices, transportation, and even in the genetic selection of animals for maximum productivity.

The Food Dialogues campaign claims to advocate consumer choice by supporting all types of farming. However, its language strongly suggests that industrial agriculture is essential to keeping food affordable. It considers organic agriculture and other sustainable faming alternatives to be no more than "niche markets." In reality, the only clear "benefit" of industrial agriculture is that it requires fewer farmers. There is no indication that industrial agriculture has produced more food than could have been produced with more sustainable methods, only that it has employed far fewer farmers. Any production-cost advantage has been more than offset by higher margins, including profits, elsewhere within the corporate food supply chain. Over the past 20 years, an era of intensive agricultural industrialization, U.S. retail food prices have risen faster than overall inflation rates.

Agricultural industrialization has had a devastating effect on the quality of rural life. Industrial agriculture has replaced independent family farmers with a far smaller number of farm workers, most of whom are paid poorly. In 1960, farmers were still more than 8% of the U.S. workforce. They are less than 1% today. Rural communities have suffered both economically and socially from this loss of traditional farm families. More than 50 years of research demonstrates that communities supported by small to mid-size family farms are better places to live, both economically and socially, than are communities dependent on large farming enterprises.

Perhaps most important, industrial agriculture has failed in its most fundamental purpose: providing food security. The percentage of "food insecure" people in the United States is greater today than during the 1960s—early in the current phase of agricultural industrialization. Furthermore, the industrial food system is linked to a new kind of food insecurity: unhealthy foods. A recent global report by 500 scientists from 50 countries suggested that "obesity is [now] a bigger health crisis than hunger." There is growing evidence that America's diet-related health problems are not limited to poor consumer food choices or processed "junk foods" but begin with a lack of essential nutrients in food crops produced on industrial farms. It's high time for fundamental change in American agriculture. The growing litany of farm/food problems today cannot be solved by redesigning the USDA "food pyramid," placing warning labels on junk foods, or imposing more stringent regulations on farmers. Today's problems are deep and systemic. They are inherent in the worldview from which industrial agriculture emerged and upon which its evolution depends.

In economic terms, industrialization allows capital and technology to be substituted for workers and managers. In other words, it allows raw materials or natural resources to be transformed into more valuable products while employing fewer, lower-skilled workers—in both labor and management positions. In a world with an abundance of natural resources and a scarcity of workers, industrialization seemed a logical strategy for economic development. With increases in populations and depletion of natural resources, the economic benefits of industrialization have declined while the negative consequences for unemployment and environmental degradation have grown.

For agriculture, the benefits of industrialization have been fewer and the costs have been greater. The reality of agriculture is in conflict with the worldview that supports industrialization. Industrialization is rooted in a mechanistic worldview: the industrial world works like a big, complex machine that can be manipulated by humans to extract natural resources and use them to meet our needs and wants. In reality, the world is an extremely complex living ecosystem, of which we humans are a part. Our well-being ultimately depends on working and living in harmony with nature rather than conquering nature. We are currently seeing the disastrous consequences of treating living ecosystems as if they were inanimate mechanisms.

Thankfully, a new kind of agriculture is emerging to meet these ecological, social, and economic challenges. The new farmers may call their farms "organic," "ecological," "biological," "holistic," or "biodynamic." Their farming methods may be called "agroecology," "nature farming," or "permaculture." They all fit under the conceptual umbrella of sustainable agriculture. They are committed to meeting the food needs of all in the present without diminishing opportunities for those who will live in the future. The strength of this movement is most visible in the growth of the organic-foods market, although some types of "organic farms," especially those mimicking industrial agriculture, may not be sustainable. Sales of organic foods grew by more than 20% per year during the 1990s and early 2000s, before leveling off at around 10%–12% annual growth following the recession of 2008. Organic foods now amount to around $35 billion in annual sales, something less than 5% of total food sales. The local food movement, as exemplified by farmers markets and "community supported agriculture," has replaced organics as the most dynamic sector of the food market, although it is only about half as large in sales.

Some question whether organic or other sustainable farms can meet the food needs of a growing global population. A comprehensive review in the journal *Nature* compared organic and conventional crop yields in "developed" countries, concluding: "Under certain conditions—that is, with good management practices, particular crop types and growing conditions—organic systems can . . . nearly match conventional yields." The challenge in the United States and the so-called developed world is to create a food system that will meet the basic food needs of all without degrading its natural and human resources. Ecological and social sustainability, not just yields, is the logical motivation for organic agriculture in the so-called developed world. Globally, industrial agriculture is not needed to "feed the world." Small, diversified farms already provide food for least 70% of the world's population and could double or triple yields without resorting to industrial production methods.

Everywhere we look, we can see the failure of the grand experiment of industrial agriculture. It's time for fundamental change. ❏

Sources: Food Dialogues, "About USFRA" (fooddialogues.com); Food Dialogues, "Faces of Farmers and Ranchers" (fooddialogues.com); U.S. Department of Agriculture Natural Resources Conservation Service and U.S. Environmental Protection Agency, "Unified National Strategy for Animal Feeding Operations," Sept. 11, 1998; Bridget Huber, "Large Livestock Farms Spread Across Iowa, Threatening Waterways" (IowaWatch.org); U.S. Center for Disease Control and Prevention, "Antibiotic Resistance Threats in the U.S. 2013" (cdc.gov); World Society for Protection of Animals, "What's on Your Plate? The Hidden Costs of Industrial Animal Agriculture in Canada," 2012 (richarddagan.com); Economic Research Service, United States Department of Agriculture, "Price Spreads from Farm to Consumer" (ers.usda.gov); Richard Volpe, "Price inflation for food outpacing many other spending categories," Economic Research Service, USDA (ers.usda.gov); Curtis Stofferahn, "Industrialized Farming and Its Relationship to Community Well-Being: an Update of the 2000 Report by Linda Lobao," North Dakota, Office of Attorney General, September 2006 (und.edu); CBS documentary, "Hunger in America," 1968 (youtube.com); Alisha Coleman-Jensen, Christian Gregory, and Anita Singh, "Household Food Security in the United States in 2013," Economic Research Report No. (ERR-173) (ers.usda.gov); Danielle Dellorto, "Global report: Obesity bigger health crisis than hunger," CNN News, Dec. 14, 2012 (cnn.com); John

Ikerd, "Foreword," in William A. Albrecht, Soil Fertility & Human and Animal Health, 2013; Organic Trade Association, "Consumer-driven U.S. organic market surpasses $31 billion in 2011" (organicnewsroom.com); Local Harvest, "Community Supported Agriculture" (localharvest.org); Verena Seufert, Navin Ramankutty, and Jonathan A. Foley, "Comparing the yields of organic and conventional agriculture," Nature, May 10, 2012 (nature.com); Parke Wilde, "Crop yields are only part of the organic vs. conventional farming debate," Grist, May 2012 (grist.org); United Nations Environmental Program, Towards a Green Economy: Pathways to Sustainable Development and Poverty Eradication, 2010 (unep.org); Fred Kirschenmann, "The challenge of ending hunger," Leopold Center for Sustainable Agriculture, Leopold letter, winter 2012 (leopold.iastate.edu); Olivier De Schutter, United Nations General Assembly, Human Rights Council, "Report submitted by the Special Rapporteur on the right to food," Dec. 20, 2010 (srfood.org).

Article 6.6

A CASE FOR PUBLIC OWNERSHIP

BY ARTHUR MacEWAN
September/October 2015

> Dear Dr. Dollar:
> *Would the U.S. economy work better if some industries were nationalized?*
> *Banks? Other industries? Which ones and why?*
> —Richard Hobbs, San Jose, Calif.

Even in a thoroughly capitalist economy, where most economic activity takes place in markets and firms are driven by profit-making, there are good reasons for some industries to be publicly owned. Indeed, a non-trivial amount of industry in the United States is already publicly owned.

For example, as Gar Alperovitz and Thomas Hanna pointed out in a July *New York Times* opinion piece, there are "more than 2,000 publicly owned electric utilities that, along with cooperatives, supply more than 25 percent of the country's electricity... In one of the most conservative states, Nebraska, every single resident and business receives electricity from publicly owned utilities, cooperatives or public power districts. Partly as a result, Nebraskans pay one of the lowest rates for electricity in the nation."

Electric utilities (and other utilities) are "natural monopolies," operating in realms of the economy which are not (or are hardly) open to multiple, competing firms. Roads, subway systems, and major water control systems are other examples of "natural monopolies." Another form of natural monopoly arises with unreproducible minerals (oil, copper, iron, etc.); public ownership could allow society in general, rather than private firms, to reap the profits from their scarce supply. Private ownership is, of course, possible in such cases, but, if it is to be socially acceptable, it must be heavily regulated or heavily taxed or both. Given the costs—and often the failures—of meaningful regulation and the ineffective taxation of large firms, public ownership can be a more effective way to go.

In other industries, where the operations of firms have large impacts beyond the firms' immediate actions, public ownership can also be the best economic option. Here is where banking provides the prime example. Because the actions of banks have such far-reaching impacts on the whole economy ("systemic impact"), they must be either publicly owned or thoroughly regulated—and, as experience of recent years has demonstrated, regulation has not worked. Also, firms outside the financial sector can have systemic impacts, and, indeed, during the Great Recession the federal government in effect nationalized large auto firms to prevent their failure from wreaking havoc throughout the economy. (However, the government played a minimal role in operating the firms and quickly moved to return them to private ownership.)

In other types of industry, firms can have large impacts beyond their immediate actions where positive "spill-over effects" ("externalities") are large. For example, the Tennessee Valley Authority and California's Water Resources Control Board (which operates as both a de facto enterprise and a regulatory agency), deliver essential services that have such large impacts. Private firms could not capture profits from all the immense social benefits that such enterprises can create. Thus the huge investments in water systems that these public agencies provide would not be undertaken by private firms.

Still another example where public operation makes economic sense is with so-called "public goods," where one individual can consume the product without reducing its availability to another individual and from which no one is excluded. Street lights are the classic example, and other municipal services—for example, fire-fighting and traffic-control systems—also fall in this category.

Clearly, it is possible for private firms to be engaged in some of these public activities. A private firm, for example, could operate the public lighting system under contract from a municipality. Garbage collection is privately operated in many locales, and road construction and repair are often contracted to private firms. Yet, when private firms are engaged, regulation and public oversight—more difficult in some realms than in others—has to be extensive.

Under present political conditions, moving to greater public ownership is not likely. Privatization, in fact, has been at the top of the agenda at many levels of government—for example, with schools, hospitals, the military, and prisons. In these cases, not only does it generally make more economic sense (in terms of costs) for the operations to be in the public sector; in addition, privatization undermines democratic control precisely in areas where it is most important. Public schools, hospitals, the military, and prisons all have their problems, sometimes severe, but placing these institutions in the private sector is neither economically nor politically beneficial.

"Public ownership" can have many forms, and certainly control of economic activity by a distant government authority does not assure democratic control. Yet, public ownership by both worker and consumer cooperatives, as well as by local governments, generally holds out more promise of democratic control as well as a greater likelihood of serving public interests. ❑

For information on public banking, see the Public Banking Institute, publicbankinginstitute.org.

Chapter 7

LABOR, UNIONS, AND WORKING CONDITIONS

Article 7.1

IS A $15 MINIMUM WAGE ECONOMICALLY FEASIBLE?

BY JEANNETTE WICKS-LIM
July/August 2012

Campaigns like 15Now and Fight for $15 are bucking convention and demanding minimum-wage hikes far larger than what has been past practice. Take, for example, the Fair Minimum Wage Act of 2007—one of the larger sets of increases in the federal minimum. This Act raised the federal wage floor by 40% in three steps: from $5.15 to $5.85 in 2007, $5.85 to $6.55 in 2008, and $6.55 to today's minimum of $7.25 in 2009. A $15 minimum wage, on the other hand, represents a more-than-100% increase in the federal minimum. The result? The fight for $15 has decisively changed the terms of today's minimum-wage debate.

The ball got rolling in 2013 with the breakthrough $15 minimum ordinance in SeaTac, a suburb of Seattle, Wash. Since then, some of the country's largest cities, including Los Angeles, San Francisco, and Seattle, have followed suit, passing their own citywide $15 minimums. In June 2015, Massachusetts passed a statewide measure covering Medicaid-funded homecare aides. Later in the fall, New York State passed a $15 minimum wage law for fast-food workers. This sea change seems to have occurred over just the past couple of years, dramatically pivoting away from President Obama's soft pitches to raise the federal minimum to $9.00 in 2013 and, more recently, to $10.10 in 2015.

These developments are certainly a remarkable political turnaround, but are these wage hikes economically feasible?

The immediate pushback against these campaigns has questioned whether it's feasible to expect businesses to adjust to a minimum-wage hike of this size without generating major negative unintended consequences. This opposition to a $15 minimum comes not only from expected corners—e.g., self-interested restaurant-industry lobbyists from the National Restaurant Association—but also from many economists. The most widely discussed of the possible unintended consequence is the large-scale loss of jobs. Such an outcome would counteract the primary intended consequence of a $15 minimum wage—to improve the living standards of low-wage workers and their families. The rationale is that, if you raise the price of anything, the quantity demanded of that thing will fall. This is how people usually interpret the basic economic principle known as the "law of demand." That raises a serious concern that raising the wages of low-wage workers will cause their employers to cut back on staff, leaving the workers worse off—either unemployed or working fewer shifts.

The current state of research on this employment question, however, finds that minimum-wage increases do not produce significant job losses. This then raises an important policy question: Why haven't there been significant job losses when minimum wages have increased?

First, the basic law of demand actually says something quite different and more specific than just "if the price of something goes up, the quantity demanded of that thing goes down." It actually says that if the price of something goes up—and nothing else changes—the quantity demanded of that something goes down. In the real world, however, other things are changing all the time. Moreover, raising the minimum wage itself causes businesses to change how they operate (more on this below). As a result, the minimum wage's actual impact on jobs depends on what other factors are changing at the same time.

Here's a specific, relevant example: Seattle's 2013 ordinance calls for a series of progressive increases in its minimum wage, up to $15 by 2021 for most businesses. At the same time that the city adopted this new policy, the local economy had been growing (and continues to grow) at a healthy clip. This helps explain why, according to the *Puget Sound Business Journal*, "six months after the first wage increase to $11 per hour took effect, the fear of soaring payrolls shows no signs of killing the appetite of ... the Seattle restaurant world—for rapid expansion." The title of the article sums it up: "Apocalypse Not: $15 and the Cuts that Never Came." Employment growth in Seattle's restaurant industry has not slowed.

The main point is that if no significant job losses result from minimum wages, then it must be the case that employers find other ways to adjust to their higher labor costs. And, in fact, past research has found that businesses often cover the costs of these higher wages by raising prices, re-directing some of their normal revenue growth into raises for their lowest paid workers, and finding savings from lower worker turnover, as higher wages strengthen workers' commitment to their jobs. A minimum-wage hike, in other words, causes both employers and workers to act differently from how they would act in the absence of a minimum wage hike. Employers adopt new strategies to increase revenue to support higher wages, and the stronger loyalty of better-paid employees frees up revenue that would have been spent on recruiting, hiring, and training new workers. Put another way, the "all else equal" clause simply does not hold in the real world. It's important to note, too, that there are disadvantages for employers if they cut their workforce—a smaller staff can make it hard for a business to maintain or improve its existing level of operation and also to retain or expand its customer base.

Even though past minimum-wage hikes have been more modest than the $15 minimum of today's political campaigns, we can use the existing body of research to develop a well-informed view of whether it's feasible for businesses to adjust to a $15 minimum wage without shedding jobs. This is exactly what my colleague Robert Pollin and I explored in our research earlier this year—we examined the question of whether the national economy could adjust to $15 minimum wage while avoiding any major negative unintended consequences.

Our analysis focuses specifically on the situation of the fast-food industry—the industry expected to require the largest adjustments. According to the U.S. Department of Labor, the two occupations that make up more than 62% of the jobs in the fast-food industry—fast-food cooks and combined food prep and serving workers—are the lowest paid occupations. Half of cooks earned less than $8.87 and half of combined food-prep and serving workers earned less than $8.85 in 2014. If fast-food firms can adjust to a $15 minimum without any major negative unintended consequences, other less-affected industries should be able to adopt a $15 minimum more easily.

In our study, we provide a detailed analysis of the labor-cost increase the fast-food industry would face as a result of a $15 minimum wage, taking as our starting point the situation as of 2013. We then use existing empirical research to make reasonable assumptions about the variety of ways firms could absorb these cost increases without shedding jobs.

We estimate that a $15 minimum, phased in over four years, would raise the overall business costs of the average fast-food restaurant by about 3.4% per year. About half of this cost increase could be covered through raising prices by 3% per year and assuming that quantity demanded will fall by about 1.5% due to the higher prices. This would mean, for example, that the average McDonald's outlet could cover about half of its total cost increase by raising the price of a Big Mac by $0.15 per year for four years—for example, from $4.80 to an eventual $5.40.

The fall in demand due to these price increases, however, is small enough that it can be more than offset by the rise in demand for fast food furnished by a healthy, expanding economy. Consumers tend to consume more fast food as their income grows. Over the past 15 years, industry sales have been growing at a slightly faster pace than the overall economy, or about 2.5% per year. As a result, even with the price increases, the fast-food industry should grow and add jobs, just at a somewhat slower pace. But note: this slower job growth is less concerning than one initially may think. Workers' gains in earnings per hour as a result of a $15 minimum wage—averaging 60% across the fast-food workforce—far outstrip the loss in earnings due to 1.5% fewer fast-food work hours added to the economy.

The remaining half of the cost increase could then be covered through cost savings due to lower turnover and by channeling more of the fast-food revenue growth generated by the growing U.S. economy toward payroll. We also found that, after these adjustments are made—increased prices, reduced worker turnover, and a more equitable distribution of the gains from growth—businesses will not have to cut into their profit rate at all. In other words, fast-food restaurants could adjust to a $15 minimum wage without laying off workers and without shrinking the industry's profit margin—the least desirable option from the perspective of employers.

There is one other possible outcome to consider: Will employers try to avoid higher labor costs, over the longer term, by replacing some workers with machines? So far, the empirical evidence of such capital-labor substitution suggests no. Preliminary research by Chicago Federal Reserve economist Daniel Aaronson and his colleague Brian Phelan indicates that jobs with a high level of routine manual work—the lion's share of low-wage positions in the fast-food industry—are unlikely to be replaced by technology in response to minimum wage hikes. This indicates that fast-food employers will tend to look first to other ways to adjust to a $15 minimum wage, before replacing their workers with robots. Since there are other ways for fast-food firms to adjust to a $15 minimum wage—as described above—it seems unlikely that employers would seek technological substitutes for their workers.

Businesses should, in other words, be able to adjust to a $15 minimum wage without having to shed jobs, as long as it is implemented at a reasonable pace. Such a policy, should provide major benefits for the lowest-paid workers in the United States. ❑

Sources: Robert Pollin and Jeannette Wicks-Lim, "A $15 U.S. Minimum Wage: How the Fast Food Industry Could Adjust Without Shedding Jobs," Political Economy Research Institute, Working Paper #373 (2015).

Article 7.2

WILL ARTIFICIAL INTELLIGENCE MEAN MASSIVE JOB LOSS?

BY ARTHUR MacEWAN
September/October 2016

Dear Dr. Dollar:

What's the story with artificial intelligence and jobs? Will the application of robotics to production really lead to massive unemployment?
—*Anonymous, via email*

In the late 1970s, my early years at the University of Massachusetts Boston (UMB), the Department of Economics had two secretaries. When I retired, in 2008, the number of faculty members and students in the department had increased, but there was only one secretary. All the faculty members had their own computers, with which they did much of the work that secretaries had previously done.

I would guess that over those thirty years, the number of departmental secretaries and other secretaries in the university declined by as many as 100, replaced by information technology—what has now become the foundation of artificial intelligence. As I started writing this column, however, I looked on the university's web site and counted about 100 people with jobs in various parts of the Information Technology Department. Neither this department nor those jobs existed in my early years at UMB. The advance in technology that eliminated so many secretaries also created as many jobs as it eliminated—perhaps more.

My little example parallels the larger and more widely cited changes on U.S. farms in the 20th century—a century when the diesel engine, artificial fertilizers, and other products of industry reduced the percentage of the labor force working on farms from 40% to 2%. No massive unemployment resulted (though a lot of horses, mules, and oxen did lose their jobs). The great expansion of urban industrial production along with the growth of the service sector created employment that balanced the displacement of workers on the farms.

Other cases are cited in debates over the impact of artificial intelligence, examples ranging from handloom weavers' resistance to new machinery in the early stages of the Industrial Revolution to a widespread concern about "automation" in the 1960s. Generally, however, the new technologies, while displacing workers in some realms of production, also raised productivity and economic growth. There has, as a result, been increased demand for old products and demand for new products, creating more and different jobs.

Historically, it seems, each time prophecies foretold massive unemployment resulting from major technological innovations, they turned out to be wrong. Indeed, often the same forces that threatened existing jobs created new jobs. The transitions were traumatic and harmful for the people losing their jobs, but massive unemployment was not the consequence.

Is This Time Different?

Today, as we move further into the 21st century, many people are arguing that artificial intelligence—sophisticated robotics—is different from past technological shifts, will replace human labor of virtually all types, and could generate massive unemployment. Are things really different this time? Just because someone, once again, walks around with a sign saying, "The world is about end," doesn't mean the world really isn't about to end!

In much of modern history, the substitution of machines for people has involved physical labor. That was the case with handloom weavers in the early 19th century and is a phenomenon we all take for granted when we observe heavy machinery, instead of hand labor, on construction sites. Even as robotics entered industry, as on automobile assembly lines, the robots were doing tasks that had previously been done with human physical labor.

"Robotics" today, however, involves much more than the operation of traditional robots, the machines that simulate human physical labor. Robots now are rapidly approaching the ability, if they do not already have it, to learn from experience, respond to changes in situations, compare, compute, read, hear, smell, and make extremely rapid adjustments ("decisions") in their actions—which can include everything from moving boxes to parsing data. In part, these capabilities are results of the extreme progress in the speed and memory capacity of computers.

They are also the result of the emergence of "Cloud Robotics" and "Deep Learning." In Cloud Robotics, each robot gathers information and experiences from other robots via "the cloud" and thus learns more and does so more quickly. Deep Learning involves a set of software that is designed to simulate the human neocortex, the part of the brain where thinking takes place. The software (also often cloud-based) recognizes patterns—sounds, images, and other data—and, in effect, learns.

While individual robots—like traditional machines—are often designed for special tasks, the basic robot capabilities are applicable to a broad variety of activities. Thus, as they are developed to the point of practical application, they can be brought into a wide variety of activities during the same period. Moreover, according to those who believe "this time is different," that period of transition is close at hand and could be very short. The disruption of human labor across the economy would happen virtually all at once, so adjustments would be difficult—thus, the specter of massive unemployment.

Skepticism

People under thirty may take much of what is happening with information technology (including artificial intelligence) for granted, but those of us who are older find the changes awe-inspiring. Nonetheless, I am persuaded by historical experience and remain skeptical about the likelihood of massive unemployment. Moreover, although big changes are coming rapidly in the laboratories, their practical applications across multiple industries will take time.

While the adoption of artificial technology may not take place as rapidly and widely as the doomsday forecasters tell us, I expect that over the next few decades many, many jobs will be replaced. But as with historical experience, the expansion of productivity and the increase of average income will tend to generate rising demand, which will be met with both new products and more of the old ones; new jobs will open up and absorb the labor force. (But hang on to that phrase "average income.")

Real Problems

Even if my skepticism is warranted, the advent of the era of artificial intelligence will create real problems, perhaps worse than in earlier eras. Most obvious, even when society in general (on average) gains, there are always losers from economic change. Workers who get replaced by robots may not be the ones who find jobs in new or expanding activity elsewhere. And, as has been the case for workers who lost their jobs in the Great Recession, those who succeed in finding new jobs often do so only with lower wages.

Beyond the wage issue, the introduction of new machinery—traditional machines or robots—often affects the nature and, importantly, the speed of work. The mechanized assembly line is the classic example, but computers—and, we can assume, robotics more generally—allow for more thorough monitoring and control of the activity of human workers. The handloom weavers who opposed the introduction of machines in the early 19th century were resisting the speed-up brought by the machines as well as the elimination of jobs. (The Luddite movement of Northwest England, while derided for incidents of smashing machines, was a reaction to real threats to their lives.)

More broadly, there is the question of how artificial intelligence will affect the distribution of income. However intelligent robots may be, they are still machines which, like slaves, have owners (whether owners of physical hardware, patents on the machines, or copyrights on the software). Will the owners be able to reap the lion's share of the gains that come with the rising productivity of this major innovation? In the context of the extremely high degree of inequality that now exists as artificial intelligence is coming online, there is good reason for concern.

As has been the case with the information technology innovations that have already taken place—Microsoft, Apple, Google, and Facebook leap to mind—highly educated or specially skilled (or just lucky) workers are likely to share some of the gains from artificial intelligence. But with the great inequalities that exist in the U.S. educational system, the gains of a small group of elite workers would be unlikely to dampen the trend toward greater income inequality.

Income inequality in the United States has been increasing for the past 40 years, and labor's share of total income has fallen since the middle of the last century—from 72% in 1947 to 63% in 2014. The rise of artificial intelligence, as it is now taking place, is likely to contribute to the continuation of these trends. This has broad implications for people's well-being, but also for the continuation of economic growth. Even as average income is rising, if it is increasingly concentrated among a small group at the top, aggregate demand may be insufficient to absorb the rising output. The result would be slow growth at best and possibly severe crisis. (See Article 1.2, "Are We Stuck in an Extended Period of Economic Stagnation?".)

Over the long run, technological improvements that generate greater productivity have yielded some widely shared benefits. In the United States and other high-income countries, workers' real incomes have risen substantially since the dawn of the Industrial Revolution. Moreover, a significant part of the gains for workers has come in the form of an increase in leisure time. Rising productivity from artificial intelligence holds out the possibility, in spite of the trends of recent decades, for a shift away from consumerism towards a resumption of the long-term trend toward more leisure—and, I would venture, more pleasant lives.

Yet, even as economic growth over the past 200 years has meant absolute gains for working people, some groups have fared much better than others. Moreover, even with absolute gains, relative gains have been limited. With some periods of exception, great inequalities have persisted, and those inequalities weigh heavily against the absolute rises in real wages and leisure. (And in some parts of the last two centuries—the last few decades in particular—gains for working people have followed from rising productivity and economic growth.)

So even though I'm skeptical that artificial intelligence will generate massive unemployment, I fear that it may reinforce, and perhaps increase, economic inequality. ❑

Sources: David H. Autor, "Whey Are There Still So Many Jobs? The History and Future of Workplace Automation," *Journal of Economic Perspectives*, Summer 2015; Johan Mokyr, Chris Vickers, and Nicolas L. Ziebarth, "The History of Technological Anxiety and the Future of Economic Growth: Is This Time Different?" *Journal of Economic Perspectives*, Summer 2015; Gill A. Pratt, "Is a Cambrian Explosion Coming for Robotics?" *Journal of Economic Perspectives*, Summer 2015; *The Economist*, Special Report on Artificial Intelligence, "The Return of the Machinery Question," June 15, 2016 (economist.com); Robert D. Hof, "Deep Learning," *MIT Technology Review*, 2016 (technologyreview.com); Andrew Figura and David Ratner, "The Labor Share of Income and Equilibrium Unemployment, Accessible Data," FEDS Notes, June 8, 2015 (federalreserve.gov).

Article 7.3

"EQUAL PAY" IS NOT SO EQUAL

BY JOHN MILLER
September/October 2016

> The latest U.S. Department of Labor data show that women working full-time make 81 percent of full-time men's wages. But this figure is both inaccurate and misleading. This statistic looks only at raw averages and does not take into account factors such as education, skills, and hours worked. After controlling for other factors, the gender pay gap practically disappears. Legislation to close the gender "wage gap" is misguided: in reality, there is no gap to close.
>
> —Diana Furchgott-Roth, "Sorry, Elizabeth Warren, Women Already Have Equal Pay," Economics21, The Manhattan Institute for Policy Research, July 27, 2016

"We believe in equal pay for equal work." That was all Sen. Elizabeth Warren (D-Mass.) said about the gender pay gap during her keynote address to July's Democratic National Convention. But it was enough to provoke a response from economist Diana Furchgott-Roth, a senior fellow at the free-market Manhattan Institute.

That's hardly surprising. Furchgott-Roth has spent two decades issuing one version or another of one basic claim: "there is no gap to close between men's and women's wages."

Publishing article after article claiming that there is no gender pay gap, however, doesn't make it so. Here's why.

No Statistical Artifact

To begin with, the gender pay gap is no statistical artifact. The most common measure of the gender pay gap compares the median earnings (wages and salaries) of full-time working women over the year to the median earnings for men. That ratio does not compare the earnings of men and women doing the same job, but rather the earnings of all men and women who work full time.

In 2014, the latest year for which data are available, men's median earnings for the year were $50,383, while women's median earnings were $39,621, or 78.6% of men's. That's where the figure that women earn 79 cents for each dollar a man earns comes from. The National Committee on Pay Equity inaugurated the tradition of using this ratio to determine the date on which "Equal Pay Day" falls each year. This year, it fell on April 12, 2016, the date by which women would have earned enough to make up the $10,762 gap between their pay and men's in 2015. (Furchgott-Roth's figure for the gender pay gap, 81% in 2015, is calculated in the same way but compares the median weekly earnings of full-time wage and salary workers.)

Whether women earn 79 cents or 81 cents for every dollar a man earns, the gender pay gap is longstanding. In 1963, the year the Equal Pay Act became law, a full-time working woman (earning the median pay for women) got 59 cents for each dollar a full-time working man received (at the median pay for men). By the first Equal Pay Day in 1996, women earned 74 cents for a dollar of men's earnings; now the figure is up to 79 cents. The gender pay gap, however, is no longer narrowing as fast as it did earlier. During the 1980s, the gap declined by more than one-quarter (28.7%), as women's earnings improved from 60 cents for every dollar a man earned to 72 cents; during the 1990s, by just 6%, as women's earnings increased from 72 cents to 73 cents for every dollar of men's earnings; in the last ten years (2004-2014), by 7.4%, as women's earnings increased from 77 cents to 79 cents for every dollar of men's earnings.

The gender pay gap is also pervasive. Regardless of her education, her occupation, her race, or her age, a full-time working woman (getting the median wage for women of that group) is paid less than a full-time working man (getting the median wage for men of that group).

Women earn less than men at every educational level. In 2015, the median weekly earnings of women without a high school diploma were 80% of their male counterparts' earnings, 77% for women with (only) a high school diploma, 75% for women with some college, 75% for women who were college graduates, and 74% for women with an advanced degree.

Women earn less than men in all but five of the 800 detailed occupations tracked by the Bureau of Labor Statistics (for which there is comparable data). Women in female-dominated occupations—from maids to secretaries to registered nurses—earn less than men do in those same jobs, as do women in male-dominated jobs—from truck drivers to retail supervisors to janitors. The same is true for women in elite jobs such as physicians, surgeons, and financial managers.

Women of all racial/ethnic groups are paid less than white men and less than men of the same race/ethnicity. In 2015, the median weekly earnings of white women working full time were 80.8% of those for white men. The weekly earnings of black women were 89% of the earnings of black men; the earnings of Hispanic women, 90% of the earnings of Hispanic men. Meanwhile, the weekly earnings of black and Hispanic women were just 62% and 67%, respectively, of the weekly earnings of white men.

Women workers of all ages are paid less than their male counterparts. Older women, however, face the largest pay gap as they are penalized for leaving the workforce more often than men for childbirth, childcare, and eldercare. In 2014, the annual median wage of women ages 18-24 who worked full time was 88% of the median wage of full-time male workers of the same age group, but 81% for women ages 35-44, and just 68% for women over 55.

Making the Unequal Look Equal

But those differences, no matter how widespread or long lasting, don't impress economist Furchgott-Roth. In her version of reality, those differences disappear once the pay gap is adjusted for gender differences in hours worked, education, experience, and choice of industry and occupation. But each of these adjustments is problematic or makes less of a difference than Furchgott-Roth and other pay gap deniers suggest.

The deniers complain that earnings differentials calculated for full-time workers, including anyone who works 35 or more hours a week, mask the fact that men work more hours (in the money economy) than women. In fact, men are almost twice as likely as women work more than 40 hours a week. But that problem can be corrected by using hourly earnings to measure the gender pay gap. In 2014, hourly earnings of full- and part-time women wage-and-salary workers were 84.6% of men's. While smaller, that gap is still quite substantial and persists at all levels of education and for all racial/ethnic groups.

Nor will making adjustments for gender differences in education and experience, two traditional measures of labor-market skills, make the gender pay gap disappear. Adjustments for education explain much less of today's gender pay gap than they did in the early 1980s. Since then, more women have graduated from college than men, and by 1999 the average full-time working woman had more years of education than her male counterpart. Gender differences in years of experience are also far smaller than they were in the past. In 1981, men had, on average, 6.8 more years of full-time labor market experience than women, but the experience gap was just 1.4 years in 2011. In their detailed study of the sources of the gender pay gap, economists Francine Blau and Lawrence Kahn estimate that, taken together, differences in education (which favor women) and differences in experience (which favor men) explained 8.2% of the gender pay gap in 2011, or just 2 cents of the 23 cent gap.

There is little disagreement that differences between women and men in terms of the industries they work in and the jobs they hold have a profound effect on the gender pay gap. Blau and Kahn, for instance, estimate that industry and occupation accounted for fully one-half (49.5%) of the gender pay gap in 2010.

But just how women ended up in particular industries and occupations and not in others is a matter of sharp debate. For gender pay gap skeptics, this is a matter of individual choice. "Women gravitate toward jobs with fewer risks, more comfortable conditions, regular hours, more personal fulfillment, and greater flexibility," argues Carrie Lukas, executive director of the Independent Women's Forum. Women, she concludes, are "willing to trade higher pay for other desirable job characteristics." But the story Lukas tells is not the empirical reality faced by most women. To begin with, women's jobs do not possess the other desirable characteristics she says compensate women for accepting lower pay. In their study of the characteristics of men's and women's jobs in 27 countries including the United States, sociologists Haya Stier and Meir Yaish found that on average the jobs held by women offered less autonomy or time flexibility and that their working conditions were more stressful and exhausting than those of men, a condition that was surely exacerbated by women bearing an inordinate share of domestic labor. (Women's jobs did require less physical labor than men's jobs.)

If individual choices of women don't explain what crowds many women into lower paying jobs, then what is responsible for gender segregation by occupation and industry? Gender discrimination that disadvantages women in the labor market and devalues their work is the more plausible answer. If you doubt that women's work is undervalued, political scientist Ellen Frankel Paul would ask you to consider this example: zookeepers—a traditionally male job—earn more than workers caring for children—a traditionally female job. The evidence that the sorting of genders into industries and occupations is shaped "by discrimination, societal norms and other forces beyond women's control," as economists Jessica Schieder and Elisa Gould argue, is compelling. For instance, it is well documented that women in better-paying male-dominated jobs have faced hostile work environments. A 2008 study found that "52% of highly qualified females working for SET (science, technology, and engineering) companies quit their jobs, driven out by hostile work environments and extreme job pressures." And gender discrimination plays a role in who gets hired in the first place. In two studies, when participants reviewed resumes that were identical except for the names, the ones with male names were more likely to be offered a job. According to another study, after five top U.S. symphony orchestras switched to blind auditions, women were 50% more likely to get past the first round. But gender norms already direct women and men toward different jobs long before they enter in the labor market. For instance, Schieder and Gould report that women arrive at college far less likely than men are to major in engineering, computer sciences, or physics, even though those fields promise lucrative job opportunities.

Most low-paying jobs, on the other hand, are female dominated. In their 2009 study, sociologists Asaf Levanon, Paula England, and Paul Allison reported that occupations with a higher percentage of women workers generally paid less than those with a lower percentage of women, even when correcting for education and skill demands. On top of that, they found evidence that when more women enter a job category, employers start paying less. For example, as jobs in parks and camps went from being male-dominated to female-dominated, between 1950 and 2000, the median hourly wages (corrected for inflation) fell by more than half.

Finally, the adjustments favored by Furchgott-Roth and other gender-gap skeptics are not enough to statistically eliminate the gender pay gap. For instance, one research study, commissioned by the Department of Labor during the George W. Bush administration, estimated a wage gap between 4.8 and 7.1 percentage points after making adjustments for other gender differences. In the Blau and Kahn study the remaining gender gap in 2010 was 8.4 percentage points when fully adjusting for differences in education, experience, region, race, unionization, industry and occupation. Those gender pay gaps, which assume that differences in occupation and industry are not evidence of ongoing gender discrimination, are much smaller than the unadjusted gap, but still substantial.

For Blau and Kahn, the unexplained portion of the gender pay gap, "suggests, though it does not prove, that labor market discrimination continues to contribute to the gender wage gap." The unexplained gender pay gap (the portion still left over after statistically adjusting for occupation, industry, or worker qualifications) has actually worsened since the late 1980s (from 7.6 cents for each dollar a man made in 1989 to 8.4 cents in 2010). In 2010, over one-third (38%) of the gender pay gap remained unexplained. If we include the portion of the gap due to gender differences in occupation and industry, a whopping 87.5%, or 18 cents of the 21 cents of the unadjusted gender gap in their study, can be interpreted as a product of continued discrimination.

Truly Equal Pay

One important step to reduce continued labor market gender discrimination would be to pass the Paycheck Fairness Act. The law would require employers to show that wage differentials are based on factors other than gender, and would strike a blow against pay secrecy by banning retaliation against employees who reveal their own wages to other employees.

But much more needs to be done to combat workplace gender discrimination. More family-friendly policies are needed. The United States is the only advanced country that does not guarantee paid maternity leave. Comparable-worth policies are needed to promote pay equity. Those policies would ensure that jobs having the same value to employers would be paid the same whether performed by women or men. Also, in order to short-circuit historical gender pay discrimination, newly passed comparable-worth legislation in Massachusetts bars employers from asking job applicants how much they earned in previous jobs. In addition, raising the minimum wage would boost the earnings of workers in low-income jobs, the vast majority of which are female-dominated. Unionization in female-dominated occupations would also reduce the gender pay gap, as it has done among public employees.

For Furchgott-Roth and the gender-pay-gap skeptics, the pay gap disappears by statistical manipulation. These policies, on the other hand, are ways to make it go away for real. ❏

Sources: Francine Blau and Lawrence Kahn, "The Gender Wage Gap: Extent, and Explanations," IZA Research Network, Discussion Paper No. 9656, Jan. 2016; Jessica Schleder and Elise Gould, "'Women's work' and the gender pay gap," Economic Policy Institute, July 20, 2016; Asaf Levanon, Paula England, and Paul Allison, "Occupational Feminization and Pay," *Social Forces*, December 2009; Hava Stier and Meir Yaish, "Occupational segregation and gender inequality in job quality," *Work, Employment, and Society*, 28(2), 2014; Marlene Kim, "Policies to End the Gender Wage Gap in the United States," *Review of Radical Political Economics*, 45(3), 2013; Emily Liner, "The Wage Gap Over Time," "A Dollar Short: What's Holding Women Back form Equal Pay?" *Third Way Report*, March 18, 2016; "An Analysis of Reasons for the Disparity in Wages Between Men and Women," A Report by CONSAD Research Corp. for the Department of Labor, 2009; Ellen Frankel, ed., *Equity and Gender: The Comparable Worth Debate* (Transactions Publishers, 1989); Corrine Moss-Racusin et al, "Science faculty's subtle gender biases favor male students," *Proceedings of the National Academy of Sciences*, Oct. 9, 2012; Claudia Goldin and Cecilia Rouse, "Orchestrating Impartiality," National Bureau of Economic Research, Working Paper 5903, January 1997; Sylvia Ann Hewlett, et al., "The Athena Factor," *Harvard Business Review*, 2008; National Committee on Pay Equity, accessed August 2016; "The Gender Wage Gap by Occupation 2015 and by Race and Ethnicity," Institute For Women's Policy Research, Fact Sheet WPR #C440; April, 2016; Janet Adamy and Paul Overberg, "Women in Elite Jobs Face Stubborn Pay Gap," *Wall Street Journal*, May 17, 2016; Stacy Cowley, "Illegal in Massachusetts: Asking Your Salary in a Job Interview," *New York Times*, Aug. 2, 2016; Kaitlin Holmes and Danielle Corley, "The Top 10 Facts About the Gender Wage Gap," Center for American Progress, April 12, 2016.

Article 7.4

THE GIG ECONOMY

The Rise of the Insecure Labor in the United States

BY GERALD FRIEDMAN
March/April 2014

Growing numbers of Americans no longer hold a regular "job" with a long-term connection to a particular business. Instead, they work "gigs" where they are employed on a particular task or for a defined time, with little more connection to their employer than a consumer has with a particular brand of chips. Borrowed from the music industry, the word "gig" has been applied to all sorts of flexible employment (otherwise referred to as "contingent labor," "temp labor," or the "precariat"). Some have praised the rise of the gig economy for freeing workers from the grip of employers' "internal labor markets," where career advancement is tied to a particular business instead of competitive bidding between employers. Rather than being driven by worker preferences, however, the rise of the gig economy comes from employers' drive to lower costs, especially during business downturns. Gig workers experience greater insecurity than workers in traditional jobs and suffer from lack of access to established systems of social insurance.

FIGURE 1: DISTRIBUTION OF THE LABOR FORCE BY CONTRACT TYPE, 1999

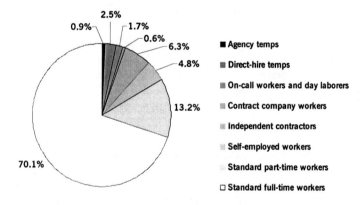

Special surveys by the Bureau of Labor Statistics in 1995, 2001, and 2005, and by the General Accounting Office in 1999, yielded widely varying estimates of the scale of the gig economy. The GAO estimated that as many as 30% of workers were on some type of contingent labor contract, including some categories of workers (self-employed and part-time workers) who are not counted as contingent workers by the BLS. Using the narrower BLS definition, 12% of workers were on contingent contracts in 1999 (similar to the number estimated from more recent surveys).

FIGURE 2: SHARE OF WORKERS ON CONTINGENT CONTRACTS, BY INDUSTRY, 2005

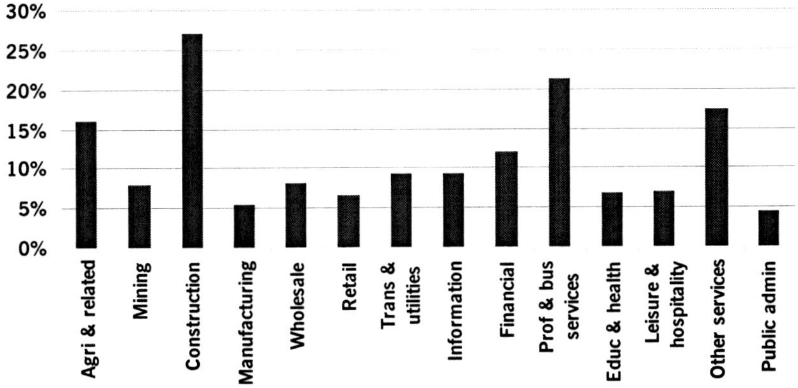

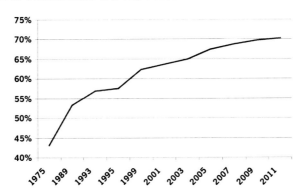

Contingent workers are employed throughout the economy, in all industries and in virtually all occupations. Using the BLS definition, which includes independent contractors, temporary workers, on-call workers, and workers provided by contract firms, contingent workers made up over 11% of the labor force in 2005. Some contingent workers do low-wage work in agriculture, construction, manufacturing, retail trade, and services; others are employed as highly paid financial analysts, lawyers, accountants, and physicians.

FIGURE 3: CONTINGENT LABOR, COLLEGE AND UNIVERSITY FACULTY

While many people may think of "day laborers" in construction or office "temps" when they think of contingent workers, few occupations have seen as sharp an increase in contingent labor as teaching in higher education. Adjunct and part-time professors now account for the great majority of college faculty nationwide. Tenured and tenure-track faculty now comprise less than a third of the teaching staff, and teach barely half of all classes. Colleges and universities hire adjunct faculty because they make it possible to more precisely match faculty to the demand for classes, and because adjuncts are paid substantially less.

FIGURE 4: AVG. EARNINGS, TRADITIONAL VS. CONTINGENT EMPLOYMENT

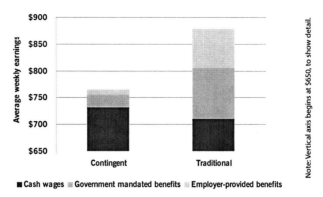

■ Cash wages ▨ Government mandated benefits ▨ Employer-provided benefits

Employers prefer contingent labor because it is more "flexible." Workers can be laid off at any time in response to a decline in sales. Employers can also pay contingent workers less by not offering benefits. By treating many contingent workers as independent contractors, employers avoid paying for government-mandated benefits (the employer's half of Social Security, unemployment insurance, workers' compensation, etc.). They also usually exclude contingent workers from employer-provided benefits such as health insurance and pensions. Counting wages and benefits, contingent workers are paid substantially less than workers in traditional jobs and are left much more vulnerable to illness or economic downturns.

FIGURE 5: NEW JOBS, TRADITIONAL VS. CONTINGENT, 1995-2013

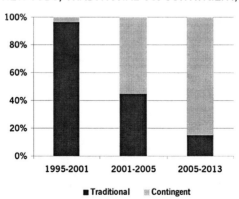

■ Traditional ▨ Contingent

While a solid majority of workers is still employed under traditional arrangements, most new jobs since 2001 have been under contingent arrangements. This is in sharp contrast to the late 1990s, when unemployment rates were low and employers had to offer workers more desirable long-term contracts. With the economic recession of the early 2000s, followed by the Great Recession and the anemic recovery (2007 to the present), however, employers have shunned long-term employment contracts and workers have had to settle. ❏

Sources: General Accounting Office (GAO), Contingent Workers: Incomes and Benefits Lag Behind Those of Rest of Workforce (gao.gov); Bureau of Labor Statistics (BLS), Contingent and Alternative Employment Arrangements, February 2005 and February 2001 (bls.gov); Sharon Cohany, "Workers in Alternative Employment Arrangements." *Monthly Labor Review* (October): 31–46; U.S. Department of Education, National Center for Education Statistics, National Study of Postsecondary Faculty; John Curtis, "Trends in Faculty Employment Status, 1975-2011" (aaup.org).

Article 7.5

THE FALLOUT FROM SUBCONTRACTING

BY ZOE SHERMAN
January/February 2017

> Dear Dr. Dollar:
> Has there ever been a study done on the economic impact of subcontract-ing on a local community? When, for example, a school district subs out its custodial work, with the obvious concomitant reduction of pay and ben-efits suffered by the employees involved, has anyone ever tried to determine the economic impact on the local community?
> — *Paul Gottleib, Montgomeryville, Penn.*

At a former workplace, I had some full-time, year-round, benefits-eligible coworkers on the janitorial and security staff. Over the years I was there, an increasing proportion of the cleaning and security work was transferred to sub-contracted cleaning and security companies.

My first impulse was to do the mental arithmetic this way: If the institution finds it more cost effective to subcontract the work rather than hire directly, they must pay the company supplying the services less than they pay their own employ-ees. In addition, the subcontracting company must take a cut. (For example, a friend who was employed by a temp agency around the same time told me her agency took a one-third cut: If a client paid the agency $15/hour for her to show up and do some work, she herself would get paid $10/hour for that work.) So that means the people actually in the building doing the work as subcontractors must be getting paid a lot less than people who were hired directly.

In addition, subcontracting raises a host of other issues, beyond just pay and benefits questions. Under a subcontracting relationship, the people who do the work are not directly employed by the institution for which they perform the assigned work tasks. Instead, subcontracting inserts an intermediary between the worker and the ultimate employer. The intermediary can in principle, and even sometimes in practice, make the process of matching workers and employers more efficient: The employer can make one call and pay one invoice and have as many workers as needed, rather than dealing with recruitment and hiring and payroll. (The intermediary who does deal with all the recruitment, hiring, and payroll can enjoy economies of scale on those tasks.) Workers, meanwhile, can be matched to any number of jobs without having to take on the costs of searching and applying for many jobs.

This sounds great, except that subcontracting reshapes power relationships in ways that keep the rewards of efficiency gains beyond most workers' grasp. A com-mon pattern identified by economist Ian Taplin in his study of the apparel industry is this: A "core" firm will subcontract out the most labor-intensive, lowest-profit-margin portions of the production process. The subcontractors are dependent on the core firm for sales and locked in intense price competition with one another.

The flexibility gained by the core firm is "squarely predicated upon deskilling, wage depression, and labor intensification," often carried out within the subcontracted companies. In other words, whatever gain subcontracting brings too often come at the expense of workers' employment security and their ability to use their voice to affect working conditions at their workplace. The labor-market intermediaries that match workers to jobs—for-profit temp agencies and the like—can make demands on workers' availability to work, but only pay them when they have a customer for that work. The intermediaries also increase the administrative distance between the workers and the people whose decisions most directly affect their working conditions. That distance weakens the social reciprocity that a direct, long-term employment relationship can sometimes foster and lessens the opportunity for collaborative problem solving. Subcontracted workers are more easily discarded and replaced, so subcontracting also weakens workers' ability to exercise voice in more combative ways, such as strikes. And subcontracting can sometimes be a cover for discriminatory employment practices, making it harder to enforce equal employment opportunity standards.

So subcontracting can be tough on the workers who are most directly affected. You asked, though, how it affects the larger community. That's a multi-headed hydra of a question.

In the example of a school district subcontracting custodial work, decent-paying employment opportunities disappear and lower-paying jobs appear in their places. Custodians' income goes down, so they buy less. Their reduction in spending means a loss of income for the people they buy things from. Now that *those* people's income is lower, *they* spend less too, and so on. This ripple effect multiplies the initial loss of income into a larger loss of aggregate income for the whole population.

In addition, many factors other than lower income for the workers cleaning the school are in play. Do the same individuals keep doing the work, but under worse conditions? Or are the subcontracted workers different people? And if the subcontracted workers are different people, what happens to the people who lost their jobs? What *does* the district do with the money it does not spend on decent pay, benefits, and working conditions for custodial workers? If budgeting in your school district looks like budgeting in my district, perhaps the district spends any money it squeezes out of the custodial services budget on maintaining comparable levels of health benefits paid to teachers in the face of rising insurance premiums. In that case the choice to subcontract custodial services reallocates income from workers who maintain school buildings to a few other recipients: to the owners and direct employees of the subcontracting company, to those who work at health insurance companies and, to the extent that teachers use their health insurance benefits to get care, to those who work in the medical sector. In the for-profit sector, subcontracting tends to concentrate economic rewards in the hands of the company at the top of the hierarchical production structure.

The intermediation and job insecurity associated with subcontracting, like the changes in income, can also have spillover effects on the community at large. There are two competing tendencies for how subcontracting and other types of what are called "flexible staffing arrangements" affect other workers. Employers could offer full-time, long-term employment to those employees they would find hardest to replace by concentrating the risk and desired flexibility on the temporary/contingent/subcontracted workers. A study of industries in Alabama in the 2000s found that this divergence within the workforce was significant: the greater an employer's use of flexible staffing arrangements to manage fluctuations in demand for their products, the greater the employment stability for a core of full-time workers. Job quality for some workers is maintained at the expense of other workers.

On the other hand, having an available employment arrangement that directly disempowers the workers who are caught in it can weaken the bargaining position of all workers. Sociologist Erin Hatton argues in her book *The Temp Economy* that the growth of the temp industry has culturally legitimated treatment of workers as disposable and shrinks the steady employment core. In other words, job quality for all workers is threatened; the interests of employers are protected at the expense of workers.

Macroeconomic data suggest that both things are happenings in the U.S. economy: overall, workers are in a weaker position and inequality between workers and owners is rising. Inequality is also rising *among* workers. A small group of well-compensated workers—often salaried professionals—occupy the rungs just below owners on the income distribution ladder while a widening swath of the population is confronted with stagnant or falling wages. There is a strong case that subcontracting and other "flexible staffing arrangements" contribute to both of those disparities. ❑

Sources: Cynthia L. Gramm and John F. Schnell, "The Use of Flexible Staffing Arrangements in Core Industrial Jobs," *Industrial and Labor Relations Review*, January 2001; Erin Hatton, *The Temp Economy: From Kelly Girls to Permatemps in Postwar America* (Temple University Press, 2011).

Article 7.6

THESE THINGS CAN CHANGE

BY DAVID BACON AND ROSARIO VENTURA
March/April 2015

In 2013, Rosario Ventura and her husband Isidro Silva were strikers at Sakuma Brothers Farms in Burlington, Wash. In the course of three months in 2013, over 250 workers walked out of the fields several times, as their anger grew over their wages and the conditions in the labor camp where they lived.

Every year, the company hires between 700 and 800 people to pick strawberries, blueberries, and blackberries. During World War II, the Sakumas were interned by the U.S. government because of their Japanese ancestry, and would have lost their land, as many Japanese farmers did, had it not been held in trust for them by another local rancher until the war ended. Today, the business has grown far beyond its immigrant roots, and is one of the largest berry growers in Washington, where berries are big business, with annual sales of $6.1 million, and big corporate customers like Häagen Dazs ice cream. Sakuma Farms owns a retail outlet, a freezer and processing plant, and a chain of nurseries in California that grow rootstock.

By contrast, Sakuma workers have very few resources. Some are local workers, but over half are migrants from California, like Ventura and her family. Both the local workers and the California migrants are immigrants, coming from indigenous towns in Oaxaca and southern Mexico where people speak languages like Mixteco and Triqui. While all farm workers in the United States are poorly paid, these new indigenous arrivals are at the bottom. One recent study in California found that tens of thousands of indigenous farm workers received less than minimum wage.

In 2013, Ventura and other angry workers formed an independent union, Familias Unidas por la Justicia—Families United for Justice. In fitful negotiations with the company, they discovered that Sakuma Farms had been certified to bring in 160 H-2A guest workers. The H-2A program was established in 1986, to allow U.S. agricultural employers to hire workers in other countries and bring them to the United States. In this program, the company first must certify that it has tried to hire workers locally. If it can't find workers at the wage set by the state employment department, and the department agrees that the company has offered the jobs, the grower can then hire workers from outside the country. The U.S. government provides visas that allow guest workers to work only for that employer, and only for a set period of time, less than a year. Afterwards, they must return to their home country. If they're fired or lose their job before the contract is over, they must leave right away. Growers must apply for the program each year. On hearing about the application, the striking workers felt that the company was trying to find a new workforce to replace them.

When I questioned someone from the company about why it needed guest workers, he said they couldn't find enough workers to pick their berries. But the farm was also unwilling to raise wages to attract more pickers. "If we [do], it unscales it for the other farmers," said owner Ryan Sakuma in an interview. "We're just robbing from the total [number of workers available]. And we couldn't attract them without raising the price hugely to price other growers out. That would just create a price war." He pegged his farm's wages to the H-2A program: "Everyone at the company will get the H-2A wage for this work."

"The H-2A program limits what's possible for all workers," says Rosalinda Guillén, director of Community2Community, an organization that helped the strikers. Community2Community, based in Bellingham, Wash., advocates for farm worker rights, especially those of women, in a sustainable food system. After the strikes, Sakuma Farms applied for H-2A work visas for 438 workers, saying that the strikers weren't available to work because they had all been fired. Under worker and community pressure, the U.S. Department of Labor (USDoL) did not approve Sakuma's application. Sakuma has still not recognized the union, and many workers feel their jobs are still in danger.

A decade ago there were hardly any H-2A workers in Washington State. In 2013, the USDoL certified applications for 6,251 workers, double the number in 2011. And the irony, of course, is that one group of immigrant workers, recruited as guest workers, is being pitted against another group—the migrants who have been coming to work at the company for many years.

Rosario Ventura: In Her Own Words

As she sat in her home in Madera, Calif., Rosario Ventura described the personal history that led her to migrate yearly from California to Washington, and then become a striker:

I came from Oaxaca in 2001, from San Martín Itunyoso. It is a Triqui town [where the indigenous language Trinqui is spoken], and that's what I grew up speaking. My mother and father were farmers, and worked on the land that belongs to the town. It was just enough to grow what we ate, but sometimes there was nothing to eat, and no money to buy food.

There wasn't much work in Oaxaca, so my parents would go to Sinaloa [in northern Mexico]. I began to go with them when I was young, I don't remember how old I was. It costs a lot of money to go to school and my parents had no way to get it. In Mexico you have to buy a uniform for every grade. You have to buy the pencils, notebooks, things the children need. My brothers went to school, though. I was the only one that didn't go, because I was a girl.

When I told my dad I wanted to come to the U.S., he tried to convince me not to leave. When you leave, it is forever—that is what he said, because we never return. You won't even call, he said. And it did turn out that way. Now I don't talk with him because I know if I do, it will bring him sadness. He'll ask, when are you coming back? What can I say?

I would like to return to live with him, since he is alone. But I can't get the money to go back. There is no money, there is nothing to eat, in San Martín Itunyoso. I thought that I would save up something here and return. But it is hard here too. It's the same situation here in the U.S. We work to try to get ahead, but we never do. We're always earning just enough to buy food and pay rent. Everything gets used up.

It is easy to leave the U.S., but difficult to come back and cross the border. When I came, it cost two thousand dollars to cross, walking day and night in Arizona. We had to carry our own water and food. Out there in the desert it is life and death if you do not have any. It took a week and a half of pure walking. We would rest a couple of hours and get up to walk again.

Those who bring children suffer the most because they have to carry water and food for them, and sometimes carry the children themselves. Thank God we all crossed and were OK. But now that I'm here I'm always afraid because I don't have papers. I can never relax or be at ease.

When I crossed the border I came alone, and then found my brothers, who were already here in Madera. They took me to Washington State to work at Sakuma Farms. I met Isidro when I was working, and we got married in 2003. He speaks Mixteco and I speak Triqui, but that did not matter to us. In those times I hardly spoke Spanish, but now I know a little more.

When I came here, they were pruning the plants. That is very hard work because you get cut and the branches hit your face. When I was in Oaxaca, thinking of coming, I was expecting a different type of work. But this is all there is. People who know how to read and write or have papers can get easier jobs. The rest of us work in the fields.

At Sakuma Farms the company was always hard on us. They would tell us, "you came to pick, and you have to make weight." If you don't make weight they won't let you work for a few days. If you still can't make weight, they pull you out of the field and fire you. But when you're working, and you take what you've picked to be weighed, they always cheat you of two or three pounds.

I've always lived in the labor camp during the picking season. We decided to continue living in Madera, and never moved to Washington permanently. When it gets really hot in the San Joaquin Valley in the summer we go to Washington, where it's cooler. Then when it gets cold there and the work runs out, we come back to Madera. We go every season.

When we go to Washington we have to rent someplace in Madera to store our belongings, like our clothes. Then when we return we have to search for a new home again. It is a hassle. This year we left the house where we'd been living with my brother instead, because he didn't go to Washington. We all live here—Isidro, my four children, my brothers and sisters, and their children. The family pays two thousand a month for the whole house, and Isidro and I pay three hundred as our share.

When we're in Washington we have to save for the winter season, because there's no work until April. I don't work in Madera because I can't find childcare. The trip to Washington is expensive—about $250 in gas and food. If we don't have enough money, we have to ask for a loan. That's what we normally do, since by then we've used up what we saved from the previous year. There is a food bank in Washington, which helps when we get there.

With the strikes last year in Washington we were out of work for almost two months. We didn't save anything, so it was very hard for us afterwards. We didn't have enough to pay the bills, and we couldn't find work. The strikes started when the company fired Federico [a coworker]. We wanted Sakuma to raise the [piece rate] price, and the company refused. They told us if we want to work, work. Then they accused Federico of starting a protest. They went to his cabin, to kick him out of the camp. That's when we stopped work, to get his job back.

We were also upset about the conditions in the labor camp. The mattress they gave us was torn and dirty, and the wire was coming out and poked us. We're accustomed to sleeping with the children, but the bed was so small we couldn't even fit on it. There were cockroaches and rats. The roof leaked when it rained. They just put bags in the holes and it still leaked. All my children's clothes were wet.

They told us they would change things, and the county inspector would come check the cabin. But the company man in charge of the camp told me: "If the inspector comes, don't show him your bed. Don't say anything or you will have a lot of problems." So when the inspector came the company man followed him and didn't let me say anything.

They always try to make us afraid to speak up. If you ask for another five cents they fire you. They threatened to remove us from the camp because of the strikes, and said they'd fire us. They are always threatening us. They fired Ramón also [the leader of the strike and union] because he talked back to them. But thank God he had the courage to talk.

I think there will be strikes again this coming year, if the company doesn't come to its senses, and as long as we have support. We can't leave things like this. There is too much abuse. We are making them rich and making ourselves poor. It's not fair. I think these things can change if we all keep at it. We won't let them keep on going like this. We have to change them. It is important that they raise wages, treat us right, and help the farmworkers. All the mistreatment, threats, everything—it isn't fair.

I want to work, to have money, to be in a better place. I want a little house and to stay in one place with my kids. That's all I'm hoping for. I'd like to see my children reach high school and maybe college. If they don't, I want to go back to Mexico, if I can save money. My kids can go to school there too. I want them to continue studying. I don't want my children to work for Sakuma. ❑

Chapter 8

POVERTY AND WEALTH

Article 8.1

INEQUALITY: THE SILLY TALES ECONOMISTS LIKE TO TELL

BY DEAN BAKER

October 2012; Al Jazeera English

There is no serious dispute that the United States has seen a massive increase in inequality over the last three decades. However there is a major dispute over the causes of this rise in inequality.

The explanation most popular in elite and policy circles is that the rise in inequality was simply the natural working of the economy. Their story is that the explosion of information technology and globalization have increased demand for highly-skilled workers while sharply reducing the demand for less-educated workers.

While the first part of this story is at best questionable, the second part should invite ridicule and derision. It doesn't pass the laugh test.

As far as the technology story, yes information technologies have displaced large amounts of less-skilled labor. So did the technologies that preceded them. There are hundreds of books and articles from the 1950s and 1960s that expressed grave concerns that automation would leave much of the workforce unemployed. Is there evidence that the displacement is taking place more rapidly today than in that era? If so, it is not showing up on our productivity data.

More germane to the issue at hand, unlike the earlier wave of technology, computerization offers the potential for displacing vast amounts of highly skilled labor. Legal research that might have previously required a highly skilled lawyer can now be done by an intelligent college grad and a good search engine. Medical diagnosis and the interpretation of test results that may have previously required a physician, and quite possibly a highly paid specialist, can now be done by technical specialists who may not even have a college education.

There is no reason to believe that current technologies are replacing comparatively more less-educated workers than highly educated workers. The fact that lawyers and doctors largely control how their professions are practiced almost certainly has much more to do with the demand for their services.

If the technology explanation for inequality is weak, the globalization part of the story is positively pernicious. The basic story is that globalization has integrated a huge labor force of billions of workers in developing countries into the world economy. These workers are able to fill many of the jobs that used to provide middle class living standards to workers in the United States and will accept a fraction of the wage. This makes many formerly middle class jobs uncompetitive in the world economy given current wages and currency values.

This part of the story is true. The part that our elite leave out is that there are tens of millions of bright and highly educated workers in the developing world who could fill most of the top paying jobs in the U.S. economy: Doctors, lawyers, accountants, etc. These workers are also willing to work for a small fraction of the wages of their U.S. counterparts since they come from poor countries with much lower standards of living.

The reason why the manufacturing workers, construction workers, and restaurant workers lose their jobs to low-paid workers from the developing world, and doctors and lawyers don't, is that doctors and lawyers use their political power to limit the extent to which they are exposed to competition from their low-paid counterparts in the developing world. Our trade policy has been explicitly designed to remove barriers that prevent General Electric and other companies from moving their manufacturing operations to Mexico, China or other developing countries. By contrast, many of the barriers that make it difficult for foreign professionals to work in the United States have actually been strengthened in the last two decades.

If economics was an honest profession, economists would focus their efforts on documenting the waste associated with protectionist barriers for professionals. They devoted endless research studies to estimating the cost to consumers of tariffs on products like shoes and tires. It speaks to the incredible corruption of the economics profession that there are not hundreds of studies showing the loss to consumers from the barriers to trade in physicians' services. If trade could bring down the wages of physicians in the United States just to European levels, it would save consumers close to $100 billion a year.

But economists are not rewarded for studying the economy. That is why almost everyone in the profession missed the $8 trillion housing bubble, the collapse of which stands to cost the country more than $7 trillion in lost output according to the Congressional Budget Office (that comes to around $60,000 per household).

Few if any economists lost their six-figure paychecks for this disastrous mistake. But most economists are not paid for knowing about the economy. They are paid for telling stories that justify giving more money to rich people. Hence we can look forward to many more people telling us that all the money going to the rich was just the natural workings of the economy. When it comes to all the government rules and regulations that shifted income upward, they just don't know what you're talking about. ❑

Article 8.2

WHAT HAPPENED TO WAGES?
How Wages Stagnated and Capital Captured Productivity Gains

BY GERALD FRIEDMAN
September/October 2014

From the dawn of American industrialization in the 19th century until the 1970s, wages rose with labor productivity, allowing working people to share in the gains produced by capitalist society. Since then, the United States has entered a new era, in which stagnant wages have allowed capitalists to capture a growing share of the fruits of rising productivity. The divergence between productivity and wages challenges orthodox economic theory, which expects employers to bid up the wages of more productive workers. What's more, the success American capitalists have had in monopolizing productivity gains undermines the social justification for capitalism: If working people no longer share the benefits of rising productivity then why should they continue to tolerate capitalist hierarchy?

FIGURE 1: PRODUCTIVITY AND WAGES, 1889-1973

— Output per worker   ········· Real wages

Productivity and wages used to rise together. For much of U.S. history, wages did rise in tandem with labor productivity. Briefly, before and after World War I, the wages of production and other workers lagged productivity. For 20 years after World War II, they rose faster than productivity. Only in the 1960s, however, did the average wages of ordinary workers begin to lag consistently behind labor productivity.

FIGURE 2: PRODUCTIVITY AND WAGES, 1970-2013

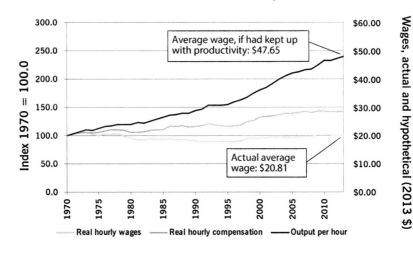

Wages have stagnated despite continued productivity growth. While productivity has increased dramatically, average hourly wages have barely kept up with inflation. Total hourly compensation (including not only wages but also the rising cost of employer-provided health insurance) has increased by just 0.8% a year, still much less than the 2.0% average annual increase in labor productivity. This rise in total compensation does not benefit most current workers, since it is mostly driven by the rising cost of health insurance and higher Social Security taxes to provide for an aging population. Had real wages kept pace with productivity, they would have risen from $19.97/hour in 1970 (in constant 2013 dollars) to $47.65/hour in 2013— more than double the actual average real wage of $20.81/hour in 2013.

FIGURE 3: PRODUCTIVITY AND PAY FOR THE HIGHEST-PAID EMPLOYEES, 1970-2012

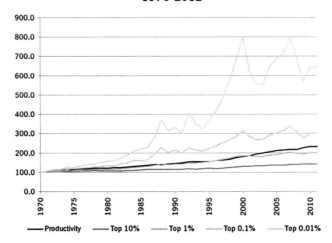

Pay has increased only for those at the very top. Pay has lagged behind productivity for all but the highest-paid employees. Even workers at the 90th percentile—those whose earnings are higher than 90% of workers—have fallen behind productivity growth. Only for employees in the top 0.5% of the pay scale has hourly pay increased as much as average productivity has. For the very highest-paid employees—the top 0.01%, just 13,000 people—pay has risen much faster than productivity. This group includes top corporate executives and other "super managers."

FIGURE 4: PRODUCTIVITY AND PROFITS, 1970-2012

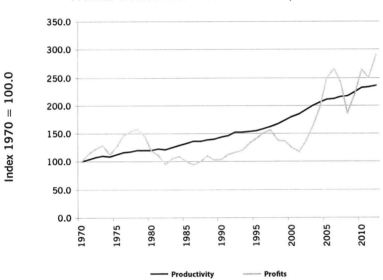

Corporate profits have risen faster than labor productivity. While workers' earnings have lagged productivity, corporate profits have grown faster than the rate of productivity growth, especially since 2000. From World War II through the early 1970s, profits rose with productivity and wages, and labor and capital shared the benefits of productivity growth. Since the recession of the early 1980s, corporate profits have soared, reaching new heights in the 21st century. Business has captured productivity gains that in earlier times went to labor in the form of rising wages—that is, business has succeeded in increasing the share of the economic "pie" going to profits.

FIGURE 5: WAGES, NON-WAGE COMPENSATION, AND PROFITS, 1970 AND 2012

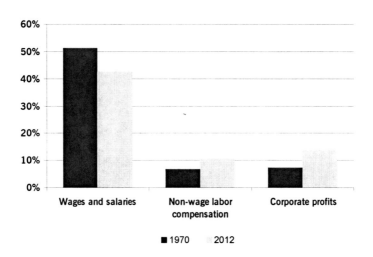

A growng share of income goes to profits, health insurance, and paying for retirement. When profits and the costs of health insurance and pensions (largely Social Security taxes but also private pensions) increase faster than productivity, it reduces the share of income available for workers' wages. Since 1970, the share of income going to wages has fallen by nearly a fifth, dropping by over 9 percentage points—from over half of GDP down to barely 42%; the share going to other forms of labor compensation has risen by almost 4 percentage points, from 7% to 11%; and the share going to corporate profits has risen by nearly 6 percentage points, from 7% to nearly 13%. ❏

Sources: Historical Statistics of the United States Millennial Edition Online; Economic Report of the President 2014; Edward Saez and Thomas Piketty, "Income Inequality in the United States, 1913-1998," *Quarterly Journal of Economics*, 118(1), 2003, 1-39; Bureau of Economic Analysis (bea.gov).

Article 8.3

NO THANKS TO THE SUPER-RICH

We don't owe them gratitude for their "superior productivity."

BY ALEJANDRO REUSS
January/February 2012

"Look at the industries that have dramatically improved over the past several decades, and you'll see a pattern: certain super-productive individuals have led the way. These individuals invariably fall under the 1% of income earners—often the 1% of the 1%. ...

"In no other country are high achievers as free to have a vision, to act on it, to reap the rewards, and to accumulate and reinvest capital—even when they are unpopular, even when 'the 99%' disagree or are resentful or envious.

"So, at a time when the 1% are the easy scapegoats, it's fitting this Thanksgiving to take a moment to thank the 1%—and to be grateful that our country rewards success. And as we approach the new year, let's resolve to keep it that way."

> —Alex Epstein, "Let's Give Thanks for the One Percent," FoxNews.com, November 23, 2011

Leave it to Fox News to publish an opinion piece, on the eve of Thanksgiving, titled "Let's Give Thanks for the One Percent." Author Alex Epstein, a former fellow of the Ayn Rand Institute, argues that most of "the 1%" (the Occupy Wall Street movement's designation of the richest 1% of the population) "earn their success—through superior productivity that benefits us all."

Is it true that the United States "fosters and rewards productivity like no other," as Epstein argues? Is greater inequality the price we pay for greater economic dynamism? As a first cut, let's compare Gross Domestic Product (GDP) per capita in different high-income countries. Here, the United States ranks second among large industrial countries (excluding small, oil-rich countries, city-states, etc.) behind only Norway. In 2010, Norway's GDP per capita was nearly $56,000, compared to just under $47,000 for the United States. This difference was not a one-year anomaly—Norway's GDP per capita has exceeded that of the United States for over twenty years. One doubts that Epstein would see Nordic social democracy as the kind of society—in which "high achievers [are] free to have a vision, to act on it, to reap the rewards, and to accumulate and reinvest capital"—that fosters high productivity. Yet the GDP figures suggest that it does just that.

Still, second place is not bad. The United States does outpace most of Western Europe on GDP per capita. So maybe Norway is an anomaly, and the more general picture is that the United States and its incentives to "high achievers" vastly outperform Western European "socialism" in fostering productivity. Here, we need to look at a more refined measure, GDP per hour worked, in place of GDP per capita. Average work hours per year vary dramatically among different countries. Workers in many Western European countries enjoy a shorter work week and much longer vacations than workers in the United States. Employed U.S. workers work an average of over 1700 hours per year. Their counterparts in France, Germany, the Netherlands, and Norway, in contrast, average just over 1400 hours. These differences in hours worked explain much of the variation in GDP per capita among these high-income countries. Shifting from GDP per capita to GDP per hour worked, we find that the United States (at about $59/hour) still ranks second to Norway (about $74/hour). The big difference in the rankings, however, is that the gap between the United States and several Western European countries all but disappears. Ireland, The Netherlands, Belgium, and France (yes, France!) all boast figures of over $57/hour, belying the idea that the United States "fosters ... productivity like no other" country (see Figure 1 below).

The idea that greater inequality fosters greater productivity is a widely held article of faith in the United States, and not only among conservatives. Even liberals may accept the idea that there is a tradeoff between equality and productivity, though they may see some loss in productivity as a price worth paying for greater equality. In fact, some countries may enjoy high labor productivity *because of*, not despite, their higher degree of economic equality (both in terms of the distribution of private incomes and the provision of public services). Near-universal access to education and health care, for example, helps people develop greater productive capabilities. Greater overall economic security (including an extensive social safety net and full-employment policies) can make it easier for people to take risks and attempt new ventures. Maybe these are some of the reasons that greater equality in many Western European countries is compatible with such high material standards of living.

While the United States does little better (or, in one case, worse) than five different Western European countries on productivity, we are clearly number one when it comes

FIGURE 1: GDP PER HOUR WORKED, HIGH-INCOME COUNTRIES

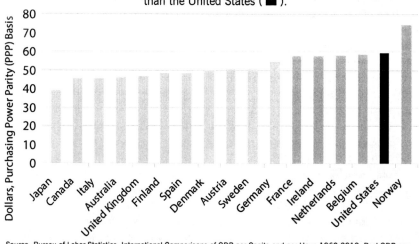

Which is the country that "fosters productivity like no other"? Five European countries (▨) have levels of GDP per hour worked very similar to or greater than the United States (■).

Source: Bureau of Labor Statistics, International Comparisons of GDP per Capita and per Hour, 1960-2010, Real GDP per hour worked, by country, 1960-2010, Table 3a. Converted to U.S. dollars using 2010 PPPs (2010 dollars).

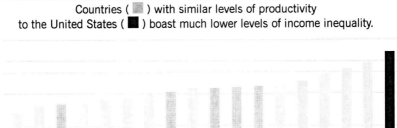

FIGURE 2: INCOME INEQUALITY—RATIO OF TOP 10% TO BOTTOM 10%

Countries (▨) with similar levels of productivity
to the United States (■) boast much lower levels of income inequality.

High-income countries, per capita income > US$30,000 PPP, 2007.

Source: United Nations Development Programme (UNDP), Human Development Report 2009, Table M: Economy and inequality, Share of income or expenditure, Richest 10%, Poorest 10%, p. 195 (hdr.undp.org/en/media/HDR_2009_EN_ Complete.pdf).

to income inequality. One way to measure income inequality is to compare the share of total income going to the top 10% of the population, by income ranking, to the share going to the bottom 10%. (Using other measures does not change the basic story.) In the United States, the top 10% receives nearly 16 times as much income as the bottom 10%. In the four countries with GDP per hour very similar to the United States'—Belgium, France, Ireland, and Holland—this ratio is less than ten to one. These countries are all in the middle of the pack, in terms of income inequality, among high-income industrial economies. Norway, the country with the highest GDP per hour, has a ratio of just six to one. By this measure, it boasts the third-lowest level of income inequality among these high-income countries (see Figure 2).

Average labor productivity in the U.S. economy, measured by output per hour in the private business sector, has nearly doubled over the last thirty years. Part of the increase is explained by an increase in the education and skills of U.S. workers; part, by the fact that they are working with more and better tools. Most of the increase in income inequality in the United States is not due to an increasing gap in incomes between highly educated (and supposedly more productive) workers and less-educated workers. It is due, rather, to an increase in incomes from property (profits, rent, dividends, interest, capital gains, etc.) at the expense of incomes from labor, and to an increase in the incomes of top corporate executives (which derive from corporate control, and should be classified as part of property income).

That one person's income is higher than another's does not prove that the former is more productive than the latter. If a particular person or group's income is rising, this does not prove that they are being "rewarded" for their increasing productivity. Gains in productivity, like those in the United States in recent decades, must go to someone or other. It is the way that these gains have been split up among different groups that explains the United States' high and rising income inequality—and that has less to do with changes in the relative productivity of different people than shifts in the balance of power between owners and workers.

That does call for a response from the majority, but it's not "thank you." ❑

Sources: Alex Epstein, "Let's Give Thanks for the One Percent," FoxNews. com, November 23, 2011; Bureau of Labor Statistics, International Comparisons of GDP per Capita and per Hour, 1960-2010, Real GDP per hour worked, by country, 1960-2010, Table 3a. Converted to U.S. dollars using 2010 PPPs (2010 dollars), (bls.gov); Bureau of Labor Statistics, Output Per Hour, Private Business Sector, Series ID number: PRS84006093 (bls.gov); United Nations Development Programme, *Human Development Report 2009*, Table M: Economy and inequality, Share of income or expenditure, Richest 10%, Poorest 10%, p. 195 (undp.org).

Article 8.4

CORPORATE CRONYISM: THE SECRET TO OVERPAID CEOS

BY DEAN BAKER
February 2014; Truthout

It's hardly a secret that the heads of major corporations in the United States get mind-bending paychecks. While high pay may be understandable when a top executive turns around a failing company or vastly expands a company's revenue and profit, CEOs can get paychecks in the tens or hundreds of millions even when they did nothing especially notable.

For example, Lee Raymond retired from Exxon-Mobil in 2005 with $321 million. (That's 22,140 minimum wage work years.) His main accomplishment for the company was sitting at its head at a time when a quadrupling of oil prices sent profits soaring. Hank McKinnel walked away from Pfizer in 2006 with $166 million. It would be hard to identify his outstanding accomplishments.

But you don't have to be mediocre to get a big paycheck as a CEO. Bob Nardelli pocketed $240 million when he left Home Depot after six years. The company's stock price had fallen by 40% in his tenure, while the stock its competitor Lowe's had nearly doubled. And then we have the CEOs in the financial industry, heads of huge banks like Lehman, Bear Stearns, and Merrill Lynch, or the insurer AIG. These CEOs took their companies to the edge of bankruptcy or beyond and still walked away with hundreds of millions of dollars in their pockets.

It's not hard to write contracts that would ensure that CEO pay bear a closer relationship to the company's performance. For example, if the value of Raymond's stock incentives at Exxon were tied to the performance of the stock of other oil companies (this can be done) then his going-away package probably would not have been one-tenth as large. Also, there can be longer assessment periods so that it's not possible to get rich by bankrupting a company.

If anyone were putting a check on CEO pay, these sorts of practices would be standard, but they aren't for a simple reason. The corporate directors who are supposed to be holding down CEO pay for the benefit of the shareholders are generally buddies of the CEOs.

Corporate CEOs often have considerable input into who sits on their boards. (Some CEOs sit on the boards themselves.) They pick people who will be agreeable and not ask tough questions.

For example, corporate boards probably don't often ask whether they could get a comparably skilled CEO for lower pay, even though top executives of major companies in Europe, Japan, and South Korea earn around one-tenth as much as CEOs in the United States. Of course this is the directors' job. They are supposed to be trying to minimize what the company pays their top executives in the same way that companies try to cut costs by outsourcing production to Mexico, China, and elsewhere.

But friends don't try to save money by cutting their friends' pay. And when the directors themselves are pocketing hundreds of thousands of dollars a year for attending four to ten meetings, there is little incentive to take their jobs seriously.

Instead we see accomplished people from politics, academia, and other sectors collecting their pay and looking the other way. For example, we have people like Erskine Bowles who had the distinction of sitting on the boards of both Morgan Stanley and General Motors in the years they were bailed out by the government. And we have Martin Feldstein, the country's most prominent conservative economist, who sat on the board of insurance giant AIG when it nearly tanked the world's financial system. Both Bowles and Feldstein were well-compensated for their "work."

Excessive CEO pay matters not only because it takes away money that rightfully belongs to shareholders, which include pension funds and individuals with 401(k) retirement accounts. Excessive CEO pay is important because it sets a pattern for pay packages throughout the economy. When mediocre CEOs of mid-size companies can earn millions or tens of millions a year, it puts upward pressure on the pay of top executives in other sectors.

It is common for top executives of universities and private charities to earn salaries in the millions of dollars because they can point to executives of comparably sized companies who earn several times as much. Those close in line to the boss also can expect comparably bloated salaries. In other words, this is an important part of the story of inequality in the economy.

To try to impose the checks that don't currently exist, the Center for Economic and Policy Research (CEPR) has created Director Watch. This site will highlight directors like Erskine Bowles and Martin Feldstein who stuff their pockets while not performing their jobs.

CEPR also worked with the Huffington Post to compile a data set that lists the directors for the Fortune 100 companies, along with their compensation, the CEOs' compensation, and the companies' stock performance. This data set is now available at the Huffington Post as Pay Pals.

Perhaps a little public attention will get these directors to actually work for their hefty paychecks. The end result could be to bring a lot of paychecks for those at the top back down to earth. ❑

Article 8.5

GLOBAL INEQUALITY

BY ARTHUR MacEWAN
November/December 2014

> Dear Dr. Dollar:
> I had thought that neoliberal globalization was making the world more unequal. But recently I have seen claims that the distribution of income in the world has become more equal. Is this true?
> —*Evan Swinerton, Brookline, Mass.*

The answer to these questions depends on what you mean by "in the world." In many countries in the world—including most of the high-income countries and the most populous lower-income countries—the distribution of income has become more unequal. If we look at the income differences among countries, however, the situation has become more equal because per capita income has generally increased more rapidly in lower-income countries than in higher-income countries—but with important exceptions. And if we look at income distribution among all the people in the world—accounting for inequality both within and between countries—it seems that in recent decades the very high degree of inequality has remained about the same.

Distribution *Within* Countries

Take a look at Figures 1 and 2, which show the changes in the distribution of income within selected countries, several high-income and several low- or middle-income, over roughly the last two decades. The measure of income distribution used in these graphs is the ratio of the total income of the highest-income tenth of the population to the total income of the lowest-income tenth of the population.

The first thing that stands out in Figure 1 is that the U.S. income distribution is substantially more unequal than those of any of the other countries. Also, the absolute increase by this measure of inequality is greatest in the United States. However, with the sole exception of Italy, all the countries in Figure 1 experienced *rising income inequality*.

Things are different in Figure 2, which includes the ten most populous lower-income countries (ten of the twelve most populous countries in the world, the United States and Japan being the other two). First, the degree of inequality is quite high in some of the countries in the graph. Brazil is the extreme case. However, Brazil and most of the other countries in Figure 2 experienced a *reduction of inequality* in this period—though several are still highly unequal. The most populous countries in Figure 2—China, India, and Indonesia—though, experienced rising inequality. These three countries are the first, second, and fourth most populous countries in the world (with the United States third).

**FIGURE 1: INCOME RATIO, TOP 10% TO BOTTOM 10%,
SELECTED HIGH-INCOME COUNTRIES**

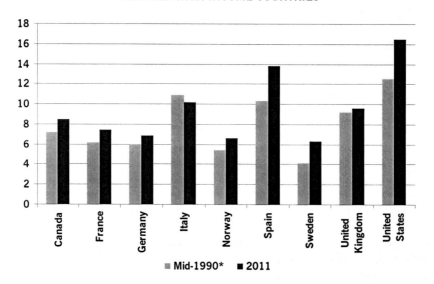

Mid-1990* ■ 2011

Note: For the U.K. the figure is for 1999; for Spain the figure is for 2004; for France the figure is for 1996. For all others the earlier figures are for 1995. The later U.S. figure is for 2012.

Source: OECD.

**FIGURE 2: INCOME RATIO, TOP 10% TO BOTTOM 10%, MOST POPULOUS
LOW- AND MIDDLE-INCOME COUNTRIES**

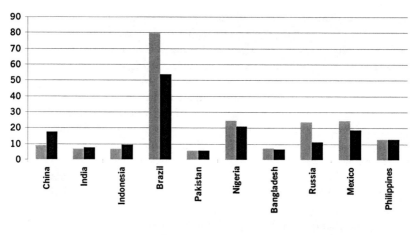

Mid-1990s ■ About 2010

Note: These countries along with the United States and Japan are the twelve most populous countries in the world. The combined population of these ten accounts for 55% of the world's population in 2014.

Source: World Bank.

The data in these two graphs illustrate the widespread rise of income inequality *within* countries, especially among high-income countries. Among lower-income countries, the picture is mixed. Although Brazil remains highly unequal, the reduction of inequality in Brazil is important because it has been achieved, at least in part, by policies directed at reducing poverty. Brazil's redistributive policies represent a trend in many Latin American countries—a backlash against the neoliberal policies of preceding decades.

Distribution *Among* Countries

Figure 3 illustrates what has been happening to income distribution *among* countries and indicates that the situation has become more equal because, in general, lower-income countries have grown more rapidly during the last two decades than have higher-income countries. For 1994 and 2013, the two columns in Figure 3 show Gross Domestic Product (GDP) per capita in the ten most populous low- and middle-income countries (listed by population) compared to GDP per capita in the United States. The comparison is in terms of purchasing power parity (PPP).

For nine of these ten countries—Mexico is the exception—GDP per capita rose more rapidly than in the United States. Taken as a group and using an average weighted by population, these ten countries in 1994 had an average GDP per capita 9% of that in the United States, but by 2013 this figure had risen to 17%. The basic result is not due simply to the remarkably rapid economic growth in China. When China is removed from the group, the weighted average still increases, over this time period, from 10% to 15%. (This general phenomenon is certainly not a universal phenomenon; several very low-income countries have fallen further and further behind.)

Warning!

There are many problems in determining the extent of income inequality. The results can differ depending on which measure of inequality we use. Also, there are data difficulties. While some of these difficulties arise from poor reporting, plenty arise from the complexity of the issues. Also, different countries collect income data in different ways and do so in different years. With one exception, I will not detail the difficulties here, but readers should keep in mind that such difficulties exits.

The one exception is how we compare incomes in different countries, where relative prices differ, currencies differ, and exchange rates (e.g., the number of Mexican pesos it takes to buy a dollar) often do not tell us accurately the buying power of income in different countries. The income data here are reported in terms of purchasing power parity (PPP) and reported in relation to the U.S. dollar. Comparing incomes in different countries using the PPP method gives us a comparison of the real buying power of income in the different countries. Calculating PPP data is complex and not precise, but the PPP figures are the best we have.

FIGURE 3: PER CAPITA GDP, MOST POPULOUS LOW-INCOME AND MIDDLE-INCOME COUNTRIES, AS PERCENTAGE OF U.S. GDP (PPP)

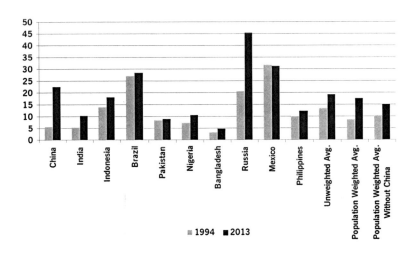

Source: World Bank.

So, if countries are our units of observation, Figure 3 illustrates how things have become more equal since the early 1990s. Going back further in time, comparing countries' incomes weighted by population shows inequality dropping pretty much continuously since 1960, and especially sharply since the early 1990s. But if the average is not weighted by population—thus removing the dominance of China, India, and some other very populous countries—the situation among countries only started to become more equal from 2000. Nonetheless, many low-income countries have been left behind in this period, most notably several countries of Africa. The dominant trend is not the exclusive trend.

Global Distribution Among People

To obtain a truly global estimate of the distribution of income, it is necessary to compare the incomes of people (or families or households) in the world. Availability of data (as well as other data problems) makes such an estimate rough, but useful nonetheless. Branko Milanovic, perhaps the leading expert on these issues, has shown that, from the mid-1980s to 2011, global inequality remained roughly constant, with a slight decline toward the end of this period—likely explained by the greater slowdown of high-income countries compared to low-income countries in the Great Recession. The relative stability of income distribution would seem to result from a rough balance between the reduction of inequality among countries (Figure 3) and the rise of inequality within countries (Figure 1 and the most populous countries of Figure 2).

Milanovic's estimate uses the Gini coefficient, a standard measure of income inequality. The Gini takes account of incomes of the whole population, unlike the measure used in Figures 1 and 2, which focuses on extremes. The Gini can vary from 0 (everyone has the same income) to 1 (all the income goes to one person). For income distribution in almost all countries, the Gini ranges from about 0.27 (Norway) to about 0.65 (South Africa).

For the global population, over the period of Milanovic's estimates, the Gini varies around 0.70—a higher figure, showing a more unequal distribution, than for any single country. However, if inequality were measured by a comparison of extremes, it is likely that inequality would be rising. There remains a large share of the world's population that continues to live in extreme poverty, while incomes at the very top have sky-rocketed in recent years. But whether the measure is the Gini or a comparison of extremes, the distribution among people in the world is very unequal.

What Matters?

Each of these measures of income inequality "in the world" matters in one way or another. For example, to understand political conflicts within countries, the changes in the distribution within countries is probably most important. To understand how the changing structures of the global economy have affected people's lives in various parts of the world, it is useful to consider all of these measures. And to understand the dynamics of international politics, the measures that focus on inequalities among countries are probably paramount.

The measurements show both some positive and negative changes in the world. On the one hand, the rapid growth of several low-income and middle-income countries has, in spite of the high (and sometimes rising) level of inequality in these countries, pulled many people out of abject poverty. On the other hand, we know that rising inequality within a country tends to undermine social cohesion and generate stress at virtually all levels of society—with damaging effects on health, education, the natural environment, and crime. Even in this era of increased globalization, it is in the national context that inequality has the primary impact on people's behavior and how they judge their well-being.

And no matter how we look at the situation, the world has long been and remains a very unequal place. ❏

Sources: Branko Milanovic, *Worlds Apart: Measuring International and Global Inequality*, Princeton University Press, 2005; Branko Milanovic, *Global Income Inequality by the Numbers: in History and Now—An Overview*, The World Bank, Development Research Group, Poverty and Inequality Team, November 2012; Christoph Lakner and Branko Milanovic, *Global Income Distribution: From the Fall of the Berlin Wall to the Great Recession*, The World Bank, Development Research Group, Poverty and Inequality Team, December 2013, WPS6719; Richard Wilkinson and Kate Pickett, *The Spirit Level: Why Greater Equality Makes Societies Stronger*, Bloomsbury Press, 2009.

Chapter 9

RACE AND CLASS

IT PAYS TO BE WHITE

Assessing how White people benefit from race-based economic inequality.

BY JEANNETTE WICKS-LIM
May/June 2016

By every major socioeconomic measure, there is an undeniable race-based hierarchy in the United States—with Black Americans sitting at or near the bot-tom. In 2014, the share of Black adults (at least 25 years old) with bachelor's or advanced degrees (22%) is notably lower than their White counterparts (32%). The official unemployment rate for Black workers is persistently double that of White workers: in 2015, 9.7% vs. 4.3%. Also in 2015, the African-American poverty rate (26.2%) stood at more than double that among White Americans (10.1%). Black Americans account for 38% of the prison population, nearly three times their share of the U.S. population. White Americans, in contrast, account for 59% of U.S. prisoners, under-representing their 77% population share.

These lopsided outcomes have, of course, two sides: by every major socioeconomic measure, White Americans sit at or near the top of the race-based hierarchy. This is an obvious point. Here's another one: if the economic odds are stacked against African Americans, the flipside is that White Americans have the odds stacked in their favor. We need to even these odds to achieve racial justice.

Current policy debates largely focus on reducing potential hurdles set in the way of African Americans. These same debates, however, overlook how race-based advantages put White Americans on an easier life path. To eliminate the United States' race-based hierarchy, we need to redirect economic resources that currently operate as a premium for being White into creating equal opportunities for African Americans and other communities of color.

Unfortunately, two policies specifically created to do so—affirmative action and reparations—only exist on the outer fringes of current policy debates.

It Pays to Be White at School

According to a 2012 study, about one-third of the nation's students attend hyper-segregated schools: schools that are 90% White or 90% non-White. Students in the nearly all-White schools benefit from $4,985 in local and state education spending per student (adjusted for regional differences in living costs), an $810 premium over the $4,176 spent on their counterparts in the nearly all-non-White schools. (All figures are inflation-adjusted to 2015 dollars.)

Over a 13-year K-12 public-school education, this White-school premium adds up to nearly $10,000 more spending on each student in nearly all-White schools compared to students in nearly all-non-White schools ($810 premium x 13 years of schooling = $10,530).

This White advantage is even more impressive when pooled together under one school's roof. Given the average school size of 500 students, this White premium scales up to an extra $2.8 million dollar investment into the elementary education in a nearly all-White school ($810 per student x 500 students x 7 years of elementary education = $2.8 million). This White school premium can translate into White students learning in better physical facilities, having access to more curriculum offerings with more and higher-quality materials, and served by greater numbers of teachers and support staff.

It Pays to Be White on the Streets

City police departments' pro-active "stop and frisk" policing techniques have come under scrutiny in recent years. The term "stop and frisk" refers to when a police officer stops and detains a person if the officer believes he or she has a reasonable suspicion that criminal activity is taking place. Controversy over "stop and frisk" policing is due to charges that officers apply the tactics unevenly— surveying and interrupting the daily routines of White Americans much less frequently than those of Black Americans.

Take, for example, the practices of the Boston Police Department (BPD). In 2010, the American Civil Liberties Union of Massachusetts and the BPD co-sponsored a study of the BPD's "Field Interrogating Observation Frisk and/or Search" (FIOS) practices. Researchers approved by both organizations examined the BPD's database of FIOS incidents from 2007–2010. The study, released in 2015, concluded that the BPD treated White neighborhoods more favorably—initiated fewer FIOS incidents, compared to Black neighborhoods, even after taking into account differences in neighborhood crime rates. In fact, the figures in the study indicate that White neighborhoods (defined here as 85% White) accumulated 2,500 fewer FIOS incidents annually compared to Boston neighborhoods with a high concentration of Black residents (85% Black).

This difference implies that if you're living in an 85% White neighborhood, chances are that you would be subject to police surveillance about once every decade. So, for example, by the age 30, such a resident might be surveyed, stopped and/or frisked twice: once at age 15 and then again at age 25. This resident's life is minimally disrupted by the BPD. If you're living in a Black neighborhood, chances are you'd have a FIOS incident every three years. In other words, by age 30, you can expect to have already had six unsolicited police encounters: at age 15, then at age 18, again at 21, again at 24, again at 27, and again at 30 years old. The situation for Whites is even better than these numbers suggest. If you're White, the police are 11% more likely to only stop and ask you questions, not frisk or search you and your belongings compared to if you're Black. This difference in frisking rates of Whites versus Blacks is the same as the BPD's differential frisking rate of non-gang members versus gang members.

What's it worth to be White on Boston's streets? It's hard to put a price tag on the ability to move around freely.

It Pays to Be White at Work

How much more do White workers benefit from paid employment than their Black counterparts? That is, what is the bonus for being White in the workplace? One way to get a handle on this is to calculate how much more the average White worker earns, over a working lifetime, compared to their Black counterpart. Note that in this exercise I do not "net out" differences in educational credentials, or any other type of possible measures of skill. This is in order to take account of how, for example, any White premium in schooling builds up into an additional White bonus at work in the form of job market preparation. In other words, the premium I calculate for being White at work includes the White bonus of better-funded educational opportunities, as well as increased access to better job opportunities, and higher rewards for work.

Take the situation of an average White male fulltime worker and compare his experience in the labor force to his Black counterpart: In 2014, the average White male full-time worker earned $10,900 more than his Black counterpart: $44,900 vs. $34,000. This average male White worker also has access to a paid job more consistently compared to his Black counterpart; the employment rate for White males is much higher than for Black males (95.7% vs. 90.3%). Their annual earnings equal $42,900 and $30,700, after accounting for their average unemployment spells. The gap is now $12,200. At this rate, this White worker could work three months less per year, and still earn more money.

What does this mean over their entire work careers? To keep things simple, let's say each continues to work until the end of his or her life. Because White men live longer than Black men, this means that the average male White worker could potentially work from 25 to 77 years old, or 52 years. Black men die, on average, five years sooner at 72 years, for a work career of 47 years. Therefore, over an entire working career, White workers get a work bonus of $790,000—$2.2 million vs. $1.4 million. It really does pay to be White at work.

It Pays to Be White When You Stumble

In 2011, the average White household held $23,000 in liquid wealth, like deposits in a checking account or a retirement account. This is more than 100 times the average amount of $200 held by African-American households. Considering all assets, including equity in a home, the average White American had more than ten times that of the average Black American, $111,740 vs. $7,113.

White people's access to wealth gives them a boost when they're down on their luck. Chances are much better that, if you're White, you can draw on some inherited asset or the assets of a family member when the proverbial chips are down. Hit with a large, unexpected medical bill? If you're White, your chances of managing this as just a bump in the road are much better than if you are Black.

Likewise, White people's greater access to wealth gives them a leg up when trying to get ahead. Starting a small business or trying to buy a house where there are good neighborhood schools? Trying to get a college degree without paying for tuition with your credit card? If you're White, your likelihood of being able to make that initial business investment, home down payment, or to cover that college bill, is far better than if you're Black. These, of course, are key steps to anyone's larger effort to enter and stay in America's middle class—by improving one's own educational and employment prospects, as well as those of one's children.

White households' outsized share of wealth is deeply tied to the country's history of racist social institutions. Public policy has built up wealth for White citizens, at the expense of any social group considered non-White, for nearly the United States' entire history. Exemplars of such public policies include, of course, enslaving Africans and African Americans and expropriating land from Native Americans.

But public policies that build up wealth for White citizens, at the expense of other social groups extend through to more recent times. Take Pres. Franklin Delano Roosevelt's New Deal programs starting in the 1930s, such as the Home Owners' Loan Corporation (HOLC) and the Federal Housing Administration (FHA), or the 1944 Servicemen's Readjustment Act (GI Bill) that provided aid to World War II veterans. These programs intervened massively in the housing market by providing federally subsidized home mortgages. From 1935 to 1953, FHA and the Veteran's Administration backed, on average, 45% of the mortgages for new construction. This support, however, focused specifically on subsidizing home ownership for Whites. White families benefited from the programs' use of restrictive covenants that required White homeowners to only sell to White buyers and from redlining that designated Black neighborhoods as undesirable areas for mortgage lending. These practices did not officially end until the 1968 passage of the Fair Housing Act. These policies effectively represented large-scale federal affirmative action programs for White Americans.

It Pays to Be White Nearly Everywhere

Growing evidence from the field of social psychology over roughly the past 20 years demonstrate how living and breathing in a world defined by an economic racial hierarchy appears to shape our most basic intuitions about the world—what is good or bad, what is dangerous or safe, what has value and what is valueless. This is the basic conclusion of social psychologists researching the phenomenon of implicit racial bias—a person's unconscious favorable or unfavorable action toward, or thoughts and feelings about, another person based on the person's race. Crucially, this bias occurs even in the absence of any consciously identified racial bias (see sidebar, next page).

Implicit racial bias helps to make sense of what economists Marianne Bertrand and Sendhil Mullainathan observed in their 2004 study, "Are Emily and Greg More Employable than Lakisha and Jamal?" They found that the answer is: yes, across a wide range of occupations and industries. For their study they sent out thousands of essentially identical resumes, with the exception of the name of the applicant. Those with stereotypically White names got callbacks for interviews 50% more frequently than resumes sent with stereotypically Black names.

Hard-pressed to find any economic rationale for this racial bias, the researchers speculate, "Employers receive so many resumes that they may use quick heuristics in reading these resumes. One such heuristic could be to simply read no further when they see an African-American name." Moreover, the shock expressed by human resource managers over Bertrand and Mullainathan's findings suggests that this heuristic operates through an implicit—rather than explicit—racial bias. That is, employers don't consciously discard resumes with Black-sounding names. More likely, employers' hold an implicit racial bias that causes them, at a glance, to consider more favorably resumes with White-sounding names.

The social environment in the United States, steeped in race-based haves and have-nots, appears to train people's gut feelings to turn positive towards White people and negative towards Black people, unconsciously and automatically. As a result, it pays to be White nearly everywhere.

Policy Implications of White Privilege

All this leads to the conclusion that if African Americans have the deck stacked against them in every major life activity, White Americans have the deck stacked in their favor. Current policy debates need to focus on the question of how to eliminate White privilege. Two examples of public policies designed to do this include affirmative action and reparations.

The explicit goal of affirmative action policies is to increase the number of people of socially stigmatized groups into positions of prestige. Affirmative action is not just a policy about diversifying the classroom or the workplace. These types of

How to Detect Implicit Racial Bias

Social psychologists have come up with clever experimental designs to detect implicit racial bias. They do this with what's called an "Implicit Association Test" (IAT). To detect implicit racial bias, the IAT measures whether a person associates, without conscious deliberation, the concept or feeling of "good" with a White person compared to a Black person.

One version of this test has a participant sit in front of a computer. Words and names alternately appear on the screen. First, the person is instructed to hit the "I" key with their right hand to indicate if a word is "good" (e.g., "joy") and the "E" key with their left hand if the word is "bad" (e.g., "pain"). When a name appears on the screen, the person is instructed to hit the "I" key if the name is typically White ("Brad") and the "E" key if the name is typically Black ("Jamal"). This set-up associates "good" with "White"— the "I" key is hit for both, and "bad" with "Black"— the "E" key is hit for both. Then the exercise is repeated but with the association reversed: the participant is instructed to hit the "I" key if the name is typically Black ("Lakisha") and the "E" key if the name is typically White ("Allison"), while the words are sorted in the same way as before. Now, the set-up associates "good" with "Black" and "bad" with "White."

Researchers have found that people sort with greater ease when the key for Black and negative are the same, and the key for White and positive words are the same— evidence of an implicit racial bias. Studies using an IAT test like this one have found evidence of implicit racial bias regardless of whether participants express any type of explicit racial bias.

policies aim to change the make-up of who holds high-ranking positions by decreasing the over-representation of members of advantaged groups.

Reparations, in the U.S. context, typically refers to a policy of providing compensation to descendants of Africans and African Americans who were enslaved in the United States. It can also refer to compensation for the damage generated by any other systematically racist public policy. Whatever the form and amount of compensation, the basic aim of reparations is to use government funds to transfer wealth to African-American households in order to correct for past government practices that transferred wealth from Black households to White households.

Implicit racial bias, however, is a major pernicious obstacle to public policies aimed at correcting for White privilege. Implicit racial bias supports the existing racial hierarchy with a gut feeling that people get what they get because that's what they deserve—in particular, that White people tend to get more because they deserve more, while Black people get less because they deserve less. This is one factor explaining the often- vitriolic political resistance to calls for reparations. Even affirmative action is currently treated as a policy debate non-starter.

Policies that require White people to give something valuable up—privileged access to a well-funded neighborhood school, an apartment or house, admission to a university, a high-paying or high-status job, a seat in Congress—become politically toxic when combined with implicit racial bias. This is the ultimate upside of race-based inequality for White Americans: it encourages White Americans to feel entitled to rebuke the policies that would end their White privilege.

What about tackling the issue of economic inequality more broadly? A flatter social hierarchy would, at minimum, limit the size of race-based gaps. Take for example, raising the federal minimum from today's $7.25 to $15.00. This policy would result in raises to 54% of Black workers and 59% of Latino workers compared to 38% of White workers.

At the same time, to uphold the moral integrity of such a political movement, and its potential broad-based political appeal, depends on coming honestly to the unifying call that "we're all in this together." This requires explicitly addressing the reality that yes, we're all in this together, but even among the 99% some get—and feel entitled to— more than their fair share.

In other words, policies that address inequality more broadly must not be used as a way to sidestep the truth about the racial hierarchy that exists in the United States. To be sure, we need social policies that address inequality more generally to build a more just economy. The United States has about 20 million poor White Americans to show for that. Still, White people—up and down the economic scale—benefit from a race-based advantage that simply does not exist for African Americans.

Promoting race-based policies, such as affirmative action or reparations, does present a political risk: it could critically weaken class-based solidarity by exacerbating race-based tensions. Such racial division can thwart efforts to hold together the needed political coalitions to fight for a more broadly just economy. In a forceful critique against calls for reparations, Black American political scientist Adolph Reed states plainly that "there's nothing (less) solidaristic than demanding a designer type policy that will redistribute only to one's own group."

At the same time, the continuing success of Donald Trump's 2016 presidential bid (as of this writing) suggests that this view may be shortsighted. Trump's racist innuendos—his "dog-whistle" politics—clearly tap into deeply felt, race-based resentments among White workers frustrated by their four-decades-long experience of economic stagnation. His stump speeches might not have such an electrifying appeal if this country ever had an honest reckoning of past and existing racist policies and practices—an honest reckoning that would reasonably call for policies such as affirmative action and reparations.

Such a reconciliation process may represent the best chance of removing Black Americans from the go-to list of scapegoats for why America is no longer great, and must be made "great again," to paraphrase Trump's slogan. In the long run, challenging White privilege head-on may open the way to secure a cross-racial, class-based, political alliance resistant to cleaving under the pressure of economic hard times.

The sobering reality is that the odds that this type of reconciliation would lead to such a positive outcome, while greater than zero, are still slim, given the country's long-standing history of racial division. However, it could very well be the only path to building a solidarity movement among the 99% resilient enough to address inequality more broadly. ❑

Sources: Marianne Bertrand and Sendhil Mullainathan, "Are Emily and Greg More Employable than Lakisha and Jamal? A Field Experiment on Labor Market Discrimination," *The American Economic Review*, September 2004; Carmen DeNavas-Walt and Bernadette D. Proctor, "Income and Poverty in the United States: 2014," *Population Reports*, September 2015; Jeffrey Fagan, Anthony A. Braga, Rod K. Brunson, April Pattavina, "Final Report: An Analysis of Race and Ethnicity, Patterns in Boston Police Department Field Interrogation, Observation, Frisk, and/or Search Reports," June 15, 2015; Federal Bureau of Prisons, March 26, 2016 (bop.gov); Leo Grebler, David M. Blank, and Louis Winnick, "The Role of Federal Aids in Mortgage Finance," in Leo Grebler, David M. Blank, and Louis Winnick, eds., *Capital Formation in Residential Real Estate: Trends and Prospects* (Princeton University Press, 1956); Anthony G. Greenwald, Debbie E. McGhee, and Jordan L. K. Schwartz, "Measuring Individual Differences in Implicit Cognition: The Implicit Association Test," *Journal of Personality and Social Psychology*, 1998; Anthony Greenwald and Mahzarin R. Banaji, "Implicit Social Cognition: Attitudes, Self-esteem, and Stereotypes," *Journal of Personality and Social Psychology*, 995; National Center for Education Statistics, "Numbers and Types of Public Elementary and Secondary Schools From the Common Core of Data: School Year 2009-10," September 2012 (nces. ed.gov); Adolph Reed,Jr.,"The Case Against Reparations," *The Progressive*, December 2000; Ary Spatig-Amerikaner, "Unequal Education: Federal Loophole Enables Lower Spending on Students of Color," Center for American Progress, August 2012; Rebecca Tippett, Avis Jones-DeWeever, May Rockeymoore, Darrick Hamilton, and William Darity, "Beyond Broke: Why Closing the Racial Wealth Gap is a Priority for National Economic Security," Center for Global Policy Solutions, 2014; United States Bureau of Labor Statistics, "Labor Force Characteristics by Race and Ethnicity," November 2015 (bls.gov); United States Census Bureau, "QuickFacts," 2015 (census. gov); United States Census Bureau, "Educational Attainment in the United States: 2014," 2015 (census.gov); Jeannette Wicks-Lim, "A $15 Federal Minimum Wage: Who Would Benefit?" PERI Research Brief, March 2016; Jiaquan Xu, Sherry L. Murphy, Kenneth D. Kochanek and Brigham A. Bastian, "Deaths: Final Data for 2013," Division of Vital Statistics, Feb. 6, 2016

Article 9.2

POVERTY CRIME, PRIVILEGED CRIME
Policing and Economic Inequality

BY KRISTIAN WILLIAMS
January/ February 2015

Police violence against Black people in the United States has set off three major waves of protest in the past year. While most analyses of Ferguson, Staten Island, and Baltimore have rightly put the spotlight on race, there is also an important economic dimension we should not forget.

A Justice Department investigation into the Ferguson police found the local apparatus of criminal law—cops, prosecutors, judges, jails—operating like a vast extortion racket, singling out Black people, charging them for minor offenses, and shaking them down for fines and fees, enforced with bench warrants and the threat of incarceration.

In New York, the police approached, and ultimately killed, Eric Garner for selling untaxed single cigarettes by the subway entrance. That is exactly the sort of low-level "public order" offense that Police Commissioner William Bratton built his career on and, like Bratton's other notable victories breaking up homeless encampments and arresting the "squeegee men" who wash windshields at traffic lights, the "crime" is practically identical with the economic status of the "perpetrator."

Meanwhile, Baltimore's riots elicited a surprising analysis from John P. Angelos, chief operating officer of Major League Baseball's Baltimore Orioles. He wrote via a series of Twitter posts that he was less concerned about "one night's property damage" than about

> the past four-decade period during which an American political elite have shipped middle class and working class jobs away from Baltimore and cities and towns around the U.S. to third-world dictatorships ... plunged tens of millions of good hard working Americans into economic devastation and then followed that action around the nation by diminishing every American's civil rights protections in order to control an unfairly impoverished population living under an ever-declining standard of living and suffering at the butt end of an ever-more militarized and aggressive surveillance state.

Angelos echoed another sports figure, basketball legend Kareem Abdul-Jabbar, whose commentary on Ferguson, appearing in *Time* under the title "The Coming Race War Won't Be About Race," argued that "we have to address the situation not just as another act of systemic racism, but as what else it is: class warfare."

Racism and poverty may be distinct modes of oppression, but in the United States—with its history of colonialism, slavery, and genocide—they are never fully separable. The complexity is demonstrated by two studies on drug enforcement. In one, New York University researchers found that both crack use and related arrests are statistically more tied to class than race: "Being poor is the true overwhelming correlate," as Dr. Joseph Palamar summarized, "not being black or a minority." African Americans, then, are over-represented in crack arrests as a side effect of poverty, which they suffer at rates twice the national average. What that analysis overlooks, however, is the racial bias implicit in the police focus on crack. In a study of drug arrests in Seattle, sociologist Katherine Beckett found that Blacks were arrested for possession at a rate 13.6 times that of Whites, and 21 times that of Whites for dealing. Beckett tested several hypotheses, but the only statistically significant factor she could identify was the police focus on crack. Of all the city's drug arrests, 72.9% were for crack, and 73.4% of crack arrests were African Americans. Looking at data concerning the frequency of drug sales, calls to police, public health considerations, and gun violence, Beckett could find no rational reason to prioritize crack enforcement. She concluded that "the focus on crack cocaine does not appear to be a function of race-neutral considerations," and it is possible that "the SPD's focus on Black suspects explains the preponderance of crack cocaine arrests," rather than the other way around.

Of course the racial politics of policing are not simply Black and White. Over the last two decades, local cops have increasingly been enlisted to enforce immigration law, often checking the status of those they arrest on minor charges. In many places, the result has been a shift in priorities: According to the ACLU, after the jail in Irving, Tex., started reporting to Immigration and Customs Enforcement, police there began arresting greater numbers of Hispanics for low-level public order offenses. Likewise, attorney Raymond Dolourtch described to the *Voice*, the digital magazine of the American Immigration Lawyers Association, a pattern he has observed in the St. Louis area: Police pull over Latino motorists, usually on some thin pretext. Undocumented immigrants, who cannot apply for a driver's license, are then arrested for driving without one. In jail, police check their immigration status—leading to possible criminal charges or deportation. In towns like Waukegan, Ill., and Rogers, Ark., police set up checkpoints for the same purpose.

Cops in California seem more interested in impounding vehicles than making arrests. They set up "sobriety checkpoints," not near bars at closing time, but on the edge of Latino neighborhoods during rush hour. According to California Watch, over a two-year period, 61% of the state's roadblocks were in areas with a Latino population of 31% or more. In 2009, police in the state made 3,200 DUI arrests at checkpoints, but seized 24,000 cars from unlicensed drivers.

Debates about immigration are raced-coded, but enforcement—like mass migration itself—is also often economically driven. As Christian Parenti argues, American capitalism needs a steady supply of immigrant labor, but needs it cheap. By criminalizing the workers, the state aims to keep them uncertain, uneasy, disorganized, and docile. The attack on immigrants, therefore, is both "[p]olitically. . . an organic expression of nativist hostility and a very useful, rational system of elite-inspired class control." Meanwhile: What about the crimes of rich White people?

In his book *The Divide*, journalist Matt Taibbi helpfully contrasts white-collar corporate fraud with a paradigmatic poverty crime, welfare fraud. On the one hand, he finds, "Twenty-six billion dollars of fraud: no charges"; on the other, the San Diego County District Attorney's office conducts 26,000 warrantless, preemptive searches every year to make sure that welfare recipients really are exactly as poor as the poverty bureaucracy demands that they be.

Even when the wealthy face arrests and prosecution—rather than administrative penalties—their punishments are typically weaker. For example, despite the reforms of the 2010 "Fair Sentencing Act," the cocaine gap persists: 28 grams of crack earn a minimum of five years in prison, as opposed to 500 grams of powder. The difference is the customer base: The NYU study found that some of the variables reducing the likelihood of crack use—full-time employment, higher income, higher education—increase the odds of using powder cocaine.

Similarly, in the mid-1980s, when legislators established harsh penalties for crack possession, they also set minimum sentences for driving under the influence. The juxtaposition is revealing. At the time, drunk driving killed about 22,000 people each year, which was more than all other drug-related deaths combined. But while crack was tagged with a five year minimum sentence, the penalty for drunk driving was typically two days in jail for a first offense, ten days for a second. The difference is that, while 93% of those convicted of possessing crack were Black, at least 78% of those arrested for drunk driving were White. What all this suggests is that the notion of crime has less to do with proscribed behaviors, or with the real consequences of such actions, than with the figure of the criminal—identified, or even defined, by race and poverty. That such a designation has persisted across decades, despite cultural and legal changes emphasizing equality, suggests that these disparities are not a result of simple prejudice, but a structural feature of our criminal legal system, reflecting in turn the basic structure of our society. ❏

Sources: Kareem Abdul-Jabbar, "The Coming Race War Won't Be About Race," *Time*, Aug. 17, 2014; Michelle Alexander, The New Jim Crow: Mass Incarceration in the Age of Colorblindness (The New Press, 2010); Katherine Beckett, *Race and Drug Law Enforcement in Seattle: Report Prepared for the ACLU Drug Law Reform Project and the Defender Association* (ACLU: September 2008); Alyssa L. Beaver, "Getting a Fix on Cocaine Sentencing Policy: Reforming the Sentencing Scheme of the Anti-Drug Abuse Act of 1986," *Fordham Law Review* 78 (2010); Amalia Greenberg Delgado and Julia Harumi Mass, *Costs and Consequences: The High Price of Policing Immigrant Communities* (ACLU of Northern California: February 2011); "The Fair Sentencing Act Corrects a Long-Time Wrong in Cocaine Sentencing," *Washington Post*, Aug. 3, 2010; Ryan Gabrielson,"Car Seizures at DUI Checkpoints Prove Profitable for Cities, Raise Legal Questions," California Watch, Feb. 13, 2010 (californiawatch.org); Anita Khashu, *The Role of Local Police: Striking a Balance between Immigration Enforcement and Civil Liberties* (Police Foundation, April 2009); Danielle Kurtzleben, "Data Show Racial Disparity in Crack Sentencing," *U.S. News and World Report*, Aug. 3, 2010; Lucy McCalmont, "Baltimore Orioles Executive Defends Freddie Gray Protesters," Huffington Post, April 27, 2015; Joseph J. Palamar, et al., "Powder Cocaine and Crack Use in the United States: An Examination of Risk Arrest and Socioeconomic Disparities in Use," *Drug and Alcohol Dependence* 149 (2015); Christian Parenti, Lockdown America: Police and Prisons in the Age of Crisis (Verso, 1999); "Powder vs. Crack: NYU Study Identifies Arrest Risk Disparity for Cocaine Use," *NYU News*, Feb. 19, 2015 (nyu.edu); Elizabeth Ricci, "D.W.U.: Driving While Undocumented," *Voice*, January/February 2011; Matt Taibbi, *The Divide: American Injustice in the Age of the Wealth Gap* (Spiegel & Grau, 2014); United States Department of Justice Civil Rights Division, Investigation of the Ferguson Police Department, March 4, 2015.

Article 9.3

WHY WE *ALL* NEED AFFIRMATIVE ACTION

BY JEANNETTE WICKS-LIM
November/December 2014

On April 22, 2014, the U.S. Supreme Court decided to allow Michigan voters to constitutionally ban the use of affirmative action in public higher education admissions. This decision adds another knot to the thick web of racial barriers operating in the United States—in this case, making Michigan's colleges and universities less accessible to students of color. But, in this age of extreme economic inequality across all races, why should we care?

After all, affirmative action primarily seeks, in the words of economist and Duke University professor William Darity, to provide "access to members of socially excluded groups to preferred positions in society." That is, as Darity points out in his 2013 paper supporting affirmative action, these policies aim for equal representation of historically disenfranchised groups at all levels of the social hierarchy. They do not aim to do anything about the relative positions of the hierarchy itself. Affirmative action is an important anti-racism tool, not a program to reduce inequality per se. A related critique of affirmative action is that the policy simply promotes already relatively advantaged individuals within a disenfranchised group (e.g., members of the African-American middle class). For these reasons, defending affirmative action feels less urgent for some than the call for reducing inequality in general.

We should care about affirmative action because recent headlines have jarred the nation's consciousness to the immediate, lethal consequences of racism. Three recent highly publicized murders of black teenagers—Trayvon Martin in 2011 in Sanford, Fla.; Jordan Davis in 2013 in Jacksonville, Fla.; and Michael Brown this year in Ferguson, Mo.—demonstrate how racism can effectively condemn someone to death.

Affirmative action policies combat racism in a critical way. By integrating "preferred positions in society," affirmative action policies undermine racist intuitions entrenched in the American psyche—intuitions that stop people from acknowledging the full humanity of black people, in particular. A common slogan on signs during the two weeks of non-stop protests over Brown's shooting stated plainly what should go without saying: "Black lives matter too." The fact that this statement had to be asserted, rather than assumed, points out the root issue.

The common link between the shootings of the three teenagers is the racial stereotyping of young black men in particular—as violent and predatory—in ways that set them up as targets. Apparently, 30-year-old self-appointed neighborhood watchman George Zimmerman gunned down 17-year-old Trayvon Martin because he looked "suspicious." Forty-seven-year-old Michael Dunn, from his car, shot teenager Jordan Davis in "self-defense" during a verbal confrontation over the volume of the music Davis and his friends were listening to. In the case of Michael Brown, police officer Darren Wilson shot the unarmed teenager while he held his hands up in the air. Ferguson residents, who are two-thirds black, were under the surveillance of a nearly all-white police force (with 50 white officers out of 53).

Shootings like these are the lethal tip of the iceberg. Many symptoms of racism, while alarming, are chronic rather than immediately deadly. For at least the last half century, for example, the African-American unemployment rate has nearly always been double (or more than double) the rate among white workers. And, in 2012, for every dollar of income the average white household brought in, the average black household brought in only 60 cents. The level of racial wealth inequality is of an entirely different magnitude: the average white household owns 6.4 times the wealth of the average African-American household. The incarceration rate among black males, on the other hand, is 6.4 times the rate among white males. More than one in three black children (37%) live in poverty, compared to one in eight white children (13%). And finally, more than one in three black children (38%) attend almost completely segregated schools.

Psychological research can tell us something about how stereotypes operate, and offers clues about how to break them down. *The Handbook of Prejudice, Stereotyping and Discrimination* describes the existence of "automatic prejudice" in American society. The handbook explains that, "[i]f the members of minority groups are consistently presented in negative social contexts (e.g., crime, terrorism, dependency, etc.) then classical and evaluative conditioning processes would certainly be expected to produce prejudiced mental associations with these groups and their members." The legacy of slavery in the United States and its present-day offshoots of racial discrimination have consistently degraded the status of being African-American. The laundry list of statistics above attests to how systematically the concept of race defines the economic and social hierarchy in the United States. This racialized hierarchy also plays out in frequent, ongoing, cultural representations of African-American people associated with negative traits that, according to the research, reinforce and deepen prejudices.

Examples abound. There are the emblematic ones. In the mid-1970s, then-presidential candidate Ronald Reagan's anti-welfare rhetoric inspired the iconic image of the "welfare queen"—an African-American woman who cheats the welfare system—and turned her into a political football. During George H.W. Bush's 1988 presidential bid came the infamous "Willie Horton" ad. The ad featured a mug shot of Horton, an African-American man who committed several felonies while out of prison on a furlough program supported by Bush's Democratic opponent, Michael Dukakis. Today, right-wing critics of President Obama, the United States' first African American president, have dubbed him the "Food Stamp" president.

And then there are the multitude of insidious micro-aggressions inflicted on the character of black men and boys in the media. In a 2011, the Pew Research Center audited mainstream news outlets in Pittsburgh for their representation of black men and boys. "Of the nearly 5,000 stories studied in both print and broadcast," they found, "less than 4 percent featured an African American male engaged in a subject other than crime or sports."

Even allegations of criminal behavior take on a uniquely negative spin when leveled against a black person. During an August 18, 2014, radio broadcast about Michael Brown and Ferguson, National Public Radio reporter Robert Siegel described a theft allegedly committed by Brown as a "pretty thuggish moment," as opposed to just a "theft," a "criminal act," or some similar combination of race-neutral words. Dr. Beverly Tatum, president of the historically Black women's college, Spelman College, describes the omnipresent feature of racism like smog:

"[S]ometimes it is so thick it is visible, other times it is less apparent, but always, day in and day out, we are breathing it in."

Psychologists have by now performed numerous experiments that document "automatic stereotype activation"—how people use racial stereotypes reflexively. Take for example evidence from a psychology experiment that timed how long white participants took to categorize positive and negative words after experiencing a visual cue of a white or black person. White participants took longer to respond—a sign of unease—when an image of a black person preceded a positive word, compared to when an image of a white person did. These patterns were not, however, related to explicitly stated prejudices. Racial stereotypes appear to unconsciously prime their minds to automatically associate a white person with positive attributes and a black person with negative attributes.

A study by the National Institute for Transportation and Communities documents a more harrowing expression of implicit pro-white and anti-black attitudes. Interested in explaining the over-representation of racial minorities among pedestrian traffic fatalities, Portland University researchers tested whether racial bias exists in the treatment of pedestrians by drivers. In predominantly white Portland, Ore., they observed that compared to white pedestrians, black pedestrians had to wait longer for drivers to yield to cross the street, and were passed by twice as many drivers. "Our findings are ... consistent," the researchers conclude, "with behavioral manifestations of implicit racial attitudes."

To reduce these implicit prejudices, the emerging psychological research prescribe frequent exposure to experiences that not only contradict the pejorative assumptions about people who are not white, but affirm positive alternative assumptions. A 2008 experimental social psychology study identified converting stereotypes into "counterstereotypes" as the key to reducing automatic negative stereotyping on the basis of race. In other words, to eradicate today's ingrained pro-white/anti-black attitudes, we need to live and breathe a world filled with counter-stereotypes. Just identifying and criticizing anti-black attitudes doesn't cut it. Affirmative-action policies are uniquely suited to break racial prejudices because these policies increase the presence of nonwhite people in preferred social positions.

Consider African-American Harvard professor Henry Louis Gates' remarkable anecdote: "No one has benefited more from affirmative action than I have. The class of '66 at Yale had six Black graduates. My class, the class of '73, had 96. And the difference was because of affirmative action." We also have more systematic, if less dramatic, evidence from the work of economist Jonathan Leonard. His empirical research linked meaningful improvements in African-American workers' employment opportunities to federal affirmative action policies. Specifically, better enforcement of affirmative action during the 1970s led to a greater share of African-American men and women in the workforces of federal contractors. These policies also increased these workers' access to better-paid white-collar and craft occupations. Changes like these can begin to normalize the association between people who have been historically discriminated against and the positive social status of holding a decent-paying job that requires specialized skills.

What affirmative action policies need to do— but have not yet achieved—is to make these associations common occurrences. When they are, people's daily experiences can chip away at the reflexive negative associations with African Americans by normalizing positive associations.

This would represent important progress toward replacing the existing set of race-based assumptions with one that permits every person to be seen as possessing a fuller range of human qualities—and ultimately the same basic human constitution—no matter his/her race. And, eventually, people may reflexively see their own humanity mirrored back in the faces of people of different racial backgrounds, instead of seeing something "less than."

Affirmative-action policies, of course, are not a panacea for racism. To substantially reduce racism, we also need a barrage of policies that address the wide range of racial disparities that exist: anti-discrimination laws in housing, economic policies that promote full employment and greater equity in the distribution of wealth, reform of school disciplinary policies and the criminal justice system. The list goes on. Affirmative-action policies, however, play a critical role in draining the power of automatic racial stereotypes.

Reducing the severity of today's economic inequality would also help reduce racism, since social tensions can be channeled into scapegoating and fuel racism. However, whether these social tensions are intense or moderated, the fact remains that a specific group of people consistently stand in their crosshairs.

Without affirmative action, in combination with other anti-racism policies, we can expect to continue to normalize—for everyone—our existing racist intuitions. And these intuitions will inevitably produce more tragic losses. Let's be clear here: that means that, as a nation, we are promising to inflict insufferable pain and loss for families that include men who are young and black. Empathy, however, may lead many more to feel the urgency for affirmative-action policies. ❑

Sources: Galen V. Bodenhausen, Andrew R. Todd, and Jennifer A. Richeson, "Controlling Prejudice and Stereotyping: Antecedents, Mechanisms, and Contexts," in *Handbook of Prejudice, Stereotyping, and Discrimination* (2009), Todd D. Nelson, ed., pp. 111-136; William Darity, "Confronting those Affirmative Action Grumbles," in *Capitalism on Trial: Explorations in the Tradition of Thomas E. Weisskopf* (2009), Jeannette Wicks-Lim and Robert Pollin, eds., pp. 215-223; Nilanjana Dasgupta and Anthony G. Greenwald, "On the Malleability of Automatic Attitudes: Combating Automatic Prejudice with Images of Admired and Disliked Individuals," *Journal of Personality and Social Psychology* 81(5) (2001), pp. 800-814; John F. Dovidio, Kerry Kawakami, Crain Johnson, Brenda Johnson, and Adaiah Howard, "On the Nation of Prejudice: Automatic and Controlled Processes," *Journal of Experimental Social Psychology* 33 (1997), pp. 510-540; Jonathan S. Leonard, "The Impact of Affirmative Action Regulation and Equal Employment Law on Black Employment," *Journal of Economic Perspectives,* 4(4) (1990), pp. 47-63; Tara Goddard, Kimberly Barsamian Kahn, and Arlie Adkins, "Racial Bias in Driver Yielding Behavior at Crosswalks," *National Institute for Transportation and Communities Report,* NITC-SS-733, April 2014; Dennis O. Ojogho, "Affirmative Reaction," *Harvard Crimson,* March 13, 2014; John Roman, "'Stand Your Ground' laws: Civil rights and public safety implications of the expanded use of deadly force," *Metrotrends Blog,* October 29, 2013 (blog.metrotrends.org); John Light, "Smart Charts: These Eight Charts Show Why Racial Equality Is a Myth in America," May 22, 2014 (billmoyers.com); Bertram Garonski, Roland Deutsch, Sawsan Mbirkou, Beate Seibt, and Fritz Strack, "When 'Just Say No' is not enough: Affirmation versus negation training and the reduction of automatic stereotype activation," *Journal of Experimental Social Psychology* 44 (2008), pp. 370-377; Beverly D. Tatum, *Why Are All The Black Kids Sitting Together in the Cafeteria?* (2003).

Article 9.4

MAPPING ENVIRONMENTAL INJUSTICE
Race, Class, and Industrial Air Pollution

BY KLARA ZWICKL, MICHAEL ASH, AND JAMES K. BOYCE
November/December 2015

East St. Louis, Ill., just across the Mississippi River from St. Louis, Mo., is not your typical American town. It has a hazardous waste incinerator, numerous chemical plants, and multiple "national priority" toxic waste sites. It's also home to 26,000 residents, 98% of them African-American. The median household income is about $21,000—meaning that half the households in the city have annual incomes even lower. The rate of childhood asthma is among the highest in the nation.

America's polluters are not color-blind. Nor are they oblivious to distinctions of class. Studies of environmental inequality have found that minorities and low-income communities often bear disproportionate pollution burdens. One of the reasons was revealed in a consultant report to the California Waste Management Board that surfaced in the 1980s: "A great deal of time, resources, and planning could be saved and political problems avoided if people who are resentful and people who are amenable to Waste-to-Energy projects [a.k.a. incinerators] could be identified before selecting a site," the report observed. It recommended that "middle and higher-socioeconomic strata neighborhoods should not fall at least within the one-mile and five-mile radii of the proposed site."

Rather than being distributed randomly across the U.S. population, pollution mirrors the distribution of power and wealth. Pollution disparities reflect conscious

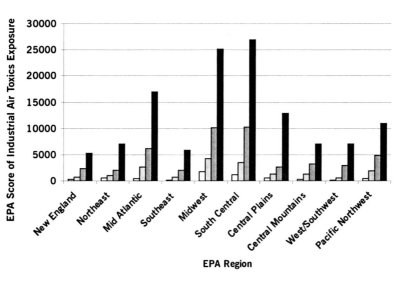

FIGURE 1: INDUSTRIAL AIR TOXICS EXPOSURE BY EPA REGION

□ 25th percentile   □ median   ▨ 75th percentile   ■ 90th percentile decisions—decisions by companies to locate hazardous facilities in vulnerable communities, and decisions by government regulators to give less priority to environmental enforcement in these communities. They can also reflect neighborhood changes driven by environmental degradation: pollution pushes out the affluent and lowers property values, while poorer people seeking low-cost housing move in, either unaware of the health risks or unable to afford alternatives. Even after accounting for differences related to income, however, studies find that racial and ethnic minorities often face higher pollution burdens—implying that disparities are the result of differences in political power as well as purchasing power.

The United States is a big, heterogeneous country. Electoral politics, social movements, industrial structure, residential segregation, and environmental policies differ across regions. So patterns of pollution may vary, too. Our recent study "Regional variation in environmental inequality: Industrial air toxics exposure in U.S. cities" examines these patterns to ask two key questions. First, is minority status or income more important in explaining environmental disparities? Second, does income protect minorities from pollution as much as it protects whites?

To tackle these questions, we used data on industrial air pollution from the U.S. Environmental Protection Agency (EPA). In the 1980s, in the wake of the deadly toxic gas release at a plant owned by the U.S. company Union Carbide in Bhopal, India, in which thousands of nearby residents were killed, environmental advocates in the U.S. demanded disclosure of information on hazards faced by communities near industrial facilities. In response, Congress passed the Emergency Planning and Community Right-to-Know Act of 1986, requiring corporations to disclose their releases of dangerous chemicals into our air, water, and lands. These are reported annually in the EPA's Toxics Release Inventory. The EPA has combined

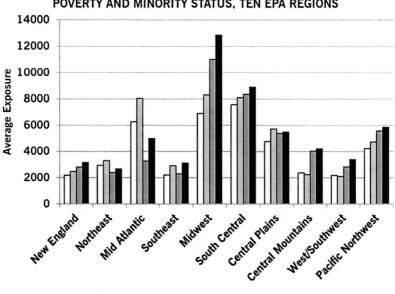

FIGURE 2: AVERAGE INDUSTRIAL AIR TOXICS EXPOSURE (EPA SCORE) BY POVERTY AND MINORITY STATUS, TEN EPA REGIONS

☐ Non-poor white ☐ Poor white ▨ Non-poor minorities ■ Poor minorities these data with information on the toxicity and dispersion of hazardous chemical releases to create the Risk-Screening Environmental Indicators (RSEI), the database we use, that estimates the total human health risks in neighborhoods across the country from multiple industrial pollution sources and chemicals.

Industrial air pollution varies greatly across regions of the country. Figure 1 shows the level of health risk faced by the median resident (in the middle of the region's exposure distribution) as well as by more highly impacted residents (in the 75th and 90th percentiles of exposure). The Midwest and South Central regions have the highest levels, reflecting historical patterns of both industrial and residential development.

Figure 2 shows average pollution exposure by region for four groups: non-poor whites, poor whites, non-poor minorities and poor minorities. Poor minorities consistently face higher average exposure than non-poor minorities, and in most regions poor whites face higher average exposure than non-poor whites. In general, poor minorities also face higher exposure than poor whites, and non-poor minorities face higher exposure than non-poor whites. But in mapping environmental injustice we do find some noteworthy inter-regional differences—for example, in the contrast between racial disparities in the Midwest and Mid-Atlantic regions—that point to the need for location-specific analyses.

Finally, Figure 3 depicts the average pollution exposure for four racial/ethnic groups across income strata at the national level. The most striking finding here is that racial disparities in exposure are much wider among people who live in lower-income neighborhoods. At the lower-income end of the scale, the average exposures of African Americans are substantially greater than those of whites. The lower average exposures for Hispanics in low-income neighborhoods are largely explained by their concentration in western and southwestern cities with

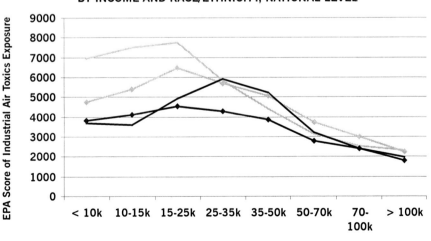

FIGURE 3: AVERAGE INDUSTRIAL AIR TOXICS EXPOSURE BY INCOME AND RACE/ETHNICITY, NATIONAL LEVEL

below-average pollution. Statistical analysis shows, however, that within these cities Hispanics also tend to live in the more polluted neighborhoods.

Pollution risk increases with average neighborhood income for all groups up to a turning point at around $25,000 per year. This can be explained by the positive association between industrialization and economic development. After that point, however, income becomes protective, and rising neighborhood income is associated with lower pollution exposure. Among these higher-income neighborhoods, racial and ethnic disparities in exposure are almost non-existent. But because of the correlation between minority status and income, minorities are more concentrated in lower-income communities whereas whites are more concentrated in upper-income communities. Based on where they live, whites may be more likely to see income as the main factor explaining disparities in pollution exposure, whereas African Americans are more likely to see the racial composition of neighborhoods as what matters most.

Environmental protection is not just about protecting nature from people: it's also about protecting people from other people. Those who benefit from industrial air pollution are the corporations that reap higher profits and their consumers, insofar as avoided pollution-control costs are passed on in the form of lower prices. Those who bear the greatest harm are the residents of nearby communities. Safeguarding the environment requires remedying this injustice and the imbalances of power that lie behind it. ❑

Sources: Michael Ash and T. Robert Fetter, "Who Lives on the Wrong Side of the Environmental Tracks?" *Social Science Quarterly*, 85(2), 2004; H. Spencer Banzhaf and Randall B. Walsh, "Do People Vote with Their Feet?" *American Economic Review*, 98(3), 2008; Vicki Been and Francis Gupta, "Coming to the nuisance or going to the barrios?" *Ecology Law Quarterly*, 24(1), 1997; James K. Boyce, "Inequality and Environmental Protection," in Jean-Marie Baland, Pranab K. Bardhan, and Samuel Bowles, eds., *Inequality, Cooperation, and Environmental Sustainability* (Princeton University Press, 2007); James K. Boyce, *The Political Economy of the Environment* (Edward Elgar, 2002); Paul Mohai and Robin Saha, "Reassessing Racial and Socioeconomic Disparities in Environmental Justice Research," *Demography*, 43(2), 2006; Rachel Morello-Frosch, et al., "Environmental Justice and Regional Inequality in Southern California: Implications for Future Research," *Environmental Health Perspectives*, 110(S2), 2002; Manuel Pastor, Jim Sadd, and John Hipp, "Which Came First? Toxic Facilities, Minority Move-In, and Environmental Justice," *Journal of Urban Affairs*, 23(1), 2001; Evan J. Ringquist, "Assessing Evidence of Environmental Inequities: A Meta-Analysis," *Journal of Policy Analysis and Management*, 24(2), 2005; Klara Zwickl, Michael Ash, and James K. Boyce, "Regional Variation in Environ-mental Inequality: Industrial Air Toxics exposure in U.S. Cities," *Ecological Economics*, (107), 2014.

Article 9.5

FUNDING BLACK FUTURES
The Movement for Black Lives policy platform targets neoliberalism.

BY BIOLA JEJE
November/December 2016

Systemic racism means that, in the United States, the threats to public safety for Black people go pretty deep. This is because none of the institutions that uphold our society were built for Black people, so even today they work to hurt Black people, whether those who take part in those institutions know it or not.

Institutional racism in the pursuit of profit has structured the so-called criminal justice system. For example, in Ferguson, Mo., before the death of Mike Brown, Black residents had long been targeted by a system of over-policing that resulted in their being fined at rates grossly out of proportion to our population. Ava DuVernay's recently released documentary 13th deftly shows how prisons today are descendants of the system of slavery supposedly abolished by the 13th amendment. The documentary correctly argues that mass incarceration is a more contemporary example of how racism in the United States works and how it is profit-driven. The math is simple, mass incarceration plus prison labor equals profit for the 1%. This has led to a policing system where it is very clear the promise to "protect and serve" does not apply to Black and Brown people.

Similarly, institutional racism in the pursuit of profit results in the denial of environmental justice. A perfect example of this is the Flint water crisis, where a predominately Black and economically struggling city was deemed unworthy of an investment in a clean water system. And the city was struggling economically because the industries that left the area years ago had decided it was more in their interests to move jobs out of the city to cut costs, depleting many of the good jobs that had formerly employed the people of this once prosperous city.

We live in a world like this because we live in a world where corporations have more power than people. The *Citizens United* ruling (which took "corporate personhood" to a whole new level) is a great example of how warped U.S. capitalism currently is. Corporations can actually argue for, and win, recognition as "people" with every right to participate in and influence politics. Meanwhile, during the Occupy protests, it became clear through the treatment of protesters that the police were there to protect the center of capital, not the people. The idea that corporations are "people," deserving of the rights and protections afforded by the state, stands in bold contrast to the many systems that disenfranchise Black people in the United States. The message is clear: Corporations are clearly people, while Black people in the United States need a grassroots movement to affirm our humanity before we can hope to be seen.

An awareness that this system is a confluence of the ruling class's need to control the working class and Black people was the spark that ignited the Movement for Black Lives (M4BL). The movement, in turn, is expanding this awareness. The issue of police brutality connects to the broader issue of systemic inequality under

202 | CURRENT ECONOMIC ISSUES

neoliberalism. Policing has always been about law and order, and that order has always been about protecting capital. There is a human cost to this.

The human cost for Black people in the United States has been the murder of Black people by law enforcement in numbers grossly disproportionate to our population, the loss of homeownership due to predatory mortgage lending, also in disproportionate numbers, a lack of access to quality higher education that actually teaches us our history, as well as over-policing, mass surveillance, and mass incarceration.

What can we do to stop this? This summer, the Movement for Black Lives released a policy platform outlining demands that, if implemented, would greatly improve the economic landscape for Black people in the United States, as well as keep us safe. Demands include the end of mass incarceration, a divestment from prisons as well as fossil fuels, and free public higher education.

In the United States today, private prisons are known to make millions by filling their cells with predominantly Black and Brown people. Prison labor is also helping other businesses drastically cut labor costs (the practice was recently parodied in the Netflix series "Orange is the New Black," where female inmates were made to stitch underwear for an unspecified lingerie company).

"It's no coincidence that the United States now imprisons more of its people than any other country in the world," write Peter Wagner and Alison Walsh of the Prison Policy Initiative. "[M]ass incarceration has become a giant industry in the U.S., resulting in huge profits not only for private prison companies, but also for everything from food companies and telecoms to all the businesses that are using prison labor to cut their manufacturing costs." Divestment from prisons would mean that the law enforcement system would no longer be predicated on profit, and the quest for profit would not drive the need for an increased inmate population.

Divestment from fossil fuels would mean that our society would not be tethered to an energy source that is incredibly harmful to our environment and ultimately unsustainable. Let's not forget that the effects of environmental pollution and disenfranchisement also disproportionately affect Black people (see Article 9.4, "Mapping Environmental Injustice"). Look at the divestment from infrastructure that would have prevented the flooding of predominantly Black New Orleans neighborhoods by Hurricane Katrina, or the lack of commitment to relief and reconstruction of the city. Now consider this contrast: Louisiana is the state with the highest incarceration rate in the nation (see Barry Gerharz and Seung Hong, "Down by Law: Orleans Parish Prison Before and After Katrina," *D&S*, March/April 2006). There is money for prisons, but not for infrastructure or human needs.

Among those human needs is education. M4BL's demand for free public higher education is also crucial (see Article 4.3, "Why Free Higher Education Can't Wait"). While it does not guarantee upward mobility anymore, education is still the basis of an engaged democracy. The City University of New York (or CUNY) began in 1847 as the Free Academy. The goal? To provide education for the working class in the hopes of having educated and engaged citizens at all class levels. Social scientists have documented the positive effects of education on the defense of democratic institutions. "As education raises the benefits of civic participation, it raises the support for more democratic regimes relative to dictatorships," find economists Edward L. Glaeser, Giacomo Ponzetto, and Andrei Shleifer.

"This increases the likelihood of democratic revolutions against dictatorships, and reduces that of successful anti-democratic coups." Free public education can be a support for our own endangered democracy today. This current election cycle, where the Republican candidate is a business owner famous for a reality TV show and a purveyor of multiple blatant -*isms*, is a prime example of why it's important to have a population that can engage critically in the political process.

Ultimately, the policy platform laid out by the Movement for Black Lives offers a concrete answer on what it would look like to #FundBlackFutures. More demands include comprehensive reparations, participatory budgeting, a universal basic income, the removal of money from politics, the elimination of barriers to voter access, net neutrality, the release of all political prisoners, the restoration of the ability to unionize, and more.

Right now, too many people are still poor, workers are still disenfranchised, and Black people are still being targeted by the police. The future remains to be written. It's how we plan to mobilize around concrete solutions that will help us create a world where Black people are safe and prioritized over corporate interests. Creating that world would be breaking a cycle that's been in place since before the founding of this country. ❑

Sources: Peter Wagner and Alison Walsh, "States of Incarceration: The Global Context," Prison Policy Initiative, June 16, 2016; Edward Glaeser, Giacomo Ponzetto, Andrei Shleifer, "Why Does Democracy Need Education?", National Bureau of Economic Research Working Paper No. 12128, April 2006; Black Youth Project 100, "BYP100&BLM DC Shutdown National Fraternal Order of Police!" byp100.org, July 20, 2016.

Chapter 10

THE GLOBAL ECONOMY

Article 10.1

THE SLOW, PAINFUL DEATH OF THE TPP

BY DEAN BAKER
November 2016

In spite of the hopes of many elite types for a last-minute resurrection, it appears that the Trans-Pacific Partnership (TPP) is finally dead. This is good news, but it took a long time to kill the deal, and the country is likely to pay a huge price for the execution.

The basic point that everyone should know by now is that the TPP had little to do with trade. The United States already had trade deals with six of the 11 other countries in the pact. The trade barriers with the other five countries were already very low in most cases, so there was little room left for further trade liberalization in the TPP.

Instead, the main purpose of the TPP was to lock in place a business-friendly structure of regulation. The deal was negotiated by a series of working groups that were dominated by representatives of major corporations. The regulatory structure was to be enforced by investor-state dispute settlement tribunals. This is an extrajudicial system that would be able to override U.S. laws with secret rulings that were not bound by precedent or subject to appeal.

In addition, the TPP would strengthen and lengthen patent and copyrights and related protections. This is protectionism: It is 180 degrees at odds with free trade. These protections can raise the price of protected items, like prescription drugs, by a factor of 10 or even 100. This is equivalent to tariffs of several thousand percent, with the same waste and incentives for corruption. Free-traders oppose such protections, if they are honest.

The dishonesty used to push the TPP continued with the post-mortems. Both the *New York Times* and the *Washington Post* gave us stern warnings about how China is likely to capitalize by pushing ahead with its own trade deal for East Asia and the Pacific. This appeal to anti-China sentiments is striking, since it completely contradicts everything that the "free traders" ordinarily say about trade.

First, we ordinarily believe that more prosperous trading partners are good for the United States. If China and other countries in the region reduce their trade barriers, it should lead to faster growth, making them better customers for U.S. exports and better suppliers of high-quality imports. This is the reason that the United States generally supported the growth of the European Common Market, and later, the European Union.

There is an argument that we may not want to see China, a country without a democratic government or respect for basic human rights, get even stronger. But it is not clear what the alternative proposal is. Furthermore, almost without exception, the current group of China fearers was 100 percent supportive of admitting China into the World Trade Organization without imposing conditions like respecting the rights of workers to organize. In other words, no one should take these people's concerns on China very seriously.

If we do want to push forward on "free trade," we should take the concept seriously and not just use trade pacts as a tool to redistribute income upward. A good place to start would be to focus on removing the barriers that prevent foreign workers in highly paid professions (e.g. doctors, dentists, lawyers) from working in the United States.

It is illegal to practice medicine in the United States unless you complete a U.S. residency program. As a result of such restrictions, our doctors earn on average more than $250,000 a year, twice as much as they get in other wealthy countries. Free trade in doctors could save us roughly $100 billion annually (around 0.6 percent of GDP). There might be comparable gains from free trade in the other highly paid professions. We can design international standards that ensure high quality, but open the door to people trained in other countries.

When it comes to technology, insted of patent and copyright monopolies, how about instead developing mechanisms for freely disbursing new innovations all over the world? There is a lot to the argument for the benefits of free trade. Let's apply it to innovations in medicine, software and other areas. We know how to develop mechanisms for financing research where the cost could be parceled out among countries.

If our trade deals were actually about free trade instead of increasing profits for the pharmaceutical, software and entertainment industries, this is the direction trade negotiators would be looking. But given the fealty of our politicians to major corporate interests, they don't even want to see alternatives to government-granted monopolies discussed. There's no time for real free trade in these people's minds.

If the politicians want to get serious about real free trade agreements, it is easy to come up with progressive directions for such deals. In the meantime, we can celebrate the well-deserved death of the TPP, which has proved to be enormously costly for the country.

The decision by proponents of the TPP to push ahead with their deal almost certainly cost Hillary Clinton the election. Trade was a big issue in swing states like Michigan and Pennsylvania, and the people who cared about trade overwhelmingly voted for Donald Trump. So the TPP might be dead, but we will have to deal with its legacy in the form of President Trump. ❑

Article 10.2

THE "EMERGING ECONOMIES" TODAY

AN INTERVIEW WITH JAYATI GHOSH
May/June 2016

The terms "emerging markets" and "emerging economies" have come into fashion, especially to refer to countries supposedly poised to make the leap from "developing" to "developed" economies. There's no definitive list, but Brazil, India, Indonesia, Mexico, Russia, South Africa, Turkey, and China are among the large countries that often headline articles on "emerging economies." Economic growth rates—as well as the drop-off in growth during the global Great Recession and the recovery since—vary widely between countries typically placed in this group.

China is by far the most prominent of the emerging economies—the most populous country in the world, with an extraordinary period of industrial growth since the 1980s, and with an enormous impact (not only as an exporter of manufactured goods but also as an importer of raw-material and intermediate inputs to manufacturing) on the world economy. The "secular stagnation" of the high-income capitalist economies and resulting growth slowdown in China, therefore, has much wider implications for the developing world. In this interview, economist Jayati Ghosh addresses the current challenges for China and other countries—and possible paths toward inclusive and sustainable development. – Eds.

Dollars & Sense: You've written about the "retreat" of emerging-market economies, which until recently had been held up as examples of robust growth, in contrast to the stagnant economies of the so-called capitalist "core." What's driving the slowdown of economic growth in the emerging economies today?

Jayati Ghosh: The emerging economies are really those that have integrated much more into the global financial system, not just the global trade system. And I think what happened during the period of the economic boom is that many people forgot that their growth was still ultimately driven by what was happening in the North. That is, the engine of demand was still the northern economies. So whether you're talking about China in particular or the range of emerging economies that was seen as more prominent in the first half of the 2000s, all of them depended on exports to the North and particularly to the United States.

It was the U.S. boom that drew in more and more of the exports from developing countries. When it came to an end—as it inevitably had to—these economies had to look for other sources of demand. There are two ways of doing this. One is to try and do a domestic demand-driven expansion based on higher domestic incomes because of wage and employment growth. And the other is the model which unfortunately seems to be the more popular one, which is to have a debt-driven kind of growth, based on both consumption and accumulation that is essentially led by taking on more and more debt. This is, of course, also what the U.S. did in the 2000s, which unraveled in 2007 and 2008. But it's also what a number of European economies did, and they're paying the price now.

Remarkably, developing countries that don't need to take this path, and can see all the problems associated with it, also took this path in the wake of the global financial crisis. In China there was a doubling of the debt-to-GDP ratio between 2007 and 2014. This reflected increases in debt to every single sector, but it was dominantly for investment. In a range of other important developing countries, from Mexico to Indonesia, Malaysia, South Korea, etc., there was a dramatic expansion of household debt, particularly real estate and housing debt. We all know that these real-estate and housing bubbles that are led by taking on more debt, these end in tears. And that's really what has been happening.

In these "emerging" economies, financial integration allowed them to break the link between productive investment and growth. It fueled a debt-driven pattern of expansion, which inevitably has to end. It's ending now. The problem is that it's ending at a time when demand from the North is slowing dramatically. So there is a double whammy for these emerging economies. The slowdown in northern markets means that China—which had become the major driver of expansion—can no longer continue to export at the same rate. That means its imports have also come down. In the past year, China's exports fell by 5%, but its imports fell by 20%. That has affected all the other developing countries. And that's in combination with this end of the debt-driven expansion model.

D&S: A number of economists have argued for quite some time that China's export-oriented growth model would inevitably reach its limits. Are we seeing it finally reach an impasse now, and if so, is there a prospect for China to make a transition from a low-wage export-oriented model to a domestic demand-driven model that would necessarily require higher wages?

JG: I think it's indisputable that the export-driven model is over for the time being, for sure, certainly for the next five years, probably the next decade. That's not a bad thing, because one of the problems with that export-driven model is that it persists in seeing wages as costs rather than as a source of internal demand that you can use to your benefit. It encourages massive degradation of nature and taking on environmental costs that are now recognized to be completely unsustainable and socially undesirable. And, overall, we know that these can't last—these export-driven models can't last.

So, yes, it has ended. It does mean that the Chinese government and authorities have to look for an alternative. Many of us have been arguing that the alternative necessarily requires much more emphasis on increasing consumption, not through debt, but by increasing real incomes. And that means encouraging more employment of a desirable type—"decent work" as it's been called—and increasing wages. Now, this doesn't mean that the rates of growth will continue as high as they have been, but that doesn't matter.

In fact, the obsession with GDP growth is becoming a real negative now in the search for alternatives. The Chinese authorities, like all the financial analysts across the world who are constantly looking at China, are obsessed with GDP: Is it going to be 6.5% annual growth? Is it going to be 6.1%? Is it going to fall below 6%? As if that's all that matters. What they should really be looking at is the incomes of, let us say, the bottom 50 or 60%. Are these growing? If these are growing at about 4 or 5%, that's fantastic. That's wonderful. And that's really what the economy needs in a sustainable way. If these are growing in combination with patterns of production and consumption that are more sustainable, that are environmentally friendly, that are less carbon-emitting, then that is of course even more desirable.

But that means the focus has to shift away from GDP growth, and away from just pushing up GDP by any means whatsoever—to one which looks at how to improve the real incomes and the quality of life of the majority of the citizens. Unfortunately, the Chinese government doesn't seem to be choosing that path just yet. There have been some moves—in terms of increasing health spending, in terms of some attempts to increase wages and social protection for some workers—but overall the focus is still once again on more accumulation, on more investment, usually driven by more debt.

D&S: When you say the export-oriented model is "over," does that mean you think sticking to this approach will no longer deliver what policymakers and elites are aiming for, in terms of growth and accumulation? (And perhaps that this will lead to an elite-driven restructuring in the near term?) Or is it that this approach just cannot plausibly deliver in terms of inclusive development—the improvement in the quality of life for the majority?

JG: Both, really. The conditions of the global economy at present are such that an economy as large as that of China (and many other smaller economies as well) cannot expect much stimulus from external demand Significant increases in exports would only be possible by increasing markets share; that is, eating into some other country's exports. So the past pattern of accumulation based on external demand is unlikely to work in the near future.

But in addition, this approach has not delivered in terms of inclusive growth over the past decade except to some extent in China, which has been able to use it to generate a "Lewisian" process (theorized by economist Arthur Lewis in the 1950s) of shifting labor out of lower productivity activities. Even in China it was successful because wages increased much less than productivity and so export prices could fall or remain low. In many other countries, export-led expansion has actually been associated stagnant or lower wages and greater fragility of incomes, along with very substantial environmental costs that are typically not factored in.

D&S: Is it possible that that kind of transition is not going to happen in China until we see the development of a robust labor movement that's capable of winning a higher share of the national income in the form of wages, and pushing up mass consumption in that way?

JG: There is probably much greater public concern about all this in China than is often depicted in the media, certainly in the Chinese media, but even abroad. We know that there are thousands, literally, tens of thousands of protests in China—often about land grabs and so on in the peasantry, but also many, many workers' protests, and many other protests by citizens about environmental conditions. They have mostly been suppressed, but I don't think you can keep on suppressing these.

I do believe the Chinese elite has recognized that there are a couple of things that are becoming very important for them to maintain their political legitimacy. One is, of course, inequality and, associated with that, corruption. That is why the anti-corruption drive of President Xi Jinping retains a lot of popularity. Then there is the fact of the environmental unsustainability. Both India and China have created monstrosities in urban areas, in terms of the pollution, congestion, degradation, which are really making many of our cities and towns unlivable. There is widespread protest about that, and about the pollution of water sources, of the atmosphere, of land quality. And there is real concern that ordinary Chinese citizens are not continuously experiencing the better life that they have grown accustomed to expect.

So I think, even without a very large-scale social mobilization, there is growing awareness in China—among officialdom, as well—that they can't carry on as before. It is likely that there's a tussle at the very higher echelons of the leadership and in the Communist Party, between those who are arguing for the slower but more sustainable and more wage-led path, and those who just want to keep propping up growth by more financial liberalization, by encouraging investors to jump in and invest even in projects that are unlikely to continue, and somehow keep that GDP growth going. It's a political tussle but of course that will determine the direction of the economy as well.

D&S: In the midst of this period of stagnation of the very high-income capitalist economies, and a resulting slowdown of growth in the so-called emerging economies, we also have an effect on countries that had primarily remained raw-material (or "primary-product") exporters. Is that boom in commodities exports now also over for the foreseeable future, and do you see those countries as now reinventing their economic development models?

JG: I think that the period of the boom was really a bit of an aberration. Since the early 20th century, these periods of relatively high commodity prices have always been outliers, and they don't last very long. They last for about five, six, maybe eight years at most, and then they they you come back to this more depressed situation relative to other prices. I have a feeling this is now going to continue, and that boom is, for the time being, over. It definitely means that the manna from heaven that many countries experienced has reduced, and therefore you have to think of other ways of diversifying your economies.

Many countries actually tried to do this but, you know, when you're getting so much income from the primary product exports it's very hard to diversify. It's actually easier to diversify when primary product prices are lower. So, once again, I think it's important for these countries to stop thinking of this as a huge loss, and start thinking of it as an opportunity—as an opportunity to use cheap primary commodities as a means of industrializing for domestic and regional markets. So it means a different strategy. The export-led obsession has to end. Without that, we're not going to get viable and sustainable strategies.

I'd like to make one other point, though, about the slowdown in China and the impact on developing countries, which is that it's also going to affect manufacturing exporters. China had become the center of a global production chain that was heavily exporting to the North but was drawing in more and more raw material and intermediate products from other developing countries. So almost every country had China become their main trade partner in both imports and exports. Many of these manufacturing economies are now going to face, once again, a double whammy. They will face a reduction, from China, in terms of lower Chinese imports of raw materials and intermediate goods for final export, and they're going to face greater competition from China in terms of their own export markets and their own domestic markets. Because China is now devaluing its currency, even though thus far it has been minor. It is looking to cheapen its exports even further, and this will definitely impact on both export markets and internal markets in developing countries.

So I think both primary exporters and manufacturing exporters are in for a bit of a bad time. They need to think of creative ways of dealing with the situation. It is not helped by believing that integration into global value chains is the only option, because these global value chains basically reduce the incomes of the actual producers. If you look at it, the emergence of global value chains and the associated trade treaties—not just the World Trade Organization (WTO) but the proliferation of regional trading agreements and things like the Trans-Pacific Partnership (TPP)—increase competition and reduce the value of the actual production stage of all commodities and goods. And they simultaneously increase the pre-production and post-production value. That is, all of the aspects that are driven by intellectual property monopolies—their values increase. So whether it is design elements or it is the marketing and branding and all of that—the intellectual property rights over which are retained by companies in the North—all of those are getting more and more value. And the actual production is getting less value because of the greater competitive pressure unleashed by these various trade agreements.

Developing countries that are seeking to get out of this really have to think of alternative arrangements—possibly regional arrangements, more reliance on domestic demand and South-South trade, which is more possible today than it has ever been—and moving away from a system that allows global and northern-led multinationals to capture all the rents and most of the profits of production everywhere.

D&S: So, in the course of this discussion, I think two major questions emerge about the way forward in so-called developing economies. One is how to square economic development—in terms of raising the quality of life for the majority—with environmental sustainability. The other is how to ensure the economic development of some countries isn't at odds with development in others. Are there ways of mutually fostering development—and in particular sustainable development—across the developing economies?

JG: Yes, I think we need to really move away from the traditional way of looking at growth and development, which is ultimately still based on GDP. As long as we keep doing that, we're going to be caught in this trap. We have to be focusing much more on quality of life and ensuring what we would call the basic needs or minimum requirements for a civilized life among all the citizenry. If we do that, then we're less in competition with one another and we're less obsessed with having to be the cheapest show in town. We then see wages and employment growth as a means of expansion of economic activity. We will see social policies as delivering not just better welfare for the people but also more employment, and therefore a better quality of life.

If we look for regional trading arrangements that recognize this, if we look to increase the value of domestic economic activity by encouraging the things that matter for ordinary people (especially, let's say, the bottom half of the population), if we focus on new technologies that are adapted to specific local requirements—in terms of being more green, more environmentally sustainable, as well as recognizing the specific availability of labor in these economies—I think we can do a lot more. It may be slower in terms of GDP growth, but really that doesn't mean anything. So we have to move away from GDP growth as the basic indicator of what is desirable. I think that's the ultimate and most essential issue. ❑

Article 10.3

AFTER HORROR, CHANGE?
Taking Stock of Conditions in Bangladesh's Garment Factories

BY JOHN MILLER
September/October 2014

On April 24, 2013, the Rana Plaza factory building, just outside of Bangladesh's capital city of Dhaka, collapsed—killing 1,138 workers and inflicting serious long-term injuries on at least 1,000 others.

While the collapse of Rana Plaza was in one sense an accident, the policies that led to it surely were not. Bangladesh's garment industry grew to be the world's second largest exporter, behind only China's, by endangering and exploiting workers. Bangladesh's 5,000 garment factories paid rock-bottom wages, much lower than those in China, and just half of those in Vietnam. One foreign buyer told *The Economist* magazine, "There are no rules whatsoever that can not be bent." Cost-saving measures included the widespread use of retail buildings as factories—including at Rana Plaza—adding weight that sometimes exceeded the load-bearing capacity of the structures.

As Scott Nova, executive director of the Worker Rights Consortium, testified before Congress, "the danger to workers in Bangladesh has been apparent for many years." The first documented mass-fatality incident in the country's export garment sector occurred in December 1990. In addition to those killed at Rana Plaza, more than 600 garment workers have died in factory fires in Bangladesh since 2005. After Rana Plaza, however, Bangladesh finally reached a crossroads. The policies that had led to the stunning growth of its garment industry had so tarnished the "Made in Bangladesh" label that they were no longer sustainable.

But just how much change has taken place since Rana Plaza? That was the focus of an International Conference at Harvard this June, bringing together government officials from Bangladesh and the United States, representatives of the Bangladesh garment industry, the international brands, women's groups, trade unions, the International Labor Organization (ILO), and monitoring groups working in Bangladesh.

How Much Change On the Ground?

Srinivas B. Reddy of the ILO spoke favorably of an "unprecedented level of ... practical action" toward workplace safety in Bangladesh.

The "practical action" on the ground, however, has been much more of a mixed bag than Reddy suggests. In the wake of massive protests and mounting international pressure, Bangladesh amended its labor laws to remove some obstacles to workers forming unions. Most importantly, the new law bars the country's labor ministry from giving factory owners lists of workers who want to organize.

But formidable obstacles to unionization still remain. At least 30% of the workers at an entire company are required to join a union before the government will grant recognition. This is a higher hurdle than workers face even in the not-so-union-friendly United States, where recognition is based at the level of the workplace, not the company. Workers in special export-processing zones (the source of about 16% of Bangladesh's exports), moreover, remain ineligible to form unions.

The Bangladesh government did register 160 new garment unions in 2013 and the first half of this year, compared to just two between 2010 and 2012. Nonetheless, collective bargaining happens in only 3% of garment plants. And employers have responded with firings and violence to workers registering for union recognition or making bargaining demands. Union organizers have been kidnapped, brutally beaten, and killed.

After protests that shut down over 400 factories last fall, the Bangladesh government raised the minimum wage for garment workers from the equivalent of $38 a month to $68. The higher minimum wage, however, fell short of the $103 demanded by workers.

The government and the garment brands have also set up the Rana Plaza Donor Trust Fund to compensate victims and their families for their losses and injuries. But according to the fund's website, it stood at just $17.9 million at the beginning of August, well below its $40 million target. Only about half of the 29 international brands that had their clothes sewn at Rana Plaza have made contributions. Ineke Zeldenrust of the Amsterdam-based labor-rights group Clean Clothes Campaign estimates that those 29 brands are being asked to contribute less than 0.2% of their $22 billion in total profits for 2013.

The Accord and the Alliance

Following Rana Plaza, a group of mostly European retail chains turned away from the business-as-usual approach of company codes that had failed to ensure safe working conditions in the factories that made their clothes. Some 151 apparel brands and retailers doing business in Bangladesh, including 16 U.S.-based retailers, signed the Accord on Fire and Building Safety in Bangladesh. Together the signatories of this five-year agreement contracted with 1,639 of the 3,498 Bangladesh factories making garments for export.

The Accord broke important new ground. Unlike earlier efforts:

- It was negotiated with two global unions, UndustriALL and UNI (Global).

- It sets up a governing board with equal numbers of labor and retail representatives, and a chair chosen by the ILO.

- Independent inspectors will conduct audits of factory hazards and make their results public on the Accord website, including the name of the factory, detailed information about the hazard, and recommended repairs.

- The retailers will provide direct funding for repairs (up to a maximum of $2.5 million per company) and assume responsibility for ensuring that all needed renovations and repairs are paid for.

- Most importantly, the Accord is legally binding. Disputes between retailers and union representatives are subject to arbitration, with decisions enforceable by a court of law in the retailer's home country.

But most U.S. retailers doing business in Bangladesh—including giants like Wal-Mart, JCPenney, The Gap, and Sears—refused to sign. They objected to the Accord's open-ended financial commitment and to its legally binding provisions.

Those companies, along with 21 other North American retailers and brands, developed an alternative five-year agreement, called the Alliance For Bangladesh Worker Safety. Some 770 factories in Bangladesh produce garments for these 26 companies.

Unlike the Accord, the Alliance is not legally binding and lacks labor- organization representatives. Moreover, retailers contribute a maximum of $1 million per retailer (less than half the $2.5 million under the Accord) to implement their safety plan and needed repairs, and face no binding commitment to pay for needed improvements beyond that. The responsibility to comply with safety standards falls to factory owners, although the Alliance does offer up to $100 million in loans for these expenses.

Kalpona Akter, executive director of the Bangladesh Center for Worker Solidarity, told the U.S. Senate Foreign Relations Committee, "There is no meaningful difference between the Alliance and the corporate-controlled 'corporate social responsibility' programs that have failed Bangladeshi garment workers in the past, and have left behind thousands of dead and injured workers."

Historic and Unprecedented?

Dan Mozena, U.S. Ambassador to Bangladesh, believes that, despite facing significant obstacles, "Bangladesh is making history as it creates new standards for the apparel industry globally."

While the Accord may be without contemporary precedent, joint liability agreements that make retailers responsible for the safety conditions of their subcontractor's factories do have historical antecedents. As political scientist Mark Anner has documented, beginning in the 1920s the International Ladies Garment Workers Union (ILGWU) began negotiating "jobber agreements" in the United States that held the buyer (or "jobber") for an apparel brand "jointly liable" for wages and working conditions in the contractor's factories. Jobber agreements played a central role in the near-eradication of sweatshops in the United States by the late 1950s. In today's global economy, however, international buyers are once again able to escape responsibility for conditions in the far-flung factories of their subcontractors.

Like jobber agreements, the Accord holds apparel manufacturers and retailers legally accountable for the safety conditions in the factories that make their clothes through agreements negotiated between workers or unions and buyers or brands. The next steps for the Accord model, as Anner has argued, are to address working conditions other than building safety (as jobber agreements had), to get more brands to sign on to the Accord, and to negotiate similar agreements in other countries.

That will be no easy task. But, according to Arnold Zack, who helped to negotiate the Better Factories program that brought ILO monitoring of Cambodian garment factories, "Bangladesh is the lynch pin that can bring an end to the bottom feeding shopping the brands practice." ❏

Sources: Arnold M. Zack, "In an Era of Accelerating Attention to Workplace Equity: What Place for Bangladesh," Boston Global Forum, July 8, 2014; Testimony of Kalpona Akter, Testimony of Scott Nova, Senate Committee on Foreign Relations, Feb. 11, 2014; Mark Anner, Jennifer Bair, and Jeremy Blasi, "Toward Joint Liability in Global Supply Chains," *Comparative Labor Law & Policy Journal*, Vol. 35:1, Fall 2013; Prepared Remarks for Rep. George Miller (D-Calif.), Keynote Remarks by U.S. Ambassador to Bangladesh Dan Mozena, Remarks by Country Director ILO Bangladesh Srinivas B. Reddy, International Conference on Globalization and Sustainability of the Bangladesh Garment Sector, June 14, 2014; "Rags in the ruins," *The Economist*, May 4, 2013; "Bangladesh: Amended Labor Law Falls Short," Human Rights Watch, July 18, 2013; Rana Plaza Donor Trust Fund (ranaplaza-arrangement.org/fund).

Article 10.4

THE HUMAN TOLL OF GREEK AUSTERITY

BY EVITA NOLKA
March/April 2016

Giannis and Lena, both in their early 30s and with MBA degrees, consider themselves lucky to be employed. Living in Thessaloniki, Greece's second largest city, located in the heart of Macedonia, Giannis is a merchandise buyer at a company that imports household items. Lena works in the export department of a pasta-producing enterprise.

"Every Greek family is experiencing the crisis their own way," Lena tells me. "Unemployment, wage and pension cuts, taxes, and increases in prices of basic goods have caused despair to millions of people."

Giannis shares a bit more. His family's income has taken a real hit. His father's wages have been reduced by one third and his mother got laid off three years ago. She used to work at a ready-made garments factory that went bankrupt soon after. For a year and a half, she hasn't been paid and she is still claiming the money she is owed.

Like so many others, Giannis had been unemployed for years. There was nothing he could do other than hope to get accepted at one of the five-month temporary work programs in the country funded by the European Union (EU). "You're being deprived of the opportunity to work during the most productive years of your life," Giannis tells me as he explains the psychological burden of unemployment. "There's a feeling that you're standing still even though the whole world keeps moving and after a while you feel numb. You accept that's how things are and you are unable to get out of the rut."

Sticking with Austerity

For six years now, Greece has lived under unprecedented austerity policies demanded by its lenders and accepted by a succession of governments. The social and political reality created by austerity was demonstrated sharply by two events on the same day in October 2015.

First, Eurostat, the European statistical service, released a report on poverty and social exclusion in Greece. The report showed that, in 2014, 22.1% of the Greek population lived in conditions of poverty, 21.5% were severely materially deprived, and 17.2% lived in families with very low work intensity. (Economists define "work intensity" as the total number of months that all working-age household members have worked as a percentage of the total number of months they theoretically could have worked. Households under 20% are considered to have "very low" work intensity.) Altogether, 36% of the population faced one or more of these terrible conditions. That figure was 7.9% percentage points higher than in 2008.

Second, the Greek parliament approved a new piece of legislation imposing further austerity measures as demanded by its creditors—primarily the EU and the International Monetary Fund (IMF)—to meet the terms of Greece's most recent (third) bailout agreement. The new package involves cutting public spending by 14.32 billion euros, while raising taxes by 14.09 billion euros, over the next five years. The measures will primarily affect privately owned businesses, homeowners, and employees close to retirement.

Austerity policies were first adopted in 2010 as a "solution" to the economic crisis that erupted in 2009–10. Severe cuts in public spending, deep reductions in wages and pensions, enormous tax increases, and a stripping back of labor protections were imposed—ostensibly—to stabilize the economy and gain the confidence of financial markets. In practice, the measures have plunged the Greek economy into a prolonged recession that has led to the disastrous results outlined by Eurostat. Unfortunately, the current Greek government, formed by the left-wing SYRIZA party, appears determined to keep the country on the same path.

The Crushing Burden of Unemployment

In the course of the recession, the Greek economy has shrunk by more than 25%. At present, more than one out of four workers is unemployed (one out of two among the nation's youth), and more than one million jobs have disappeared. The prospects for improvement, given the austerity policies imposed under the third bailout agreement, are dim at best. "No legislation can guarantee even the most basic labor rights," Lena says in describing the way employers have used the specter of unemployment to further reduce wages. "It's no wonder," she adds, "that so many well-educated young people choose to leave the country."

Since the unemployment rate for people with higher education is nearly 20%—the highest in the world—more than 200,000 young Greeks have left the country in search of better opportunities abroad. I discussed Greece's brain drain with Victoria, 18, a first-year electrical and computer engineering student at the University of Thessaly. "Don't be mistaken," she says, "all those young people that seek a better life abroad care deeply for Greece and won't hesitate to return once things have improved." Victoria herself is already considering leaving Greece once she finishes her studies. Who can blame her? She is highly unlikely to find a job in her field after graduation.

Collapse of Production

Austerity policies have also led the country's productive sector to near collapse, with industrial production in 2015 down by a staggering 35% compared to its level in 2008. Industrial production currently represents less than 10% of Greece's GDP, an exceptionally low level historically for the country, as well as for the eurozone today.

To be sure, the deindustrialization of the Greek economy started a lot earlier, in the early 1980s. The country's new development model, after its integration into the European Community and the emerging Single Market, systematically favored the tertiary (services) sector and ignored the primary (agriculture, mining, etc.) and secondary (manufacturing) sectors. Greek industries, accustomed to the heavy protectionist measures of the post-war period and poorly prepared for the requirements of market integration and the liberalization of trade, failed to adapt. The massive influx of European funds to the tertiary sector (mainly tourism) shaped a services-centered economy (the services sector contributes over 80% to the country's GDP), while weakening the country's competitiveness and contributing decisively to the dismantling of its industrial base.

Things got immeasurably worse after 2009. During the recession, about 250,000 small and medium-sized enterprises closed down. Many more have been forced to the verge of closure due to reduced revenues and increased financial obligations to social security funds, tax offices, and banks. Thousands of small business owners have opted to relocate to neighboring Balkan countries, which offer lower labor costs and corporate tax breaks.

"Reality has shown that the austerity measures applied across Europe are not the most effective response to the crisis," says Costas, a civil engineer from Patra, Greece's third largest city, in the southern region of the Peloponnese. Costas is 45 years old and a former member of SYRIZA, the current governing party. "No other country in the eurozone has had to impose such far-reaching austerity programs," he says, "and I just don't see how Greek society can sustain the burden of yet another bailout."

The policy is simply not working, even on its own terms. After five years of austerity and three bailout agreements, Greece's national debt of 320 billion euros is right where it was in 2010. But its debt-to-GDP ratio has shot up to 175% (compared to 150% in 2010), and the European Commission projects that it will rise to 200% in 2016. The country's destroyed economy will never be able to repay this huge volume of debt.

SYRIZA U-Turn, Popular Disillusionment

Originally elected in January 2015 on a vehement anti-austerity platform, Greek Prime Minister Alexis Tsipras subsequently made a complete U-turn. Ignoring the popular outcry against austerity, loudly expressed in a referendum on July 5, he has given in to the creditors' demands. In August, SYRIZA and the creditors signed a new bailout agreement, including not only another round of austerity measures but also neocolonial restrictions on Greece's national sovereignty. No legislation related to the objectives of the bailout, however minor, can be taken by Greece's political institutions without the prior approval of its creditors. The creditors thus have the right to monitor the Greek government and to wield veto power over virtually all policy measures in Greece.

And yet, on September 20, Tsipras won a new election, again forming a government. The result seemed to vindicate his capitulation. It appears that Greek voters, confronted with a narrative presenting the new agreement as inescapable, opted to give the governing party a second chance. "This wasn't a vote of hope," says Costas, the civil engineer from Patra, "but a vote for the 'lesser evil' within the limits of a 'nothing can really change' mentality."

Costas is even convinced that if there were another general election soon, the governing party would still emerge victorious. Greek voters appear to think that there is no credible alternative to austerity. "Ever since the PM marginalized any voices in SYRIZA that tried to show a different way and declared there was no alternative," he says, "Greek society, having lost its morale, has come to accept its fate."

Defeat and Apathy

To fully understand the popular mood, one must look at the abstention rates in the recent election. Turnout plummeted, with a record-high abstention rate of 45%. In addition, blank ballots reached an extraordinary 2.5%. The message is quite clear:

the Greek people's disappointment has led to a massive rejection of the political process altogether. Victoria tells me that most of her friends either cast a blank ballot or didn't bother to vote at all since "they didn't believe any of the existing political parties could actually make a difference."

The low turnout was not an isolated incident. During the past few years, social unrest and frustration over the austerity measures have given rise to widespread discontent and large-scale demonstrations. But the decline of the struggle as unemployment began to bite and, especially, SYRIZA's betrayal of popular hopes have led to a wholesale rejection of politics by broad layers of the population. The sense of defeat and indifference is pronounced among workers, and especially the young.

"Wishful thinking," says Costas about SYRIZA's hopes to overturn austerity by creating a domino effect in the countries of the European periphery. The balance of power has proven not that easy to change and now people feel that Greece is being punished for daring to question Europe's neoliberal policies.

European Union officials have categorically ruled out any possibility of a debt write-down. Restructuring in the form of a lengthening of maturity or perhaps a lowering of interest rates is still on the table, but it would have very debatable long-term results. Greece would probably be given more time to get back on its feet, but this would not eliminate short-term financing problems. Besides, even though Greek aid loans are very long-term (over thirty years) and interest rates have already been lowered several times (lower than 1%), the country's national debt is still considered unsustainable.

As for the SYRIZA government's current promise to implement a "parallel" social program that would ease the burden of harsh new austerity policies on poorer Greeks, it has already been forced to withdraw the intended bill following severe objections by the country's creditors. Many of the proposed measures lacked required budget-impact estimates. There were also concerns about the program's compatibility with the conditions of the third bailout agreement. "Parallel" programs running alongside austerity measures are not what the EU has in mind, nor would they be possible to implement within the strict framework of the latest bailout.

The Prospect of Change

The only real question for Greece at the moment is: Could there be an alternative path?

Not everyone has given in to despondency and apathy. In a school building in central Athens, I meet Georgia, a young teacher and mother of three, who offers extra classes to underprivileged students free of charge. "People would take to the streets because they hoped they could make an actual difference," she says. "Now it is clear that our hopes were false." Nonetheless, she tells me, the economic crisis has made her more politically aware. She now chooses to spend much of her time and energy in political and social movements and social solidarity structures, where she can actually feel useful.

Popular Unity, a new political front including SYRIZA's left wing, which split from the party by refusing to accept the new bailout, has so far offered the only coherent argument about how Greece could adopt an anti-bailout strategy. Its radical program includes the introduction of a new national currency, a deep national debt write-off, a lifting of austerity measures, and a restructuring of the productive

ENKLO: Life, Death—and Rebirth?

A case in point of Greece's manufacturing decline is provided by United Textiles (ENKLO), a 140-year-old company operating in Central Macedonia and Thrace with a strong presence in international markets, a skilled workforce, advanced technology, and excellent product quality. The company closed down in 2009, sinking under a debt burden of 350 million euros due mostly to poor management decisions and the expansion of its business activities beyond the textiles industry.

Ever since its shutdown, the laid-off workers, unable to find other jobs and refusing to accept that the company would never operate again, have been maintaining the equipment and guarding the buildings in order to prevent theft. "We are here night and day to make sure that the machines remain unharmed," says Petros, who has worked as an electrician for 25 years.

Instead of the scheduled liquidation of the company's property, the workers now propose its revival by converting its debts into stockholders' equity, taking advantage of the country's bankruptcy code. It is an ambitious business plan that aspires to utilize the existing equipment and the invaluable expertise of the workers.

No public funds are needed to re-start production. All that's required is a government intervention that would settle any legal complications that may arise. With the government's support, Petros argues, the company could operate the very next day.

sector and the welfare state. However, Popular Unity has so far failed to convince Greek voters, and did not gain parliamentary representation in the last elections.

Social injustice has spurred new modes of resistance far from political parties and trade unions. As the state becomes ever more hostile to the Greek people, many choose to self-organize by forming neighborhood assemblies and solidarity networks that support basic human rights, organizing micro-economies without middle-men, and setting up "solidarity clinics" providing free health care.

This is a period of reflection and finding alternative forms of resistance that could potentially be the basis for something new to emerge in the future. All hope is not yet lost that Greece may regain some economic stability and find a development policy in the interest of its people. "People feel exhausted, defeated and betrayed," says Georgia, "but many refuse to give up." ❑

Sources: Eurostat news release 181/2015 (ec.europa.eu/eurostat/documents); Eurostat dataset (ec. europa.eu/eurostat), "Youth unemployment rate," "Long-term unemployment rate," "Production in industry—manufacturing," "Production in industry—total (excluding construction)," "Production in industry—annual data, percentage change," "General government gross debt—annual data"; "Young, gifted and Greek: Generation G—the world's biggest brain drain," *The Guardian* (theguardian.com); C. Pitelis & N. Antonakis (2003), "Manufacturing and competitiveness: the case of Greece," *Journal of Economic Studies*, Vol. 30, Issue 5, pp. 535—547; H. Louri and I. Pepelasis Minoglou (2002), "A hesitant evolution: industrialisation and de-industrialisation in Greece over the long run", *Journal of European Economic Studies*, Vol. 31, No. 2, pp. 321-348; M. Nence, "Greek entrepreneurship after crisis—investment abroad, the easiest solution" (pecob.eu); Kathimerini, "Crisis wipes out a quarter of Greece's SMEs" (ekathimerini.com); September 2015 official election results (ekloges.ypes.gr)..

Article 10.5

INVERSION ACCELERATION

More and more U.S. corporations are sending their headquarters offshore to reap immense tax savings.

BY ROGER BYBEE
May/June 2016

Corporate "inversions"—the fast-accelerating phenomenon of major U.S. firms moving their official headquarters to low-tax nations through complex legal maneuvers—are causing an annual loss of about $100 billion in federal tax revenues.

But new rules imposed in early April by the U.S. Treasury Department scuttled the mammoth $162 billion deal between pharmaceutical giant Pfizer and Allergan, based on relocating the official headquarters to low-tax Ireland. The Treasury rules are designed to inhibit "serial inverters"—corporations that repeatedly shift their official headquarters to cut U.S. taxes—and to discourage "earnings stripping," where firms use loans between their American units and foreign partners to reduce U.S. profits subject to federal taxation. The collapse of the Pfizer-Allergan inversion suggests that the Treasury regulations may constitute a major barrier to some future inversions. However, with firms like Johnson Controls and Tyco moving ahead with their inversion plans, stronger measures will clearly be needed to halt the tide.

U.S. corporations have pulled off about 60 inversions over the last two decades, according to *Fortune*. In the last five years alone, corporations have executed 40 inversions, the *New York Times* stated.

This fast-rising dimension of corporate globalization has immense implications for Americans. The industrial powerhouse Eaton Corp. (#163 on the Fortune 500), Medtronic, Accenture (formerly the consulting wing of Arthur Andersen), Burger King, and AbbVie (the world's 11th-largest drug maker) are among the firms that have repudiated their U.S. nationality and shifted their official headquarters to low-tax nations. The annual toll to the U.S. Treasury from corporate inversions is about $100 billion, based on the studies of Reed College economist Kimberly Clausing. This impact is likely to worsen significantly in the near future. Another dozen or more inversions are currently under consideration, according to conservative *New York Times* business columnist Andrew Ross Sorkin.

Fortune senior writer Allan Sloan, who has been outraged by inversions despite his overall pro-corporate stance, points to powerful vested interests who stand to gain: "There's a critical mass of hedge funds, corporate raiders, consultants, investment bankers, and others who benefit from inversions." (The collapse of the Pfizer-Allergan deal could cost just the major banks as much as $200 million, the *New York Times* reported.) These interests and their political allies have incessantly claimed that American-based multinational corporations are driven to repudiate their U.S. nationality in order to escape "burdensome" U.S. corporate tax rates that they call "the world's highest."

In reality, actual federal corporate taxes on 288 profitable corporations —as distinguished from the official 35% rate almost all firms easily avoid—were actually only 19.4% in the 2008-2012 period, a 2014 Citizens for Tax Justice (CTJ) report revealed. This placed the United States 8th lowest among the advanced nations in the Organization for Economic Cooperation and Development (OECD), the CTJ found (see sidebar).

A just-released CTJ study went further in its scope and included state and local taxes as well as federal levies in comparing the United States with other OECD countries. It found combined U.S. corporate taxes at 25.7%, ranking 4th lowest in the OECD, based on U.S. Treasury figures. The OECD average is 34.1%. Only Chile, Mexico, and South Korea had a lower total burden as a share of GDP.

Incessant Talk of 35% Tax "Burden" Diverts Focus from Minimal Taxes

Elite debate about corporate taxes is dominated by the notion that U.S. corporations are afflicted by the highest official corporate tax rate in the world. In fact, the 35% official rate is easily avoided by almost all corporations. *Effective* U.S. corporate taxes—what corporations actually end up paying—are among the lowest in the advanced world. This represents a huge drain on the U.S. Treasury's revenues needed for public services.

- A 2014 study by Citizens for Tax Justice found an *effective* average tax rate of only 19.4% for major, consistently profitable corporations. This places the United States at 8th-lowest among the 34 OECD nations in terms of the effective federal tax rate.

- The most recent study on corporate taxes by the CTJ, released in April 2016, went further in its scope and included state and local taxes as well as federal levies. It found combined U.S. corporate taxes at 25.7%, ranking 4th-lowest in the OECD (above only Chile, Mexico, and South Korea). The OECD average is 34.1%.

- Strategies for tax avoidance have been particularly effective for the very largest members of the Fortune 500. Corporations studied by CTJ included 26—such as Boeing, General Electric, Priceline.com, and Verizon—that paid no federal income tax whatsoever over the five-year period.

- Boeing, which depends heavily on federal contracts, had an effective federal tax rate of negative 2%, despite earning $26.4 billion in profits 2008-2013. It also collected a record $13.2 billion in state-level tax breaks and subsidies in 2013. About one-third of the corporations—93 of the 288 studied by CTJ—paid an effective tax rate of less than 10% between 2008 and 2013. And contrary to claims that U.S. corporate taxes are far higher than those facing their foreign competitors, two-thirds of those corporations with significant offshore profits paid higher corporate tax rates to foreign governments for their overseas operations than they paid in the United States on their U.S. profits.

Source: Citizens for Tax Justice, "The Sorry State of Corporate Taxes," 2014 (ctj.org).

Despite this reality of low corporate taxes, a growing number of large multinational firms have concluded that repudiating their U.S. "citizenship" and inverting is the most effective means of cutting their tax burdens, avoiding possible reforms that could potentially hike their tax bills, and most importantly, gaining direct and unregulated access to untaxed "offshore" funds.

The 35% Myth

The fundamental realities of U.S. taxes on multinational corporations are obscured by an elite debate fixated on the official statutory rate of 35%, which is relentlessly cited as a barrier to U.S. competitiveness.

House Republican James Sensenbrenner (R-Wisc.), for example, wrote in a recent *Milwaukee Journal Sentinel* opinion piece, "The current rate paid by American companies is 35 percent—the highest corporate tax rate among developed countries."

This narrative—endlessly recited by leading corporate and media elites, along with virtually all Republicans and a number of Democrats, has come to dominate much of the national dialogue. Robert Pozen, a senior fellow at the liberal Brookings Foundation, urgently called for a sharp cut in the 35% statutory rate, claiming broad bi-partisan support in Congress. "If there's one policy agreement between Republicans and Democrats, it's that the 35% corporate tax rate in the United States should be reduced to 28% or 25%," he asserted. "The current rate, highest in the advanced industrial world, disincentivizes investment and encourages corporations to relocate overseas."

Even President Barack Obama, while an outspoken foe of inversions, perversely weakened his own case against them by speaking of "companies that are doing the right thing and choosing to stay here, [and] they get hit with one of the highest tax rates in the world. That doesn't make sense," as he told a Milwaukee audience in a typical comment.

Obama has thus inadvertently reinforced the conventional wisdom among U.S. elites that is used to justify inversions, as outlined by John Samuels of the International Tax Foundation. "Today, with most of their income and almost all of their growth outside the United States, U.S. companies have a lot more to gain by relocating their headquarters to a foreign country with a more hospitable tax regime," declares Samuels. "And conversely they have a lot more to lose by remaining in the United States and having their growing global income swept into the worldwide U.S. tax net and taxed at a 35% rate."

Why Inversions?

The crucial motive in transferring corporations' "nationality" and official headquarters to low-tax nations is that inversions shield the "foreign" profits of U.S. corporations from federal taxation and ease access to these assets. This protects total U.S. corporate profits held outside the United States—a stunning $2.1 trillion—from any U.S. corporate taxes until they are "repatriated" back to the United States.

Major corporations benefit hugely from the infinite deferral of taxes purportedly generated by their foreign subsidiaries. "If you are a multinational corporation, the federal government turns your tax bill into an interest-free loan," wrote David Cay Johnston, Pulitzer-Prize winning writer and author of two books on corporate tax avoidance. Thanks to this deferral, he explained, "Apple and General Electric owe at least $36 billion in taxes on profits being held tax-free offshore, Microsoft nearly $27 billion, and Pfizer $24 billion."

Nonetheless, top CEOs and their political allies constantly reiterate the claim that the U.S. tax system "traps" U.S. corporate profits overseas and thereby block domestic investment of these funds. But these "offshore" corporate funds are anything but trapped outside the United States. "The [typical multinational] firm ... chooses to keep the earnings offshore simply *because it does not want to pay the U.S. income taxes it owes*," explains Thomas Hungerford of the Economic Policy Institute. "This is a very strange definition of 'trapped'."

In fact, these offshore profits can be, and are, routed back into the United States through the use of tax havens. (Tax havens, where corporations and super-rich individuals place an estimated $7.6 trillion, were thrust into the international spotlight with the recent release of the Panama Papers. See William K. Black, "Business Press Spins Elite Tax Fraud as 'Good News'," p. 5.) "'Overseas' profits are neither overseas nor trapped," explained Kitty Rogers and John Craig. "It is true that for accounting purposes, multinational corporations keep these dollars off of their U.S. books. But in the real world, the money is often deposited in U.S. banks, circulating in the U.S."

However, the "overseas" profits come with some significant constraints on their use, pointed out David Cay Johnston. "The funds can only be accessed for short-term loans back to the U.S., and are not useful for major investments like new factories or long term R&D, or for investment outside the U.S.," said Johnston. But inversions eliminate these restrictions on how such funds can be used. "By inverting and then using a variety of tax avoidance schemes, the firms can have access to these earnings virtually free of U.S. taxes," notes Hungerford. "This is undoubtedly the primary motivation to invert."

The inversion route is not the only means for U.S. corporations to radically slash their U.S. taxes and gain access to offshore earnings. Any particular company's tax-avoidance strategy is dependent on the specific conditions it faces. As tax expert Johnston notes, "Every company has its own unique issues so it will decide what works for it."

Some giant multinational corporations, like Apple, Microsoft, and Google, have chosen to bypass inverting. Instead, they utilize immensely complex shifts of their revenue to minimize their taxes and maintain access to their offshore earnings. These maneuvers have gained exotic names like "Double Dutch Irish Sandwich," reflecting the multiple transfers of capital that they employ. The corporations involved are able to avoid the public backlash brought on by jettisoning their U.S. nationality. On the other hand, such ploys require careful planning and execution, compared to the simple, direct step of inverting.

Corporate inversions also head off the possibility of higher rates being imposed in the United States, an idea with very broad public support as shown by polling. But in addition to the vast political resources that corporations bring to any fight in Congress on corporate taxes, inversions remind U.S. public officials that their policies can be undermined by CEOs' unilateral decisions to relocate anywhere on the globe. Companies use this trump card to weaken the push for increases in corporate taxes and instead build momentum for further federal concessions.

Johnson Controls: The Ugly Truth

The most recent inversion deal, orchestrated by Johnson Controls—called the "latest and quite possibly the most brazen tax-dodger" in a *New York Times* editorial—explodes the myths underlying the standard rationale for inversions. Johnson Controls, which has been based in the Milwaukee area for 131 years, is the 66th largest firm in the United States.

Much media coverage has focused on the $149 million in annual tax savings that Johnson Controls will purportedly reap by jettisoning its U.S. identity and moving its official "domicile" to Ireland, where the tax rate is 12.5%. This is a tidy sum, but not because Johnson Controls was victimized by paying the statutory rate of 35%.

On the contrary, Johnson Controls has already been benefitting handsomely from a U.S. tax system that is remarkably generous to major corporations. As Matthew Gardner of the Institute on Tax and Economic Policy pointed out, "Between 2010 and 2014, Johnson Controls reported just over $6 billion in U.S. pretax income, and it paid a federal income tax rate averaging just 12.2 percent over this period." Significantly, "This is actually *lower* than the 12.5 percent tax rate Ireland applies to most corporate profits."

Far more central to Johnson Controls' inversion is the virtually tax-free status that it will gain over its vast pile of profits accumulated offshore, Gardner argues. Digging beneath the surface, Gardner found, "At the end of 2014, Johnson Controls disclosed holding $8.1 billion of its profits as permanently reinvested foreign income, profits it has declared it intends to keep offshore indefinitely."

The tax stakes for Johnson Controls are therefore much higher than the annual savings so often cited. "Reincorporating abroad would allow Johnson Controls to avoid ever paying a dime in U.S. income tax on profits currently stashed in tax havens," Gardner stated.

Johnson Controls is using the common inversion strategy of arranging for a smaller corporation based in a low-tax nation to purchase a much larger firm operating in the United States. In this case, the Ireland-based Tyco International (itself an inverted firm which had long been based in the United States) is buying Johnson Controls. Tax expert Edward Kleinbard describes this as a "minnow swallowing a whale" scenario that characterizes many inversions.

The Johnson Controls-Tyco deal qualifies as a so-called "super inversion," as *Fortune* put it, because it evades a number of new ownership regulations set by the U.S. Treasury Department to discourage inversions. "Tyco shareholders will own 44% of the deal after it is done, avoiding any penalties the Treasury Department has tried to impose on these deals," *Fortune* reported. "The Treasury Department had set an ownership requirement in 2014 of 40% for foreign firms involved in inversion deals with U.S. corporations, in an effort to discourage inversions."

The deal with Tyco will change virtually nothing for Johnson Controls International except for its slightly modified name—"Johnson Controls plc."—and its ability to manipulate the U.S. tax system. The company's new domicile will officially be Cork, Ireland, but it will retain its real operating headquarters in its present site near Milwaukee. It will continue to be listed on the S&P 500 stock index. Johnson Controls will still be protected by the vast legal architecture safeguarding U.S. firms, like those on securities, intellectual property, and patents.

The corporation's CEO Alex Molinaroli insists that the firm is simply acting to best serve its shareholders: "It would be irresponsible for us as a company to not take advantage of the opportunities that come along." The inversion will also provide some advantages to the CEO himself, with *Fortune* observing, "Molinaroli will receive at least $20.5 million and as much as $79.6 million for doing the deal over the next 18 months."

Johnson Controls also stands to retain other advantages. It will remain eligible for U.S. government and state contracts under current law, as have Accenture and other firms which have staged inversions. Between 2010 and 2014, Johnson and its subsidiaries received more than $1 billion in federal contracts—more than $210 million a year, according to ITEP's Gardner. Furthermore, Johnson Controls' ability to gain federal and state tax incentives for job creation will apparently continue.

The Pushback

In an age of fast-eroding economic security, corporate inversions have stirred vast public anxieties and outrage over corporations that seem both rootless and ruthless. Public anger over inversions is mounting, as household incomes continue to fall for tens of millions of Americans and worry about the offshoring of capital and jobs becomes more widespread. An August 2014 poll by Americans for Tax Fairness revealed that more than two-thirds of likely voters disapprove of corporate inversions—86% of Democrats, 80% of independents, and 69% of Republicans.

Surprisingly, one of the loudest voices to emerge against inversions has been *Fortune*'s Allan Sloan. Sloan penned a cover story titled "Positively Un-American," warning, "We have an emergency, folks, with inversions begetting inversions." Even though Sloan advocates long-term changes that would tilt the tax system further in a pro-corporate direction, he called for immediate action by the Congress and President Obama to stem the tide of inversions. "I still think we need to stop inversions cold right now," he wrote, "to keep our tax base from eroding beyond repair."

Besides the drain to the U.S. tax base, Sloan expressed concern about the impact of inversions on Americans' view of corporate America: "It also threatens to undermine the American public's already shrinking respect for big corporations."

The recently announced Johnson Controls inversion dealt a major blow to public trust in America's largest corporations, reflected in calls by Democratic presidential candidates Bernie Sanders and Hillary Clinton for stiff regulation on inversions.

Johnson Controls' announcement gave Sanders and Clinton a chance to tap a strong vein of public sentiment. Lashing out at the company in a January 25 media release, Sanders called it and its new partner Tyco "corporate deserters." Sanders declared, "Profitable companies that have received corporate welfare from American taxpayers should not be allowed to renounce their U.S. citizenship to avoid paying U.S. taxes."

Clinton blasted Johnson Controls on January 27 at an Iowa campaign stop, stating "I will do everything I can to prevent this from happening, because I don't want to see companies that thrive, use the tax code, the gimmicks, the shenanigans ... to evade their responsibility to support our country." She also began using a TV commercial aired in Michigan and elsewhere, showing her speaking in front of the Johnson Controls headquarters to denounce the corporation's inversion.

A Cure Worse Than the Disease

Up until now, conservative Republicans' control of the House of Representatives has blocked even modest legislation from gaining any traction, despite public outrage against inversions. Using the standard Republican soundbite about the high corporate tax rate driving U.S. firms and jobs overseas, Sensenbrenner, wrote in an op-ed in the *Milwaukee Journal Sentinel*: "Despite the negative effects the departures of these companies are having on the American economy, it is difficult to blame corporate leaders when you crunch the numbers."

Similarly, influential hedge-fund tycoon Carl Icahn, although acknowledging the dislocation and insecurity generated by inversions, exempted corporations from any obligation to the United States and laid the blame at the feet of Congress for failing to cut corporate taxes. "Chief executives have a fiduciary duty to enhance value for their shareholders," he argued in a *New York Times* opinion piece. "The fault does not lie with them but with our uncompetitive international tax code and with our dysfunctional Congress for not changing it."

Icahn expressed hope that the public's sense of urgency about stopping inversions could be shunted away from its current anti-corporate trajectory and instead stampede Congress into lowering corporate tax rates this year. He wrote in the *New York Times*, "How will representatives and senators, with an election year approaching, explain to their constituents why they are out of work because their employers left the country, when it could so easily have been avoided?"

In pressing for lower corporate taxes in the name of heading off more inversions, corporate and financial figures like Icahn and Republicans are backed by some influential Democrats and self-described liberals who share an elite consensus on corporations' absolute "right" to switch their nationalities and to offshore jobs and capital. *New York Times* business columnist Jeffrey Sommer summarized this consensus in 2014, inadvertently illustrating the vast gulf between elite opinion and majority sentiment. "At this stage of globalization," Sommer declared, "... most American consumers, investors and politicians have tacitly accepted that if a company is profitable, doesn't violate the law and produces appealing products and services, it can operate wherever and however it likes."

Treating corporate investment decisions as sacrosanct regardless of their impact on the public welfare, key Democratic figures like Sen. Charles Schumer (D-N.Y.) and Senate Minority Leader Harry Reid (D-Nev.) are calling for a "tax holiday" on the foreign profits of U.S. corporations. They essentially seek to replicate the holiday declared in 2004 to encourage corporations to "repatriate" foreign profits to the United States by giving them a radically discounted tax rate.

The "tax holiday" idea is a particularly counter-productive measure. First, tax holidays reinforce corporations' use of tax deferrals as they create an incentive for the companies to wait for Congress to capitulate and offer discounted tax rates. Second, these top Democrats' backing of a new corporate-tax holiday is particularly indefensible given the disastrous outcome of the 2004 holiday. "Advocates said it would create 660,000 new jobs," pointed out David Cay Johnston. "Didn't happen. Pfizer brought home the most, $37 billion, escaping $11 billion in taxes. Then Pfizer fired 41,000 workers."

A Real Solution

If corporate tax avoidance is to be stopped, the most immediate step is ending corporations' ability to endlessly defer taxes on income which they claim to have generated overseas.

Offshore tax havens enable corporations to routinely engage in a practice called "profit-stripping." With this practice, taxable earnings in the United States are stripped—with costs allocated to the U.S. units and earnings attributed to firms' foreign subsidiaries. "This kind of accounting alchemy actually works, turning the black tax ink of profit into red ink of debt," Johnston explained. "You appear as a pauper to government but valuable to investors."

"Most of America's largest corporations maintain subsidiaries in offshore tax havens," reported Citizens for Tax Justice. "At least 358 companies, nearly 72 percent of the Fortune 500, operate subsidiaries in tax haven jurisdictions as of the end of 2014."

This means a loss of an additional $90 billion to the Treasury, according to Citizens for Tax Justice, apart from the cost of inversions.

It is relatively easy to envision reforms that would give the U.S. tax code a badly needed updating—suited to the current era dominated by the global operations of multinational corporations—to foreclose maneuvers like inversions and the deferral of taxes on foreign earnings.

But serious action on inversions and major loopholes will likely prove impossible as long as our political democracy continues to be eroded by a torrent of campaign contributions from the multinational corporations exploiting the existing tax system.

Until that link—between those who write the big campaign checks and those who write our laws and tax code—is irrevocably broken, our political system will remain impervious to majority sentiment for stiffer taxes and restrictions on corporations' inversions and the offshoring of capital and jobs. ❑

Sources: Matt Gardner, "Johnson Controls Attempts a Snow Job," Tax Justice Blog, Jan. 26, 2016 (taxjusticeblog.org); Citizens for Tax Justice "The Sorry State of Corporate Taxes," 2014 (ctj.org); Citizens for Tax Justice, "Offshore Shell Games," Oct. 5, 2015 (ctj.org); Jesse Drucker and Zachary R. Mider, "Tax Inversion: How U.S. Companies Buy Tax Breaks," BloombergView QuickTake, Nov 23, 2015 (bloombergview.com); David Cay Johnston, "Corporate Deadbeats: How Companies Get Rich Off Of Taxes," *Newsweek*, Sept. 4, 2014; Andrew Ross Sorkin, "A Tidal Wave of Corporate Migrants Seeking (Tax) Shelter," Dealbook, *New York Times*, Jan. 26, 2016; David Cay Johnston, "The Shocking Numbers Behind Corporate Welfare: Boeing and Its Stockholders Fly High on Tax Dollars,"

Al Jazeera America, Feb. 25, 2014 (america.aljazeera.com); Kimberly Clausing, "3 Myths About Inversions and U.S. Corporate Taxes," Fortune, Jan. 30, 2016; Carl Icahn, "How to Stop Turning U.S. Corporations Into Tax Exiles," *New York Times*, Dec. 14, 2015; Allen Sloan, "How to Stop Companies from Deserting America before It's Too Late," *Fortune*, Aug. 11, 2014; Thomas Hungerford, "Policy Responses to Corporate Inversions: Close the Barn Door Before the Horse Bolts," Economic Policy Institute Issue Brief #386, Sept. 8, 2014 (epi.org); James Sensenbrenner, "Tax Reform Is Critical For American Economic Prosperity," *Milwaukee Journal Sentinel*, Feb. 8, 2016; Philip Mattera, "Subsidizing the Corporate One Percent: Subsidy Tracker 2.0 Reveals Big-Business Dominance of State and Local Development Incentives," Good Jobs First Subsidy Tracker, February 2014 (goodjobsfirst.org/subsidy-tracker); Roger Bybee, "Corporate 'Consensus' on Offsourcing, Inversions," *Progressive Populist*, Nov. 1, 2014 (populist.com); Chris Matthews, "Why Washington is Tackling the Tax Inversion Problem All Wrong," *Fortune*, Nov. 25, 2015; Thomas Content and Cary Spivak, "After getting taxpayers' help, Johnson Controls packs its bags," *Milwaukee Journal Sentinel*, Jan. 30, 2016; Stephen Gandel, "You Won't Believe How Much Johnson Controls' CEO Is Making on the Tyco Deal," *Fortune*, Jan. 25, 2016; Roger Bybee, "Manufacturing Revival a Worthy Goal, but Obama's Timid Plans Won't Get Job Done," Working in These Times blog, Feb. 20, 2012 (inthesetimes.com); "The Corporate Tax Dodge Continues," *New York Times*, Jan. 29, 2016; Eileen Applebaum, "No Tax Holiday for Multinational Corporations," Truthout, June 11, 2011 (truthout.org); Geoff Colvin, "Tyco-Johnson Controls Gives Us a Window into the Business World's Hardest Challenge," *Fortune*, Jan. 27, 2015; Allan Sloan, "Positively Un-American," Fortune, July 7, 2014; Allan Sloan, "Corporate Tax Dodgers Leave the Rest of Us to Foot the Bill," *Washington Post*, July 12, 2014; "U.S. Polling Shows Strong Opposition to More of the Same U.S. Trade Deals from Independents, Republicans and Democrats Alike," Public Citizen, July 2015 (citizen.org); James O'Toole, "GAO: U.S. corporations pay average effective tax rate of 12.6%," CNN, July 1, 2013 (cnn.com); Jesse Drucker and Zachary R. Mider, "Tax Inversion: How U.S. Companies Buy Tax Breaks," BloombergView, updated Nov. 23, 2015 (bloombergview.com); Michael Henigan, "IMF explains 'Double Irish Dutch Sandwich' Tax Avoidance," FinFacts Ireland, Oct. 11, 2013 (finfacts.ie); Elizabeth Warren, "Enough Is Enough: The President's Latest Wall Street Nominee," Huffington Post, Nov. 19, 2014 (huffingtonpost.com); David Sell, "Here and in New York, CEOs Talk Tax Inversion—or Don't," *Philadelphia Inquirer*, Sept. 3, 2014 (philly.com); Cliff Taylor, "Explained: The Upside Down World of Corporate Tax Inversions," *Irish Times*, Nov. 23, 2015 (irishtimes.com); Orsolya Kun, "A Broader View of Corporate Inversions: The Interplay of Tax, Corporate and Economic Implications," Bepress Legal Series, Sept. 26, 2003 (law.bepress.com); Americans for Tax Fairness, "Tax Fairness Coalition Sees Poll Results on Corporate Inversions as a Sign that the Issue Will Be Hot this Election Season," Aug. 5, 2014 (americansfortaxfairness.org); Citizens for Tax Justice, "Memo to Senate Permanent Subcommittee on Investigations: US Corporations Already Pay a Low Tax Rate," July 30, 2015 (ctj.org); Citizens for Tax Justice, "The U.S. Is One of the Least Taxed Developed Countries," April 2016 (ctj.org);Robert C. Pozen, "35 Percent Is Way Too High For Corporate Taxes," Brookings Institution," Jan. 29, 2016 (Brookings.edu); Leslie Picker, "Pfizer And Allergan Advisers Lose Out On $200 Million In Fees," *New York Times* Dealbook, April 6, 206; Diana Furchtgott-Roth, "Free Pfizer!: Why Inversions are Good for the U.S.," *New York Times*, April 7, 2016; Oxfam, "An Economy for the 1%,", Jan. 18, 2016.

Article 10.6

IN THE WAKE OF BREXIT, WILL THE EU
FINALLY TURN AWAY FROM AUSTERITY?

BY DEAN BAKER
June 2016

Voters in the United Kingdom caught almost everyone by surprise with their decision to leave the European Union. The push for Brexit was driven by nationalistic, xenophobic and racist sentiments. There is no point in putting a pretty face on it. But this vote is now a fait accompli. The question is how the leadership of the European Union chooses to respond.

In the lead up to the Brexit vote, there was much discussion of punishment. Wolfgang Schauble, the finance minister of the European Union, had made several comments implying that the UK would be punished if its people voted to leave the European Union. The idea was that if they don't want to be in the European Union, then Schauble and his colleagues would impose substantial trade barriers following the country's departure. Since the UK is so heavily dependent on trade with the EU, large trade barriers would impose real costs on the British economy.

Of course, such trade barriers would also impose costs on the EU. The costs would not be as large on the block as a whole since the UK is less important to the EU than vice-versa, but the costs would nonetheless be a big hit for the countries that have the most trade with the UK. In effect, the EU leadership would be imposing costs on its people in order to punish voters in the UK for wanting to leave.

Some of the drive for punishment seems like a spurned lover story. Having been rejected by UK voters, the EU leadership is now intent on making them suffer. That's not the sort of attitude that should determine economic policy.

But there is a more serious angle. The UK is hardly the only country where much of the public is unhappy with the EU. If the UK can engineer a relatively painless departure, then other countries may wish to follow its lead. From this vantage point, punishment is important since it will show the rest of Europe that leaving the EU really hurts.

It would be unfortunate if the EU went this direction. The better path would be to ask why it is that so many people are unhappy with the EU. It isn't too hard to find answers. Part of this is the bureaucracy, which is widely viewed as bloated and unresponsive to the European people. However, what is probably more pressing for most voters is the state of Europe's economy.

Many countries in the EU still have not recovered their pre-recession level of output and employment. For example, GDP is still down from its 2007 level by almost 6.0% in Portugal and 8.0% in Italy. Employment in Spain is down by more than 2 million, which is more than 10 percent of its pre-recession employment. In Greece, employment and GDP are both down by more than 20%, a track record that makes the Great Depression look mild by comparison.

This bleak economic performance was not dictated by the gods. It was the result of the conscious decision by the EU leadership to turn toward austerity in 2010, long before the economy was close to having recovered. Rather than using fiscal policy to steer economies toward full employment and address needs in infrastructure, clean energy, education and health care, the EU leadership demanded that governments move toward balanced budgets. This meant cutbacks in spending and tax increases that worsened and prolonged the downturn.

The EU leadership apparently likes balanced budgets. It may be something their parents told them. But the EU and the world can no longer be governed by folk wisdom handed down from prior generations; it needs to use real economics. And in real economics, the message is clear, they need to run larger budget deficits to boost economies and reduce unemployment.

The logic here is straightforward. If a deficit is too large it pushes up interest rates. And if central banks accommodate large deficits to keep interest rates down, then it leads to inflation.

Well, interest rates are about as low as they can be. In fact, the interest rate on Germany's 10-year bond is now negative. You have to pay the German government to lend it money. Inflation is also nowhere in sight. The inflation rate has been barely positive for most of the last five years and certainly well below the European Central Bank's 2.0% target. It's hard to see a serious harm if interest rates rose to more normal level and inflation increased to the level that the European Central Bank targets.

In short, there is no argument against spending more money to both boost growth to create jobs and meet real needs.

The proper response to the Brexit vote would be for the EU leadership to finally embrace reality and adopt an economic policy that will push the continent toward stronger growth and full employment. If it goes this path, the rest of the EU will not be anxious to follow the UK's lead.

If the EU leadership instead goes the route of tit for tat and tries to punish Britain, Brexit will be the first round of a very unhappy story. ❑

Chapter 11

MIGRATION

Article 11.1

WHAT TRUMP CAN AND CAN'T DO TO IMMIGRANTS

BY DAVID BACON
January/February 2017

> People make their own history, but they do not make it as they please; they
> do not make it under self-selected circumstances, but under circumstances
> existing already, given and transmitted from the past.
> —*Karl Marx, "The Eighteenth Brumaire of Louis Bonaparte," 1852*

While the government officials developing and enforcing U.S. immigration policy will change on January 20, the economic system in which they make that policy will not. As fear sweeps through immigrant communities in the United States, understanding that system helps us anticipate what a Trump administration can and can't do in regard to immigrants, and what immigrants themselves can do about it.

Over the terms of the last three presidents, the most visible and threatening aspect of immigration policy has been the drastic increase in enforcement. President Bill Clinton presented anti-immigrant bills as compromises, and presided over the first big increase in border enforcement. George W. Bush used soft rhetoric, but sent immigration agents in military-style uniforms, carrying AK-47s, into workplaces to arrest workers, while threatening to fire millions for not having papers. Under President Barack Obama, a new requirement mandated filling 34,000 beds in detention centers every night. The detention system mushroomed, and over 2 million people were deported.

Enforcement, however, doesn't exist for its own sake. It plays a role in a larger system that serves capitalist economic interests by supplying a labor force employers require. High levels of enforcement also ensure the profits of companies that manage detention and enforcement, who lobby for deportations as hard as Boeing lobbies for the military budget.

Immigrant labor is more vital to many industries than it's ever been before. Immigrants have always made up most of the country's farm workers in the West and Southwest. Today, according to the U.S. Department of Labor, about 57% of the country's entire agricultural workforce is undocumented. But the list of other industries dependent on immigrant labor is long—meatpacking, some construction trades, building services, healthcare, restaurant and retail service, and more.

During the election campaign, candidate Donald Trump pledged in his "100-day action plan to Make America Great Again" to "begin removing the more than two million criminal illegal immigrants from the country" on his first day in office. In speeches, he further promised to eventually force all undocumented people (estimated at 11 million) to leave.

In a society with one of the world's highest rates of incarceration, crimes are often defined very broadly. In the past, for instance, under President George W. Bush federal prosecutors charged workers with felonies for giving a false Social Security number to an employer when being hired. He further proposed the complete enforcement of employer sanctions—the provision of the 1986 Immigration Reform and Control Act that forbids employers from hiring workers without papers. Bush's order would have had the Immigration and Customs Enforcement agency (ICE) check the immigration status of all workers, and required employers to fire those without legal immigration status, before being blocked by a suit filed by unions and civil rights organizations.

Under President Obama, workplace enforcement was further systematized. In just one year, 2012, ICE audited 1600 employers. Tens of thousands of workers were fired during Obama's eight years in office. Given Trump's choice of Alabama Senator Jeff Sessions as Attorney General, greater workplace enforcement is extremely likely. Sessions has been one of the strongest advocates in Congress for greater immigration enforcement, and has criticized President Obama for not deporting enough people. Last year he proposed a five-year prison sentence for any undocumented immigrant caught in the country after having been previously deported.

Industry Needs Immigrants

Both deportations and workplace firings face a basic obstacle—the immigrant workforce is a source of immense profit to employers. The Pew Hispanic Center estimates that, of the presumed 11 million people in the country without documents, about 8 million are employed (comprising over 5% of all workers). Most earn close to the minimum wage (some far less), and are clustered in low-wage industries. In the Indigenous Farm Worker Survey, for instance, made in 2009, demographer Rick Mines found that a third of California's 165,000 indigenous agricultural laborers (workers from communities in Mexico speaking languages that pre-date European colonization) made less than minimum wage.

The federal minimum wage is still stuck at $7.50/hour, and even California's minimum of $10/hour only gives full-time workers an annual income of $20,000. Meanwhile, Social Security says the national average wage index for 2015 is just over $48,000. In other words, if employers were paying the undocumented workforce the average U.S. wage it would cost them well over $200 billion annually. That wage differential subsidizes whole industries like agriculture and food processing. If that workforce were withdrawn, as Trump threatens, through deportations or mass firings, employers wouldn't be able to replace it without raising wages drastically.

As president, Donald Trump will have to ensure that the labor needs of employers are met, at a price they want to pay. The corporate appointees in his administration reveal that any populist rhetoric about going against big business was just that—rhetoric. But Hillary Clinton would have faced the same necessity. And in fact, the immigration reform proposals in Congress from both Republicans and Democrats over the past decade shared this understanding—that U.S. immigration policy must satisfy corporate labor demands.

During the Congressional debates over immigration reform, the Council on Foreign Relations (CFR) proposed two goals for U.S. immigration policy. In a report from the CFR-sponsored Independent Task Force on U.S. Immigration Policy, Senior Fellow Edward Alden stated, "We should reform the legal immigration system so that it operates more efficiently, responds more accurately to labor market needs, and enhances U.S. competitiveness." He went on to add, "We should restore the integrity of immigration laws, through an enforcement regime that strongly discourages employers and employees from operating outside that legal system." The CFR, therefore, coupled an enforcement regime—with deportations and firings—to a labor-supply scheme.

This framework assumes the flow of migrating people will continue, and seeks to manage it. This is a safe assumption, because the basic causes of that flow have not changed. Communities in Mexico continue to be displaced by 1) economic reforms that allowed U.S. corporations to flood the country with cheap corn and meat (often selling below the cost of production—known as "dumping"—thanks to U.S. agricultural subsidies and trade agreements like NAFTA), 2) the rapacious development of mining and other extractive concessions in the countryside, and 3) the growing impoverishment of Mexican workers. Violence plays its part, linked to the consequences of displacement, economic desperation, and mass deportations. Continuing U.S. military intervention in Central America and other developing countries will produce further waves of refugees.

While candidate Trump railed against NAFTA in order to get votes (as did Barack Obama), he cannot—and, given his ties to business, has no will to—change the basic relationship between the United States and Mexico and Central America, or other developing countries that are the sources of migration. Changing the relationship (with its impact on displacement and migration) is possible in a government committed to radical reform. Bernie Sanders might have done this. Other voices in Congress have advocated it. But Trump will do what the system wants him to do, and certainly will not implement a program of radical reform.

H-2A Guest Workers

The structures for managing the flow of migrants are already in place, and don't require Congress to pass big immigration reform bills. In Washington State alone, for instance, according to Alex Galarza of the Northwest Justice Project, the Washington Farm Labor Association brought in about 2,000 workers under the H-2A guest worker program in 2006. In 2013, the number rose to 4,000. By 2015, it grew to 11,000. In 2016, it reached 16,000. That kind of growth is taking place in all states with a sizeable agricultural workforce.

The H-2A program allows growers to recruit workers outside the country for periods of less than a year, after which they must return to their country of origin.

Guest workers who lose their jobs for whatever reason—whether by offending their employer, or not working fast enough, for example—have to leave the country, so joining a union or protesting conditions is extremely risky. Growers can only use the program if they can show they can't find local workers, but the requirement is often unenforced.

The program for foreign contract labor in agriculture is only one of several like it for other industries. One study, "Visas, Inc.," by Global Workers Justice, found that over 900,000 workers were brought to the United States to work every year in similar conditions. The number is growing.

In the context of the growth of these programs, immigration enforcement fulfills an important function. It heralds a return to the *bracero* era, named for the U.S. "guest worker" program that brought millions of Mexican farmworkers to the United States between 1942 and 1964. The program was notorious for its abuse of the *braceros*, and for pitting them against workers already in the United States in labor competition and labor conflict. In 1954 alone, the United States deported over a million people—while importing 450,000 contract workers. Historically, immigration enforcement has been tied to the growth of contract labor, or "guest worker" programs.

Arresting people at the border, firing them from their jobs for not having papers, and sending people to detention centers for deportation, all push the flow of migrants into labor schemes managed to benefit corporations. The more a Trump administration pushes for deportations and internal enforcement, the more it will rely on expanding guest worker programs.

The areas where programs like H-2A are already growing were heavy Trump supporters. In eastern Washington, a heavily Trump area, immigration agents forced the huge Gebbers apple ranch to fire hundreds of undocumented workers in 2009, and then helped the employer apply for H-2A workers. While the undocumented workers of eastern Washington had good reason to fear Trump's threats, employers knew they didn't have to fear the loss of a low-wage workforce.

Deportations and workplace enforcement will have a big impact on unions and organizing rights. Immigrant workers have been the backbone of some of the most successful labor organizing of the last two decades, from Los Angeles janitors to Las Vegas hotel workers to Republic Windows and Doors in Chicago. At the same time, the use of the E-Verify database under President Obama often targeted workers active in labor campaigns like Fight for $15, as did earlier Bush and Clinton enforcement efforts.

Unions and immigrant communities have developed sophisticated tactics for resisting these attacks, and will have to use them effectively under Trump. Janitors in Minneapolis fought the firing of undocumented fast-food workers in Chipotle restaurants. The International Longshore and Warehouse Union (ILWU) teamed up with faith-based activists, immigrant-rights groups, and environmentalists to stop firings of undocumented workers in Bay Area recycling facilities, winning union representation and higher wages as a result. The same unions and community organizations that have fought enforcement in the workplace have also fought detentions and deportations.

These efforts will have to depend on more than a legal defense. The Supreme Court has already held that undocumented workers fired for organizing at work can't be rehired, and their employers don't have to pay them back pay.

Border Enforcement

Trump's threatened enforcement wave extends far beyond the workplace. He promised increased enforcement on the U.S./Mexico border, expanding the border wall, and increasing the number of Border Patrol agents beyond the current 25,000. Immigration enforcement already costs the government more than all other federal law enforcement programs put together.

Trump proposed an End Illegal Immigration Act, imposing a two-year prison sentence on anyone who re-enters the U.S. after having been deported, and five years for anyone deported more than once. Under President Obama, the United States deported more than two million people. Hundreds of thousands, with children and families in the United States, have tried to return to them. Under this proposed law, they would fill the prisons.

One of Trump's "first day" commitments is to "cancel every unconstitutional executive action, memorandum and order issued by President Obama." This promise includes Obama's executive order giving limited, temporary legal status to undocumented youth brought to the United States by their parents (Deferred Action for Childhood Arrivals, or DACA). DACA has been attacked by the right-wing ideologues advising Trump's transition team since Obama issued his order.

The 750,000 young people who gained status under DACA—the "Dreamers"—have been one of the most active sections of the U.S. immigrant-rights movement. But they had to give the government their address and contact information in order to obtain a deferment, making them vulnerable to deportation sweeps. Defending them will likely be one of the first battles of the Trump era.

Trump further announced that on his first day in office he will "cancel all federal funding to Sanctuary Cities." More than 300 cities in the United States have adopted policies saying that they will not arrest and prosecute people solely for being undocumented.

Many cities, and even some states, have withdrawn from federal schemes, notably the infamous "287(g) program," requiring police to arrest and detain people because of their immigration status. Trump's proposed order would cancel federal funding for housing, medical care, and other social services to cities that won't cooperate. As attorney general, Sessions can be expected to try to enforce this demand. After the election, many city governments and elected officials were quick to announce that they would not be intimidated.

The Dreamers especially see direct action in the streets as an important part of defending communities. In the push for DACA, youth demonstrations around the country sought to stop deportations by sitting in front of buses carrying prisoners to detention centers. Dreamers defended young people detained for deportation, and even occupied Obama's Chicago office during his 2012 re-election campaign.

In detention centers themselves, detainees have organized hunger strikes with the support of activists camping in front of the gates. Maru Mora Villapando, one of the organizers of the hunger strikes and protests at the detention center in Tacoma, Wash., says organizers cannot just wait for Trump to begin his attacks, but have to start building up defense efforts immediately. She advocates pressuring the

Obama administration to undo as much of the detention and deportation machinery as possible before leaving office. "We don't want him just to hand over the keys to this machine as it is right now," she warns.

The success of efforts to defend immigrants, especially undocumented people, depends not just on their own determination to take direct action, but on support from the broader community. In Philadelphia, less than a week after the election, Javier Flores García was given sanctuary by the congregation of the Arch Street United Methodist Church after being threatened by federal immigration agents. "Solidarity is our protection," urged the Reverend Deborah Lee of the Interfaith Movement for Human Integrity in California. "Our best defense is an organized community committed to each other and bound together with all those at risk. ... We ask faith communities to consider declaring themselves 'sanctuary congregations' or 'immigrant welcoming congregations.'"

But while many workers may have supported Trump because of anger over unemployment and the fallout from trade agreements like NAFTA, they also bought his anti-immigrant political arguments. Those arguments, especially about immigrants in the workplace, even affect people on the left who opposed Trump himself. Some of those arguments have been made by Democrats, and used to justify enforcement measures like E-Verify included in "comprehensive immigration reform" bills. One union activist, Buzz Malone, wrote a piece for *In These Times* arguing for increased enforcement of employer sanctions, although he envisioned them more as harsher penalties for employers who hire the undocumented. "Imprison the employers ... and all of it would end," he predicted. "The border crossings would fizzle out and many of the people would leave on their own."

What Is to Be Done?

To defeat the Trump enforcement wave, immigrant activists in unions and communities will have to fight for deeper understanding and greater unity between immigrants and U.S.-born people. Workers in general need to see that people in Mexico got hit by NAFTA even harder than people in the U.S. Midwest—and their displacement and migration isn't likely to end soon. In a diverse workforce, the unity needed to defend a union or simply win better conditions depends on fighting for a country and workplace where everyone has equal rights. For immigrant workers, the most basic right is simply the right to stay. Defending that right means not looking the other way when a coworker, a neighbor or a friend is threatened with firing, deportation, or worse.

The rise of a Trump enforcement wave spells the death of the liberal centrism that proposed trading increased enforcement and labor supply programs for a limited legalization of undocumented people. Under Trump, the illusion that there is some kind of "fair" enforcement of employer sanctions and "smart border enforcement" will be stripped away. Sessions will have no interest in "humane detention," with codes of conduct for the private corporations running detention centers. The idea of guest worker programs that don't exploit immigrants or set them against workers already in the United States will face the reality of an administration bent on giving employers what they want.

So in one way the Trump administration presents an opportunity as well—to fight for the goals immigrant rights advocates have historically proposed, to counter inequality, economic exploitation, and the denial of rights. To Sergio Sosa, director of the Heartland Workers Center in Omaha, Nebr., "we have to go back to the social teachings our movement is based on—to the idea of justice." ❏

Sources: "Donald Trump's Contract with the American Voter" (donaldjtrump.com); Chico Harlan, "The private prison industry was crashing—until Donald Trump's victory," Wonkblog, *Washington Post*, Nov. 10, 2016 (washingtonpost.com); U.S. Immigration and Customs Envorcement, "Delegation of Immigration Authority Section 287(g) Immigration and Nationality Act" (ice.gov); Interfaith Movement for Human Integrity (im4humanintegrity.org); Community Initiatives for Visiting Immigrants in Confinement, "End the Quota" (endisolation.org); Jens Manuel Krogstad, Jeffrey S. Passel, and D'Vera Cohn, "Five facts about illegal immigration in the U.S.," Pew Research Center, Nov. 3, 2016 (pewresearch.org); Bureau of Labor Statistics, "Foreign-Born Workers: Labor Force Characteristics, 2016," May 19, 2016 (bls.gov); Jie Zong and Jeanne Batalova, "Frequently Requested Statistics on Immigrants and Immigration in the United States," Migration Information Service, April 14, 2016 (migrationpolicy.org); "Selected Statistics on Farmworkers," Farmworker Justice, 2014(farmworkerjustice.org); "Indigenous Mexicans in California Agriculture," Indigenous Farmworker Study (indigenousfarmworkers.org); "U.S. Immigration Policy Task Force Report," Council on Foreign Relations, Aug. 2009 (cfr.org); "Visas, Inc.: Corporate Control and Policy Incoherence in the U.S. Temporary Foreign Labor System," Global Workers Justice Alliance, May 31, 2012 (globalworkers.org); "H-2A Temporary Agricultural Workers," U.S. Citizenship and Immigration Services (uscis.gov); Buzz Malone, "Stop Blaming Immigrants and Start Punishing the Employers Who Exploit Them," Working *In These Times*, Nov. 15, 2016 (inthesetimes.com); David Bacon, *Illegal People* (Beacon Press, 2008); David Bacon, *The Right to Stay Home* (Beacon, 2013); David Bacon, author interviews with Alex Galarza, Maru Mora Villapando, Deborah Lee, and Sergio Sosa (2016); Mae M. Ngai, *Impossible Subjects: Illegal Aliens and the Making of Modern America* (Princeton University Press, 2004); Ronald L. Mize and Alicia C. Swords, *Consuming Mexican Labor: From the Bracero Program to NAFTA* (University of Toronto Press, 2010).

Article 11.2

WALLED OFF FROM REALITY

Trump's claims about immigration economics are without merit.

BY JOHN MILLER
November/December 2015

> Mexico's leaders have been taking advantage of the United States by using illegal immigration to export the crime and poverty in their own country. The costs for the United – States have been extraordinary: U.S. taxpayers have been asked to pick up hundreds of billions in healthcare costs, housing costs, education costs, welfare costs, etc. ... "The influx of foreign workers holds down salaries, keeps unemployment high, and makes it difficult for poor and working class Americans—including immigrants themselves and their children—to earn a middle class wage.
> —"Immigration Reform That Will Make America Great Again," Donald Trump campaign website

Donald Trump's immigration plan has accomplished something many thought was impossible. He has gotten mainstream and progressive economists to agree about something: his claims about the economics of immigration have "no basis in social science research," as economist Benjamin Powell of Texas Tech's Free Market Institute put it. That describes most every economic claim Trump's website makes about immigration: that it has destroyed the middle class, held down wages, and drained hundreds of billions from government coffers. Such claims are hardly unique to Trump, among presidential candidates. Even Bernie Sanders has said that immigration drives down wages (though he does not support repressive nativist policies like those proposed by Trump and other GOP candidates).

Beyond that, even attempting to implement Trump's nativist proposals, from building a permanent border wall to the mass deportation of undocumented immigrants, would cost hundreds of billions of dollars directly, and forfeit the possibility of adding trillions of dollars to the U.S. and global economies by liberalizing current immigration policies. That's not counting the human suffering that Trump's proposals would inflict.

No Drag on the Economy

Even the most prominent economist among immigration critics, Harvard's George Borjas, recognizes that immigration has had a large positive effect on the U.S. economy. By his calculations, immigrant workers (documented and undocumented) add $1.6 trillion to the U.S. economy each year, or 11% of Gross Domestic Product (GDP). The great bulk that additional income (97.8% according to Borjas) goes to immigrant workers. But that still leaves what he calls an "immigrant surplus" of $35 billion a year, which goes to non-immigrants, including workers, employers, and other users of services provided by immigrants.

Others have emphasized the disproportionate impact that immigrants have had on innovation in the U.S. economy. A study for the Kauffman Foundation found that, in 2006, foreign nationals residing in the United States were named as inventors or co-inventors in over 25% of all U.S. patent applications. Around the same time, another study found that immigrants were the founders of over half of all Silicon Valley startups and almost one-third of Boston startups.

Immigrants Didn't Do It

U.S. workers have undoubtedly fallen on hard times. The reasons are manifold: slow economic growth; pro-rich, anti-worker, anti-poor policies; the decline of unions; "free-trade" globalization; and so on. But immigration isn't one of those reasons, especially when it comes to "the middle class." Not only has immigration benefitted the U.S. economy, but economists find no evidence that immigration causes a widespread decrease in the wages of U.S.-born workers.

Estimates vary, but the best economic studies point to the same conclusion: over the long run, immigration has not caused the wages of the average U.S. born worker to fall. Immigration critic Borjas calculated that, from 1990 to 2010, immigrant labor pushed down the wages of (pre-existing) U.S. workers by 3.2% in the short run. But even he conceded that over the long run, wages of native-born and earlier immigrant workers recovered to their previous level. Other economists find immigration to have a positive long-run effect on wages. Gianmarco Ottaviano and Giovanni Peri found that, from 1990 to 2006, immigration reduced wages of native-born workers in the short run (one to two years) by 0.7%, while over the long run (ten years) immigration into the United States boosted wages 0.6%.

Neither Ottaviano and Peri's nor even Borjas's estimates of the wage effects of immigration are consistent with Trump's claim that immigration is destroying the middle class. But what happens when we look at the wages of native-born workers by level of education? The Ottaviano-Peri study shows, in the long run, immigration is associated with an increase in wages across all education levels. Borjas's study reports that immigration has negative effects on the wages of native-born college graduates and especially on workers with less than a high-school education (those at the "bottom" of the labor market, mostly in low-wage jobs), even in the long run. But again concedes a positive effect for the 60% of U.S. workers with either a high school degree or some college (but no degree).

These results are probably a headscratcher for anyone who has taken introductory economics. After all doesn't increasing the supply of labor, through immigration, drive down its price (the going wage)? Well, no.

Immigrant workers do add to the supply of labor. But the economic effects of immigration do not stop there. Immigrants largely spend their wages within the U.S. economy. Businesses produce more—and hire more workers—to meet the increased demand. The cost savings from hiring cheaper immigrant labor also frees up businesses to expand production and hire more workers overall. Both those effects increase the demand for labor, offsetting the effects of added labor supply.

Economist David Card concludes that, taking into account these demand-side effects, "the overall impacts on native wages are small—far smaller than the effects of other factors like new technology, institutional changes, and recessionary macro conditions that have cumulatively led to several decades of slow wage growth for most U.S. workers."

Complements or Substitutes?

The effect of immigration on native-born workers with less than a high-school education remains a matter of dispute. Borjas insists that the costs of immigration are visited disproportionately upon those with the least education (and, to a lesser extent, those with the most education). He estimates, in a couple of different studies, that over the long run the wages of native-born high school dropouts fell 3-5% due to immigration.

But these estimates rely on the assumption that immigrant and native-born workers are substitutes for each other, and therefore compete for the same jobs. But, in fact, their skills differ in important ways. The first is their command of English. The Immigrant Policy Institute found that approximately one-half of the 41 million immigrants ages five and older speak English less than "very well." In addition, immigrant workers often have culture-specific skills— from cooking to opera singing to soccer playing, to cite examples given by Ottaviano and Peri—that differ from those of native-born workers.

When Ottaviano and Peri accounted for the imperfect substitutability between immigrants and natives, the negative of effect of immigration on native high school dropouts disappeared, and their wages were shown to rise by 0.3% over the long run.

Giving More Than They Get

Nor is there a credible case that undocumented immigrants are draining the public coffers by consuming more public services than they pay for. Immigrants migrate to jobs, not to welfare, and are disproportionately of working age. They are not major beneficiaries of the most generous U.S. welfare-state programs— Social Security and Medicare, which serve the elderly, not the young or the poor. And undocumented immigrants are already ineligible for most government benefits. (Even documented immigrants are ineligible for many federal programs, at least for some years after their arrival.)

On top of that, immigrants, both documented and undocumented, do pay taxes. They pay sales taxes, payroll taxes, and often income taxes. And they pay far more in taxes than they receive in benefits. That puts Trump's outrage over $4.2 billion in "free tax credits … paid to illegal immigrants" in a different light. In 2009, the federal government did in fact pay $4.2 billion in child tax credits to low-income tax filers using an Individual Taxpayer Identification Number (ITIN), the vast majority of them undocumented immigrants. But that same year, those ITIN filers paid an estimated $12 billion into a Social Security system from which they are not eligible to collect any benefits.

Trillions Left on the Sidewalk

Before the 1882 Chinese Exclusion Act, the United States allowed completely free immigration into our country. Immigration from elsewhere remained unrestricted until the eve of World War I. And immigrants flooded into the country and contributed mightily to its economic development.

Liberalizing immigration policies, unlike Trump's proposed border wall or mass deportations, could once again benefit the U.S. economy. Economists Angel Aguiar and Terrie Walmsley found that deporting all undocumented Mexican immigrants from the United States would reduce U.S. GDP by about $150 billion, while granting legal status to unskilled, undocumented Mexican workers (without additional effective border enforcement) would raise it by nearly that amount. And the potential gain for the global economy from liberalizing immigration policies is far greater. In fact so large that economist Michael Clemens likens liberalizing immigration to picking up "trillion-dollar bills on the sidewalk."

Such policies would also specifically improve conditions for workers, immigrant and native, in the United States. Immigrant workers, especially the estimated eleven million undocumented immigrants, tend to have less bargaining power than native-born workers. A policy granting undocumented immigrants legal status would make it easier for them to insist on their rights at work, and to organize and form unions. That's why the AFL-CIO and unions like UNITE HERE and SEIU now favor it.

For those who remain concerned about the effects of immigration on U.S. born low-wage workers, there are obvious policies that would improve the lot of all low-wage workers: Boosting the minimum wage, making it easier for workers to organize unions, and making the welfare state more generous and inclusive, so people don't have to accept whatever lousy job they can find. These are the policies that are called for, not keeping immigrants out. ❑

Sources: George Borjas, "Immigration and the American Worker: A Review of the Academic Literature," Center for Immigration Studies, April 2013; Vivek Wadhwa, Foreign-Born Entrepreneurs: An Underestimated American Resource," Kauffman Foundation, Nov. 24, 2008; Michael A. Clemens, "Economics and Emigration: Trillion-Dollars Bills on the Sidewalk?" *Journal of Economic Perspectives*, Summer 2011; Gianmarco Ottaviano and Giovanni Peri, "Rethinking the Effects of Immigration on Wages," National Bureau of Economic Research, August 2006; Gianmarco Ottaviano and Giovanni Peri, "Immigration and National Wages: Clarifying the Theory and Empirics," National Bureau of Economic Research, August 2008; Gianmarco Ottaviano and Giovanni Peri, "Rethinking the Effect of Immigration on Wages," *Journal of the European Economic Association*, February 2012; George Borjas and Lawrence Katz, "The Evolution of the Mexican-Born Workforce n the United States," in George Borjas, ed., Mexican Immigration to the United States, 2007; Benjamin Powell, "Why Trump's Wrong on Immigration," Independent Institute, Sept. 15, 2015; Angel Aguiar and Terrie Walmsley, "The Importance of Timing in the U.S. Response to Illegal Immigrants: A Recursive Dynamic Approach," Global Trade Analysis Project, Working Paper No. 75, 2013; David Card, "Comment: The Elusive Search For Negative Wage Impacts of Immigration," *Journal of the European and Economic Association*, February 2012; Glenn Kessler, "Trump's Immigration plan include many claims that lack context," *Washington Post*, Aug. 20, 2015; Linda Qiu, "Trump's says illegal immigrants get $4.2B in tax credits but doesn't count their taxes paid," PolitiFact, Aug. 18, 2015; Michael Greenstone and Adam Looney, "What Immigration Means for U.S. Employment and Wages," Brookings on Job Numbers, May 4, 2012; Jie Zong and Jeanne Batalova, "Frequently Requested Statistics on Immigrants and Immigration in the United States," Migration Policy Institute, Feb. 26, 2015.

Article 11.3

EQUAL TREATMENT FOR IMMIGRANTS

BY ALEJANDRO REUSS

July 2013, Washington Spectator

In this age of mass migration, U.S. immigration policy has mixed relative openness to immigration (since 1965) with nativist hostility toward immigrants. On the state level, we have seen a wave of anti-immigrant legislation (like the Arizona "papers, please" law); on the federal level, the militarization of the U.S.-Mexico border coupled with spasms of workplace immigration raids. Recent reform proposals, including a bill passed by the Senate, have coupled "guest worker" provisions with still more military-police-prisons immigration enforcement. Nativist fantasies of walling off the United States, it is clear, are doomed to fail. Given the harm that such measures cause in both economic and human terms, moreover, it would be bad if they succeeded.

Immigration today is inextricably bound up with globalization. The international movement of people, no less than international trade or investment, connects different countries economically. Globalization in its current form, however, has been shaped by the wealthy and powerful to their own advantage. This is obvious when we compare the treatment of the international movement of capital to the international movement of people.

Under the guise of "equal treatment of investors in similar circumstances"—as put by the World Bank's "Guidelines on the Treatment of Foreign Direct Investment"—international trade-and-investment agreements have guaranteed corporations' ability to invest abroad without fear of unfavorable government intervention. A NAFTA tribunal, for example, notoriously decided against Mexico in a case where the government had blocked foreign investment in the form of a toxic-waste dump.

International agreements, in contrast, have varied dramatically in their treatment of international migration. The European Union, for all its shortcomings, allows nearly unencumbered migration between member countries. NAFTA, on the other hand, has created a three-country zone where goods and capital can move with little restriction, but people face harsh barriers to migration.

The U.S.-Mexico border is one of the most militarized in the world—lined with razor-wire, armed patrols, and even drone aircraft—and undocumented immigrants live in constant peril of arrest and deportation. A recent article in *The Economist* paraphrases University of California-San Diego economist Gordon Hanson on the results of U.S. immigration policy: "inflicting economic self-harm by spending so much to keep workers out." The self-harm hardly compares to that inflicted on undocumented migrants.

We can see the operation of unequal power here in three ways.

First, undocumented immigrants lack political power. In addition to being denied formal political rights, like the vote, their insecure status poses an additional obstacle to legal social protest. On the other hand, the increasing significance of Latinos as an electoral constituency is a political counterweight. Many Latinos rightly see attacks on "illegal immigration" as thinly veiled attacks on them, so immigrant-bashing politicians risk an electoral backlash. That's why some Republicans are talking immigration reform now.

Second, labor wields far less political influence than capital. It is employers, not labor, who have gotten what they wanted from trade-and-investment agreements (mainly the ability to locate operations where labor costs are low and government regulation lax). While organized labor has not always (or typically) championed immigrants' rights, U.S. unions have turned more pro-immigrant in recent years, especially as they have come to see immigrant workers as crucial to their own futures.

Third, global corporations have powerful governments on their side. The U.S. government fights for agreements protecting the interests of U.S.-based companies. The governments of many lower-income countries advocate in favor of their nationals abroad, but they have less muscle on the international political scene. Unsurprisingly, these efforts have been less successful.

Today, discrimination on the basis of national origin is a central principle of immigration law. Even though U.S. labor laws, on their face, cover all workers regardless of immigration status, everyone knows this is a fiction because undocumented immigrants' precarious status keeps them from reporting violations to the authorities.

Imagine, instead, that the contours of political power were reversed. Instead of untrammeled freedom for globetrotting corporations, we would have guarantees for people of the right to move, live, and work where they wish. Instead of the "equal treatment" for global investors under trade-and-investment agreements, we would have equal treatment for workers, regardless of nationality, wherever they worked. That would be good not only for immigrants, but also for workers in general, by reducing labor-market competition and strengthening workers' overall bargaining power. As the late legal scholar Anna Christensen put it, in the context of Europe, "Equal treatment of foreign and domestic workers ... is no threat to the position of domestic labor. If anything, the reverse is true."

That is a far cry from the current situation. Indeed, it is a far cry from the Senate bill, which includes still more money for coercive enforcement measures, plus guest-worker provisions that would leave immigrant workers largely at the mercy of their employers.

Equal treatment, however, is the immigration reform we need. ❏

Article 11.4

ENFORCEMENT OF PUERTO RICO'S COLONIAL DEBT PUSHES OUT YOUNG WORKERS

"Compromise" protects vulture funds, not Puerto Rico.

BY JOSÉ A. LAGUARTA RAMÍREZ
JULY/AUGUST 2016

At least 23 of the 49 people killed in the mass shooting that took place at Pulse nightclub in Orlando on June 12 were born in Puerto Rico. While the horrendous hate crime targeted LGBT people of all ethnicities, the large proportion of island-born casualties is not surprising, as the central Florida city has become a preferred destination of Puerto Rican migrants over the past two decades. Steadily growing since the onset of the island's current "fiscal" crisis in 2006, yearly out-migration from Puerto Rico now surpasses that of the 1950s. The island's total population has begun to decline for the first time in its history.

Nearly a third of the island-born victims of the Orlando massacre were 25 or younger, most of them students employed in services or retail. This is the population group that will be hit hardest when the ironically named Puerto Rico Oversight, Management, and Economic Stability Act (PROMESA) comes into effect. Among its other "promises" for working-class Puerto Ricans, PROMESA will cut the minimum wage in Puerto Rico for those under 25, from the current federally mandated $7.25 to $4.25 per hour, and scale back the federal nutritional assistance program on the island. Purportedly aimed at "job-creation," these measures will likely intensify the outflow of able-bodied "low-skilled" workers. Ongoing out-migration has already decimated the number of available healthcare and other professionals on the island. Puerto Rico's 2013 median household income of $19,183 was barely half that of Mississippi, the poorest U.S. state (at $37,479), despite a cost of living that rivals that of most major cities in the United States. Inequality on the island is also greater than in any of the states.

The U.S. House of Representatives approved PROMESA on the evening of June 9, following a strong endorsement by President Barack Obama. The bill, which would also impose an unelected and unaccountable federal oversight board and allow court-supervised restructuring of part of the island's $73 billion debt, now awaits consideration by the Senate. Its advocates hope the president can sign PROMESA into law before July 1, when $1.9 billion's worth of Puerto Rico general obligation bonds will come due. Unlike those issued by public utility corporations and certain autonomous agencies, general obligation bonds, under Puerto Rico's colonial constitution, must be repaid before any further public spending for the following fiscal year is authorized. Puerto Rico's government has partially defaulted three times within the past year, but not on general obligation bonds. Puerto Rico is not the only place, under the global regime of austerity capitalism, to face predatory creditors and the imposition of unelected rulers—as illustrated by cases like Argentina, Greece, and post-industrial U.S. cities such as

Flint, Mich.—but its century-old colonial status has made it particularly vulnerable and defenseless.

The House vote followed a concerted, carefully timed media push by the Democratic establishment, on the premise that "despite its flaws" PROMESA represents a bipartisan compromise that is, in Obama's words, "far superior to the status quo." Among similar statements, a *New York Times* editorial on May 31 claimed that PROMESA "offers the island its best chance of survival." However, following the bill's approval, Republican House Speaker Paul Ryan tweeted in almost identical terms that PROMESA is "the best chance," but for something quite different —"for American taxpayers to be protected from a bailout of Puerto Rico." The threat of a taxpayer-funded "bailout" (which has never been on the table) has been deployed in anonymous scare ads, probably financed by high-risk/yield-seeking "vulture funds" that hold Puerto Rican bonds and so oppose PROMESA's mild restructuring provisions.

PROMESA's oversight board, which will be staffed by San Juan and Washington insiders with the bondholders' best interests at heart, is sure to continue to impose draconian austerity measures that have already slashed much-needed social services. (Former Puerto Rico governor Luis Fortuño, a Republican who enacted legislation laying off up to 30,000 public employees in order to appease credit rating agencies, has been mentioned as a likely appointee.) Democratic support for the bill was forthcoming despite the fact that neither the oversight provisions nor those reducing the minimum wage were removed.

Most U.S. observers reduce Puerto Rico's debt crisis to a result of "mismanagement" by its local administrators. (A Google search of the terms "Puerto Rico," "debt," and "mismanagement" yields pieces articulating this narrative from Bloomberg, CNN, USA Today, the National Review, and the Huffington Post, among others, within the top 10 hits.) This view conveniently erases the historical and structural roots of the crisis.

U.S. troops occupied Puerto Rico in 1898 and the Supreme Court quickly declared it an "unincorporated territory" subject to the authority of the U.S. Congress and federal courts system, without voting representation in Congress. Although U.S. citizenship was extended to individuals in 1917, and a local constitution was authorized and adopted in 1952 (not without significant amendments by Congress), the juridical fact of colonialism has remained unaltered, as reiterated by the Court on the very day of the House vote on PROMESA. (See Puerto Rico v. Sánchez Valle, a criminal case on double jeopardy, in which the Court reminds Puerto Rico's local government that unlike states, it is not legally considered a "sovereign" separate from Congress.) In the mid-1970s, Puerto Rico's comparative advantage as the only low-wage tax haven with direct access to the U.S. market waned. Washington's solution to the colony's economic stagnation was Section 936 of the Internal Revenue Code, which granted federal tax exemptions to U.S. corporations on products made in Puerto Rico, in addition to local tax breaks in place since the 1940s. The local government, in turn, pursued massive debt-fueled investment in infrastructure, whose use by these corporations it heavily subsidized. The resulting debt addiction spiraled out of control in the 1990s, fed by easy credit, and exacerbated after Congress began a ten-year phase out of Section 936 in 1996. Meanwhile, profits continue to leave the island to the tune of $30 billion annually.

In international law, the term for debt incurred by colonial, corrupt, or authoritarian regimes is "odious debt." A prominent example of its application was the cancellation of Cuba's colonial debt when that country achieved its independence from Spain, following the so-called Spanish-American War of 1898. The U.S. government's argument at the time, which Spain never formally accepted but most of Cuba's creditors eventually did, was that the debt was incurred neitherwith the consent of the Cuban people nor to their benefit. Although odious debt is a grey area of international law, with sufficient political resolve Puerto Rico's leadership could use it to bolster a claim to refuse payment. In 2008, Ecuador invoked the doctrine as part of a largely successful audit and partial default. Such a course would necessarily put Puerto Rico on a collision course with colonialism, as it would need to refuse to recognize any resulting lawsuits in U.S. courts.

This is precisely the type of outcome that PROMESA is designed to prevent. It is one which Puerto Rico's current administrators have proven entirely unwilling to pursue. Yet it is a path that is not alien to U.S. political history: one of the grievances that led to the thirteen colonies' Declaration of Independence was the imposition of new taxes—largely to pay debts incurred by Britain in the Seven Years' War. An independent Puerto Rico, released of an illegitimate debt burden incurred to profit U.S. corporations, could better focus on serving the needs of its poor and working-class majority. A movement capable of leading such a process has yet to materialize, but with U.S. statehood farther away than ever and housing and labor markets in migrant destinations becoming increasingly saturated, the matter is far from decided.

As living conditions on the island continue to deteriorate under PROMESA (and they surely will), young Puerto Rican students and workers will continue to flood those places where family connections, climate, the price of airfare, and job opportunities pull them. Not all will be targeted for physical violence because of their multiple identities, as the Orlando victims were. Their fate, however, will continue to be a haunting reminder of the ways in which invisible forces pattern seemingly random events in the lives of individuals and communities. ❑

Article 11.5

NATIVISM
As American as (Rotten) Apple Pie

BY GERALD FRIEDMAN
November/December 2016

> [W]hy should the Palatine Boors be suffered to swarm into our settlements, and by herding together establish their languages and manners to the exclusion of ours? Why should Pennsylvania, founded by the English, become a colony of Aliens, who will shortly be so numerous as to Germanize us instead of our Anglifying them, and will never adopt our language or customs, any more than they can acquire our complexion?
> —*Benjamin Franklin,* Observations Concerning the Increase of Mankind *(1751)*

While one of the first American nativists, Benjamin Franklin was far from the last. Instead, he inaugurated a tradition that has persisted in American society and politics, occasionally rearing its ugly head to threaten our society. From Franklin, to the Protestant nativists who warned against Irish and German immigrants in the 1850s, to the anti-Chinese crusaders of the 1880s, it was a short step to the Ku Klux Klan movement of the 1920s, which was anti-Catholic and anti-Jewish in addition to being anti-Black. And, of course, to Donald Trump today.

Since the United States is largely populated by people who came here from Africa, Asia, and Europe—of course, most who came from Africa were kidnapped and brought involuntarily—it should seem odd for Americans to disparage "aliens." The founding documents of the United States welcomed immigrants. The Declaration of Independence proclaims the equality of all, the Constitution provides that immigrants are to be accorded equal rights with those born here with only minor restrictions, and the first naturalization laws provided for a short and easy path to citizenship open to all without restriction. Unlike other countries, the United States has no official language or religion, and all citizens, regardless of place of birth, are guaranteed all the "privileges or immunities of citizens of the United States" and cannot be deprived of "life, liberty, or property" or "equal protection of the laws" without due process.

Indeed, Americans have often maintained an open and welcoming attitude towards immigrants. Through the 19th century, many states allowed all residents to vote without regard for citizenship, and schools and public services were offered in languages other than English. Native English speakers learned German, Spanish, Yiddish, and other languages so that they could do business with their non-English-speaking neighbors. Even now, in the midst of a new nativist surge, public-opinion polls report that a majority of Americans (in contrast with residents of most European countries) believe ethnic and cultural diversity makes the country better. This view attracts significant support across the political spectrum (ranging from nearly half of self-described "conservatives" to over three-fourths of "liberals").

Against such welcoming attitudes has been a stubborn and resilient nativism which has periodically found political expression.

Waves of Immigration and Waves of Nativism

Sometimes, nativism has been linked with national security scares. Fear of a French invasion in 1798, for example, prompted Congress to pass the so-called Alien and Sedition Acts—including the Naturalization Act, which increased the period of residence required for immigrants to become full citizens from just five years to 14. Another law authorized the president to expel without hearing or judicial recourse any noncitizen deemed "dangerous to the peace and safety" of the United States. And the Alien Enemies Act authorized the president to arrest, imprison, or banish any resident alien hailing from a country against which the United States has declared war.

These anti-immigrant measures were defended by Federalist politicians who warned against inviting "hordes of Wild Irishmen, nor the turbulent and disorderly of all the world, to come here with a basic view to distract our tranquility." The passing of the war scare and the defeat of the Federalists in the elections of 1800 led to repeal of two of the Alien Acts in 1801. After the repeal, political nativism was weakened for the next few decades—possibly as a result of embarrassment at this experience. Widespread nativist politics only returned in the 1850s, after famine and civil war led to a dramatic increase in European immigration. Compared to previous decades, annual immigration to the United States increased four-fold in the 1840s , including an annual influx of over 150,000 fleeing the Irish famine. While each year's immigration equaled barely 1% of the population of the United States, and the Irish were less than half of that, the concentration of Irish immigrants in a few localities had large economic and political effects.

Fears of labor-market competition have also stoked nativist movements. In cities like Boston and New York, Irish immigrants quickly came to dominate the market for common laborers, including construction workers and domestic servants. Often desperate for money and food, the Irish took any work they could find: cleaning stables, unloading ships, digging trenches.

While avoiding the southern states with slave labor and agricultural economies, the new immigrants spread throughout the Northern states. In New England, the Irish would settle in Lynn to work in the shoe factories, or in Lowell and Lawrence to operate looms in the textile mills and build the dams that powered the factories. Around Boston, as throughout the United States, Irish immigrants built the roads and laid the track for the network of railroads that came to tie together the United States after 1850. Not that their work was appreciated by all of their neighbors.

The Native American Party (renamed the "American Party" in 1855 but better known as the "Know Nothings") ran candidates on an anti-Catholic and anti-immigrant platform. At its peak, in the mid-1850s, the Know Nothings dominated the Massachusetts legislature and elected mayors in Philadelphia, Chicago, and other cities. The Know Nothings were more than an electoral vehicle. In 1854, election-related violence led to the deaths of 22 people in Louisville, Ky., and the burning of a Catholic church in Bath, Me., among other incidents.

After 1854, the Know Nothings faded quickly when "Bleeding Kansas" and slavery replaced immigration as the major political issues. For decades after the Civil War, the prominent role that many Irish- and German-born soldiers played in the Union cause may have contributed to the sharp decline of nativism. When nativism returned in the 1880s, its center had moved west to the Pacific coast, and it had a new focus with attacks on Asian immigrants, especially the Chinese.

Like the Irish before them, Chinese immigrants took many of the hardest and dirtiest jobs, working in laundries, in construction gangs building railroads, and in mines. Chinese workers dug much of the gold during the California Gold Rush, and many died building the First Transcontinental Railroad. Competition for work and the use of Chinese workers as strike-breakers certainly contributed to the anti-Chinese campaign. Formed in 1876 to "rid the country of Chinese cheap labor," the Workingmen's Party of California was led by an Irish immigrant, Denis Kearney, who liked to end his speeches with the phrase: "Whatever happens, the Chinese must go!"

Nativist movements have been opposed by advocates of equal rights (though not always successfully). While some Republicans and most Democrats joined Kearney in his racism, most Republicans, especially radicals and former abolitionists, defended the Chinese and other immigrants. The great Massachusetts abolitionist Sen. Charles Sumner (R) insisted on equal rights for the Chinese: it is, he said, "the question of the Declaration of Independence and whether we will be true to it. 'All men are created equal' without distinction of color." Sen. Samuel Pomeroy, a Kansas Republican, agreed and pragmatically warned that denying equal rights to the Chinese would threaten the rights of all: "If you deny citizenship to a large class, you have a dangerous element; you have an element that you can enslave; you have an element in the community that you can proscribe."

Such warnings fell on deaf ears after the end of Reconstruction. The return of Democrats to power in the South brought to Congress a large racist block just when anxious northern Republicans feared to push an aggressive equal-rights agenda. A united Democratic Party was joined by enough Republicans to enact racist laws against the Chinese. In 1875, Congress, with a newly elected Democratic majority, enacted the Page Act preventing Chinese women from entering the United States on the assumption that they were prostitutes. And, in 1878, Congress passed a Chinese Exclusion Act. Vetoed by Republican President Rutherford B. Hayes, it was eventually signed into law by Chester A. Arthur in 1882.

As memories of the Civil War and emancipation struggles faded, and migration from southern and eastern Europe surged, nativism spread. In 1894, three Harvard graduates, Charles Warren, Robert DeCourcy Ward, and Prescott Farnsworth Hall, met in Boston to form the Immigration Restriction League (IRL). Arguing that these recently arrived "undesirables" were inherently unable to participate in self-government or to adopt American values, the IRL sought to "arouse public opinion to the necessity of a further exclusion of elements undesirable for citizenship or injurious to our national character."

The IRL quickly attracted a large membership, including many prominent scholars and philanthropists. On its behalf, Sen. Henry Cabot Lodge (R-Mass.) sponsored a literacy bill to prohibit the entry of immigrants unable to read at least

40 words in any language. In 1896, Congress enacted the Lodge proposal only to have it vetoed by Pres. Grover Cleveland as contrary to traditional American policy and values. The failure of immigration restriction left the golden door open to new waves of immigrants from southern and eastern Europe: Jews to work in New York's apparel industry, Slavs for the Pennsylvania coal fields and steel mills, and Italians, Greeks, Poles, and others to build and to operate America's growing industries. Re-introduced repeatedly, the proposed literacy test became law only in 1917, during World War I, when Congress overrode President Woodrow Wilson's third veto.

And once again, fears of foreign "subversives" fueled nativism. The war inaugurated a new period of American nativism, one fed less by fear of economic displacement than by fear of subversion and anger at foreign ideas and involvements. The fear was fed by terrorist incidents. On June 2, 1919, for example, followers of the Italian-born anarchist Luigi Galleani exploded bombs in seven cities, including at the homes of John D. Rockefeller and of U.S. Attorney General A. Mitchell Palmer. A progressive Democrat with a pro-labor record in Congress, Palmer met the bombing campaign with a wave of arrests of radicals and by deporting immigrants and others. Called the "Red Scare," Palmer's attacks targeted immigrants as much as anarchists and communists. The Palmer raids resulted in the arrest of over 10,000 labor activists, radicals, and liberals and the deportations of 556 resident aliens. The warrantless arrests and deportations were widely denounced as "utterly illegal" and led to the establishment of the American Civil Liberties Union. Nearly all the resulting arrests were ultimately voided.

The involvement of immigrant radicals and of immigrant workers in the great strike wave of 1919-20 fed nativist fears. Eastern and Southern Europeans were condemned as incapable of assimilation and incapable of responsible self-government because they were genetically inferior. A broad coalition formed around a program of immigration restriction focused on limiting the admission of immigrants from the "lower races" seen as threats to the nation's gene pool, its democratic institutions, and the American "way of life." Immigration laws enacted in 1921 and 1924 created a national-origins quota system, restricting the absolute number of immigrants and the number from southern and eastern Europe.

Legislation restricting immigration did not end the culture war. Nativists flocked to a revived Ku Klux Klan seeking to limit the rights of African-Americans and of immigrants, especially Catholics and Jews. The rise of the Klan in the 1920s was inspired by one of Hollywood's first full-length epics, D.W. Griffith's 1915 "Birth of a Nation." With its story of how the Klan saved white Americans from African-American rapists and corrupt politicians, the firm brought renewed attention to the Klan. Reborn at a rally at Stone Mountain, Ga., shortly after the film's release, the "second era" Klan soon grew beyond its southern base. By 1924, the KKK had four million members, and professed to control over 24 of the nation's 48 state legislatures. The KKK claimed that it prevented Al Smith, the progressive governor of New York State, from winning the Democratic presidential nomination. While this may be an exaggeration, the Klan may have contributed to the wave of lynchings in the early 1920s.

Beset by corruption and internal dissension, the KKK soon lost most of its new membership. The nativist cause was taken up by others. The industrialist Henry

Ford financed the dissemination of the notorious anti-Semitic forgery, *The Protocols of the Elders of Zion,* and for ninety-one consecutive issues beginning May 22, 1920, his weekly newspaper, the *Dearborn Independent,* published articles describing an international Jewish conspiracy. Broadcasting from his Detroit parish, the Catholic priest Charles Coughlin added economic populism to Ford's anti-Semitism. Coughlin reached a radio audience estimated in the tens of millions with a message that blamed the economic crisis on financiers and communists, especially Jews, who have "murdered more than 20 million Christians" and have stolen "40 billion [dollars] ... of Christian property." Inspired by the success of the German Nazis, he founded a Christian Front to defend the country from communists and Jews and he urged his listeners to "buy Christian."

Coughlin's support for Nazi Germany was his undoing. The association of nativism and racial supremacism with Nazi genocide discredited such ideas. By the 1960s, the United States abandoned the system of national preferences in immigration, opening the country to new waves of immigrants from China, Asia, Africa, and Latin America, as well as the southern and eastern Europeans who had been targeted by the 1921 and 1924 laws.

The (Not So) New Nativism

The repeal of the system of national preferences opened the door to renewed immigration with the number of documented immigrants tripling between the 1960s and 1990s. While the number of immigrants is comparable to past waves, as a share of the much larger population of the 21st century United States, the new immigration wave is much smaller than those of the past. As in the past, however, the new immigration wave has brought migrants from countries previously little represented in the United States. American cities are now filled with immigrants from Africa, Asia, and Latin America, and this is true not only of traditional immigration centers on the East and West Coasts like Boston, New York, and San Francisco, but also big cities in the South and West, like Atlanta and Houston, and small towns throughout the country with motels managed by Indian-Americans, and restaurants and other small businesses run by migrants from throughout the world.

Like the Irish and Germans of the 1840s or the Jews, Italians, and Slavs of 1900, the new immigrants of today are helping to build a new American economy while changing and enriching our culture. And like their predecessors, the new immigrants face racists and nativists. In 1994, California Republicans rode to state-wide victory on their support of Proposition 187, touted as a way to stop undocumented immigration by requiring local police and social services agents to report suspected immigrants. While passed with nearly 60% of the vote, Proposition 187 was never enforced because of challenges in the courts.

Political nativism has found renewed strength after the terrorist attacks of September 11, 2001, and, even more, with the economic crisis beginning in 2007. Again, we are seeing the familiar political and economic fears underlying the surge in nativism. While most Americans continue to support allowing immigrants into the United States and allowing those here to become citizens, a very boisterous minority has emerged calling for a restrictive, even punitive, policy like that in Proposition

187. Particularly active in Republican Party politics, nativists have won some signal victories, including the primary defeat of Republican House Majority Leader Eric Cantor. (Cantor, the only Jewish Republican in Congress, supported reforms that would have provided for a path toward citizenship for undocumented migrants.) Cantor's defeat killed immigration reform in the Republican-led Congress, and pointed the way for Donald Trump's successful campaign for the Republican presidential nomination on a nativist program—including a wall on the Mexico border, mass deportation of undocumented immigrants, and "extreme vetting" of immigrants from Islamic countries—not too different from that of the Know Nothings of the 1840s, or the KKK of the 1920s. ❑

Sources: Benjamin Franklin, "Observations Concerning the Increase of Mankind" (1751) (archive.org); John Higham, *Strangers in the Land: Patterns of American Nativism, 1860-1925* (Rutgers University Press, 1988); Alexander Saxton, *The Indispensable Enemy: Labor and the Anti-Chinese Movement in California* (University of California Press, 1995); Gwendolyn Mink, *Old Labor and New Immigrants in American Political Development: Union, Party, and State, 1875-1920* (Cornell University Press, 1986); Jennifer Ludden, "In Rural Wisconsin, German Reigned For Decades" (NPR.org); Bruce Drake, "In Views of Diversity, Many Europeans Are Less Positive than Americans," Pew Research Center, July 12, 2016 (pewresearch.org); Philip Chin, "The Path to the Chinese Exclusion Act: 1868 to 1882," Chinese American Heroes (chineseamericanheroes.org); "Constitution of the Immigration Restriction League" (1894) (ocp.hul.harvard.edu); "Charles E. Coughlin," United States Holocaust Memorial Museum (ushmm.org); Alan Brinkley, *Voices of Protest: Huey Long, Father Coughlin, & the Great Depression* (Vintage, 1983); Steven Camarota, "Immigrants in the United States, 2010: A Profile of America's Foreign-Born Population," Center for Immigration Studies (cis.org); Frank Newport, "Americans Widely Support Immigration Reform Proposals" (gallup.com); Sara Goo, "What Americans Want to Do about Illegal Immigration," Pew Research Center, August 24, 2015 (pewresearch.org); Samantha Smith, "Trump Supporters Differ from Other GOP Voters on Foreign Policy, Immigration Issues," Pew Research Center, May 11, 2016 (pewresearch.org).

CONTRIBUTORS

Frank Ackerman is principal economist at Synapse Energy Economics in Cambridge, Mass., and a *Dollars & Sense* Associate.

Eileen Appelbaum is a senior economist at the Center for Economic and Policy Research and a visiting professor at the University of Leicester, UK

Michael Ash is an associate professor of economics at the University of Massachusetts-Amherst.

David Bacon is a journalist and photographer covering labor, immigration, and the impact of the global economy on workers. He is author of several books, including *Illegal People: How Globalization Creates Migration and Criminalizes Immigrants* (Beacon Press, 2009).

Dean Baker is co-director of the Center for Economic and Policy Research.

Rosemary Batt is the Alice Hanson Cook Professor of Women and Work at the Industrial and Labor Relations School, Cornell University, and a *Dollars & Sense* Associate.

James K. Boyce is a professor of economics at the University of Massachusetts-Amherst and co-director of the Political Economy Research Institute (PERI) Program on Development, Peacebuilding, and the Environment.

Jeremy Brecher is author of *Strike!* (revised, expanded, and updated edition 2015) and *Climate Insurgency: A Strategy for Survival* (2015), and co-founder of the Labor Network for Sustainability (www.labor4sustainabiconlity.org).

Chris Brooks, a native of Chattanooga, Tenn., is a former organizer for the Tennessee Education Association and currently a staff writer-organizer for Labor Notes in New York City.

Sasha Breger Bush is an assistant professor of political science at the University of Colorado-Denver and author of *Derivatives and Development: A Political Economy of Global Finance, Farming, and Poverty* (Palgrave Macmillan, 2012).

Rober Bybee is a Milwaukee-based writer on labor issues whose has contributed frequently to *Dollars & Sense, The Progressive*, Working In These Times (workinginthesetimes.com), and *Z Magazine*.

James M. Cypher (co-editor of this book) is a research professor in the doctoral program in development studies, Universidad Autónoma de Zacatecas (México).

Gerald Friedman is a professor of economics at the University of Massachusetts-Amherst.

Jayati Ghosh is professor of economics and chairperson at the Centre for Economic Studies and Planning, School of Social Sciences, Jawaharlal Nehru University, New Delhi, India.

John Ikerd is professor emeritus of agricultural economics at the University of Missouri-Columbia and author of several books, including *The Essentials of Economic Sustainability* (Kumarian Press, 2012).

Biola Jeje is a cofounder of New York Students Rising, a statewide student network at state and city colleges, and now works as a full-time digital media organizer in the labor movement.

José A. ("Josean") Laguarta Ramírez is a scholar-activist and educator born in San Juan, Puerto Rico and trained in anthropology, law, and comparative politics. His recent doctoral dissertation from the CUNY Graduate Center explores the 2010-2011 University of Puerto Rico student strike against austerity.

Rob Larson (co-editor of this book) is an instructor of economics at Tacoma (Wash.) Community College. His book *Bleakonomics* was published by Pluto Press in 2012.

Arthur MacEwan is professor emeritus of economics at the University of Massachusetts-Boston and is a *Dollars & Sense* associate.

John Miller is a member of the *Dollars & Sense* collective and professor economics at Wheaton College.

Evita Nolka is a political theorist from Greece.

Robert Pollin is a professor of economics and co-director of the Political Economy Research Institute (PERI) at UMass-Amherst

Alejandro Reuss (co-editor of this book) is co-editor of *Dollars & Sense* and author of *Labor and the Global Economy* (*Dollars & Sense*, 2013). He is also an instructor of labor studies at the University of Massachusetts-Amherst.

Belinda Rodriguez is a climate justice activist and organizer. She sits on the board of the Energy Action Coalition and most recently served as Training Director at United States Student Association.

Geoff Schneider is a professor of economics at Bucknell University and co-author of *Introduction to Political Economy*, 8th ed. (*Dollars & Sense*, 2016).

Zoe Sherman is an assistant professor of economics at Merrimack College and a member of the *Dollars & Sense* collective.

Chris Sturr (co-editor of this volume) is co-editor of *Dollars & Sense* and a lecturer on Social Studies at the Committee on Degrees in Social Studies, Harvard University.

Rosario Ventura is a migrant farm worker, moving between California and Washington State.

Jeannette Wicks-Lim is an economist and research fellow at the Political Economy Research Institute at the University of Massachusetts-Amherst.

Kristian Williams is author of *Our Enemies in Blue*, whose third edition, from which this article is adapted, was released in August 2015. He is also the author of *Fire the Cops! Essays, Lectures, and Journalism* (Kersplebedeb, 2014).

Marty Wolfson teaches economics at the University of Notre Dame and is a former economist with the Federal Reserve Board in Washington, D.C.

Klara Zwickl is a postdoctoral researcher at the Vienna University of Economics and Business.

CPSIA information can be obtained
at www.ICGtesting.com
Printed in the USA
FFOW02n0531040118
44341894-44011FF